Universal Banking in The United States

Universal Banking in The United States

What Could We Gain?
What Could We Lose?

Anthony Saunders

Ingo Walter

New York   Oxford
OXFORD UNIVERSITY PRESS
1994

Oxford University Press

Oxford   New York   Toronto
Delhi   Bombay   Calcutta   Madras   Karachi
Kuala Lumpur   Singapore   Hong Kong   Tokyo
Nairobi   Dar es Salaam   Cape Town
Melbourne   Auckland   Madrid

and associated companies in
Berlin   Ibadan

Library of Congress Cataloging-in-Publication Data
Saunders, Anthony.
Universal banking in the United States: what could we gain? What
could we lose? / Anthony Saunders and Ingo Walter.
p. cm.
Includes bibliographical references and index.
ISBN 0-19-508069-6
1. Universal banks—United States.
2. Universal banks.
3. Banks and banking—United States—State supervision.
4. Banks and banking—State supervision.
5. International finance.
I. Walter, Ingo.   II. Title
HG1588.S27 1994   332.1'0973—dc20
92-41473

1 3 5 7 9 8 6 4 2

Printed in the United States of America
on acid-free paper

Preface

The basic regulatory framework for the U.S. financial services industry has been in place for 60 years in the face of profound changes in the economic environment, in the structure of the national and international financial markets, and rapid technological change. In this span of time ordinary industries, especially those confronting global competition, would have transformed themselves almost unrecognizably in their efforts to survive and prosper over the years. Not so in the American financial services sector, stuck in a 60-year-old regulatory structure that has placed the burden of responding to the needs of market-driven structural change on the shoulders of the regulators and the courts in a constant search for loopholes in the law. In fundamentally reforming the rules to bring them into alignment with market realities, the Congress has consistently failed to act in the national interest. In its latest and best opportunity to do so, responding to 1991 U.S. Treasury initiatives, the Congress once more failed to produce meaningful change.

The purpose of this book is to examine the case for and against eliminating the barriers that have so long existed between banking and other types of financial services in the United States.

- Why should banks be barred from selling or underwriting insurance if they can do it better and more efficiently than traditional suppliers?
- Why should banks be restricted in creating and selling mutual funds, underwriting and dealing in all kinds of securities, bro-

kering real estate or running consulting companies if competitive conditions suggest this might be profitable?

- Why should banks not be allowed to hold significant equity stakes in industrial companies if a combination of lender/shareholder relationships offers a chance for superior economic performance and risk-sharing?

- Why should insurance companies or industrial companies be barred from owning shares in banks if the synergies or capital strength they bring to the table promises to strengthen the performance of their banking affiliates?

- Beyond constraints on their lines of business, why shouldn't banks be able to operate nationally without restrictions, just as other business firms are allowed to do?

All of these issues have long been controversial in the United States and many financial services firms have developed high stakes in the status quo or in very specific changes in the rules that favor themselves and impede their competitors. Few dispassionate voices speak for the national interest, although all protagonists argue that the national interest is identical to their own views. Indeed, it is curious that the United States is virtually alone in clinging to a financial system that effectively prevents market conditions from determining the optimal structures and organizational forms of its financial institutions. Americans preach market reforms around the world, yet in this critical area fail to practice it at home.

This book is about *universal banking* as a model for reforming the U.S. system of financial regulation. Universal banking is an institutional arrangement under which most of the aforementioned barriers would be scrapped. It is also an arrangement that is practiced in one form or another in most of the major economies of the world. What are the pros and cons of universal banking? How important are they, and what are the potential risks to the financial system in allowing functional and geographic interpenetration in financial services in the United States?

In this book we revisit and reevaluate old arguments and raise a number of new ones regarding this critical issue. We also carry out some new empirical and simulation analyses in order to support or refute the central hypotheses on which the arguments rest.

Overall, we suggest that barriers to market access, whether geography- or activity-based, erode the static and dynamic efficiency and global competitiveness of the U.S. financial system and its contribution to the national economic welfare. The barriers also erode the financial system's stability, by limiting financial institutions' access to capital and their ability to effectively diversify exposures and profit streams, thereby placing the taxpayer at risk, given the existing design of the bank safety net. In this sense, the existing U.S. bank regulatory structure seems to embody a triple threat to the national interest in being comparatively inefficient, uncompetitive, and unsafe, all at the same time.

This project began in 1989, at the start of the most recent round of national debate on these issues, and was completed in 1992, following the weak conclusion in the passage of the Federal Deposit Insurance Corporation (FDIC) Improvement Act of 1991.

We are grateful to a number of professional colleagues with whom we have discussed and debated these issues. They include George Benston, Roy Smith, Ernest Bloch, Tom Pugel, Greg Udell, Mitch Berlin, Tony Santomero, Bill Haraf, Dick Herring, Jean Dermine, Tom Huertas, William Garvin, Jorge Urrutia and Irwin Vanderhoof. We are equally grateful to Hugh Thomas, now at McMaster University, who co-authored Chapter 3; to Nils Pällmann, who provided the research assistance for Chapter 6; and to Gayle DeLong, who did much to edit-down an excessively lengthy manuscript and (together with Mark Herlitz-Ferguson) updated much of the statistical material. For help in accessing data, we are grateful to the New York Representative Office of the Deutsche Bundesbank, to Michael O'Connor of the Federal Reserve Board, and to John Leonard of Salomon Brothers Inc. Last but certainly not least, Ann Rusolo and Robyn Vanterpool capably and efficiently handled the often complex chores of manuscript preparation. To all we owe a debt of thanks although, as always, none can be held responsible for any remaining errors of fact or judgment.

New York   A.S.
July 1993   I.W.

Contents

Universal Banking in The United States

1

Introduction: Banking Structure and Global Competition

Few topics in economics and finance have been as hotly debated as the "optimum" structure and regulation of the banking system. The objective is always the same: maximum static and dynamic efficiency within a politically and economically tolerable framework of stability and equity. Gains in efficiency often come at a cost in terms of stability and equity. More stable and equitable financial systems often require sacrifices in terms of efficiency. Coupled to these basically *national* considerations is *global competitiveness*—of the national financial services industry and of the national economy more generally. The four benchmarks against which the ultimate performance of national financial systems must invariably be measured are stability, equity, efficiency, and competitiveness.

Financial services as an industry has become one of the most rapidly changing sectors of the global economy, with massive shifts in information transmission and processing, financial innovation in products and processes, and intense competition among institutions—and between them and many of their clients. As the industry and its role in the economy changes, it stands to reason that the regulatory structure ought to be reexamined periodically as well. In the United States, major pieces of the regulatory structure—such as the McFadden Act and Glass-Steagall Act—were put in place some six decades ago, and despite the dramatic reconfiguration of the financial intermediation process little change has occurred in the legislative overlay. Decades of political lethargy, coupled with powerful vested interests capable of suppressing national welfare considerations, has left it to the regulators and the courts to bend the regulatory system as much as possible to the economic realities. Observers in Europe and Japan occasionally remark that the United States has managed to create a system that is inefficient, unstable, and uncompetitive—all at the same time. To many, U.S. "financial reform" has become an oxymoron.

Of the various dimensions of the financial regulatory structure in the United States, as elsewhere, none is more controversial than *activity limits*—restrictions on the kinds of businesses financial institutions can undertake, and how they can undertake them. The United States had few such limits in place during its period of most rapid growth and industrialization in the late nineteenth and early twentieth century, with broadgauge financial institutions heavily involved in banking, commerce, and industry. Such limits have prevented banks, in the interest of stability, from engaging in commerce and industry (and vice versa) no matter how closely these activities were associated with the competitive viability and comparative advantages of the players. No other major industrial countries, except perhaps Japan, have such limits—although all have regulations as to *how* multifunctional financial activities may occur—and even Japan avoids some of the regulatory constraints through industrial and financial crossholdings, and is systematically relaxing the activity limits that do remain in force in a deregulatory process no less heavily politicized than the United States.

Activity Limits and the National Interest

In the pervasive economic restructuring that goes on in response to changing consumer and industrial demand patterns, capital and other resource costs, international competition, and perceived economies of scale and scope, individual business firms in search of maximum shareholder value constantly reassess the activity span of their strategies. *Vertical* integration to secure sources of supply or downstream distribution may serve this purpose, for instance. *Horizontal* expansion to acquire market share, complementary product lines, or risk spreading may be attempted for the same reason, sometimes successfully, sometimes not.

When management appears to be on the wrong track, the financial markets provide appropriate signals leading to further corporate restructuring or retrenchment. When the firm's objectives collide with the overriding public interest in keeping markets functioning efficiently or in achieving various noneconomic objectives—even at some cost to the economy—external constraints are imposed in the form of antitrust, environmental, employment, consumer protection, or other types of legislation, along with appropriate enforcement measures. These constraints involve a delicate balancing act to insure that the social *benefits* of regulation justify their *costs*, which come in the form of less efficient use of resources and possibly slower growth. Within the bounds of such constraints, industrial restructuring and shifting forms of business organization in market-oriented economies are allowed to be driven mainly by the underlying economic fundamentals.

Progressive economic restructuring in the financial services sector is conceptually no different than restructuring in any other industry. The financial services sector comprises deposit taking, lending, underwriting, and distribution of new issues of debt and equity securities, securities trading and brokerage, investment management, fee-based advisory activities, insurance, foreign exchange transactions, and a range of derivative instruments related to the management of risk (such as forward contracts, futures, and options). Market forces may dictate *vertical positioning* somewhere on the spectrum from the ultimate consumer to the wholesale financial markets or *horizontal positioning* ranging in breadth of activities from the highly focused financial specialist to *Allfinanz* or *Bankassurance*—the respective German and French terms for providing the full range of financial services under one roof.

As in other industries, the nature of the functions to be performed, alongside the underlying demand and supply characteristics in a highly competitive market, ought to dictate the optimum size, scope, and form of the organizations that compete in the open marketplace.

At the same time, it has been argued extensively and often passionately, that financial services firms are *special*—either in view of their fiduciary and other responsibilities to clients or in terms of the macroeconomic role performed by banks at the core of the national and international payments system [Walter, ed., 1985]. Firm or systemwide failure can impose costs on those insufficiently informed to make rational financial choices or on society at large. Alternatively, or in addition, the degree of control that financial firms exercise over other parts of the economy may be deemed in a political context to be excessive. And financial firms have a highly sensitive fiduciary role with regard to their clients, so that conflicts of interest, malfeasance, and standards of conduct are ever-present concerns.

Specialness can be considered in both a narrow and a broad sense. In the narrow sense, specialness is considered to bear only the deposit/loan and monetary policy dimensions, and therefore applies only to "commercial banks" under the traditional U.S. institutional definition—but not to a broad and growing array of other types of financial services firms. However, to the extent that either of these dimensions bear on other types of financial services firms as well (e.g., thrift institutions, insurance companies, and investment banks) they too can be considered *special*. Kane [1987] and others have argued that all financial services firms vulnerable to crises of confidence or failure-related negative externalities could be considered special, and therefore be subject to certain assistance and regulatory treatment on the part of the public sector that need not apply to other types of firms such as industrial companies.

A variety of constraints ranging from capital adequacy standards to liquidity requirements and periodic compliance reviews are usually set in place in order to mitigate concerns related to specialness. Each constraint may involve economic costs by displacing financial firms' activities from those dictated by competitive factors, and may therefore erode the static and/or dynamic efficiency properties of the financial services industry. Whether the social gains in terms of improved firm and industry stability and fiduciary performance exceed these costs is a complex and difficult matter for debate.

Moreover, since improvements in stability and fiduciary performance can only be measured in terms of events that *did not occur* and costs that were successfully *avoided*, the argument is invariably based on "what if" hypotheticals. There are no definitive answers with respect to optimum financial regulatory structures. There are only "better" and "worse" solutions as perceived by the electorate and their representatives and those who serve them. Consequently, collective risk aversion and political reaction to past regulatory failures in the financial services sector can easily produce overregulation. This is also reflected in the reward system of bureaucrats charged with operating the regulatory structure, which may cause them to be excessively risk averse and therefore prone to overregulation [Kane 1987].

In addition to conventional forms of fiduciary and stability-oriented regulation, the financial services industry in some countries—most notably in the United States and Japan—has been subject to activity limitations that constrain access to geographic markets, services, or clients. In the United States, these are anchored in the Glass-Steagall provisions of the Banking Act of 1933, the Bank Holding Company Act of 1956 and its 1970 Amendments, and the McFadden Act of 1927. Within the financial services sector, they have traditionally prevented or limited cross-penetration between banking and securities activities and between banking and insurance, but *not* between the insurance and the securities business. Likewise, they have prevented or inhibited geographic cross-penetration in banking, but *not* in the securities industry or (despite fragmented state-level regulation) in insurance. And they have prevented cross-penetration between banking and commerce but *not* between commerce and the securities or insurance sectors—including long-term shareholdings by the latter.

Although Congress in 1991 attempted to enact a comprehensive overhaul of banking regulation, the result was little more than a stopgap measure to prevent the deposit insurance system from becoming insolvent. Congress debated intensively the merits of allowing banks to operate on a nationwide basis as well as to engage in areas such as securities and insurance. Unable to reach a consensus, Congress merely passed an act—the Federal Deposit Insurance Corporation (FDIC) Improvement Act—that recapitalized the Bank Insurance Fund, which insures depositors in U.S. banks, and detailed specific interventionist actions regulators must take when the capital levels of banks fall below particular levels. The question of restructuring the banking industry remained largely unresolved and open.

Critics of allowing banks to engage in nontraditional activities point to the savings and loan disaster. They contend that the problems in that industry developed as a result of allowing savings and loans (S&Ls) to engage in nontraditional activities, after the passage of the 1982 Garn-St. Germain Act, where they did not have proper experience or resources. In the end, many S&Ls had to be liquidated at great cost to the U.S. taxpayer. Critics of universal banking maintain that the same consequences await the commercial banking industry if banks are permitted to engage in nontraditional activities such as securities and insurance. However, the fact that the FDIC was technically insolvent in 1991—when activity constraints were present—might suggest that such constraints themselves may be part of the problem. That is, restrictions on diversification of bank activity may *enhance* insolvency risk.

Activity Limits and Global Markets

The key question is whether activity limitations imposed on financial services firms in today's environment represent a *necessary* regulatory component, in order to achieve a politically acceptable degree of financial stability and fiduciary performance. Dramatic changes in the conduits of financial intermediation, information technologies, and the global competitive environment may well have altered the balance to the point where such limitations have become increasingly dysfunctional from the standpoint of public policy. In particular, the changing structure and extent of competition in the financial services industry has focused the spotlight on whether the costs associated with traditional U.S. activity limitations may have risen in relation to their presumed benefits in a world in which there is keen rivalry among regulators, as well as among financial firms [Kane 1987]. If so, then a reexamination of these barriers may well be in order.

The competitive dynamics of the major world financial markets over the past quarter century have been powerfully affected by financial product and process innovation and by technological change. *Product* innovations usually involve creation of new financial instruments (e.g., caps, futures, options, swaps) along with the ability to replicate certain instruments by bundling existing ones (synthetic securities) or to highlight only a single financial attribute by unbundling an existing instrument. *Process* innovations have included contract design (e.g., cash settlement futures contracts), methods of settlement and trading, methods for efficient margin calculation, methods of contract pricing, passive or index-based portfolio investment techniques, and a range of others. Technological change, primarily in telecommunications and information processing, has greatly facilitated the drive to create and broaden the market for both product and process innovations.

Financial firms as well as the users of financial services today have access to a broad range of location choices—including a variety of foreign or offshore operations. Only some functions still need to be carried out near the client; most others seek the most cost-effective site. This is certainly true at the wholesale end of the industry, and it is becoming more true at the retail end of the financial spectrum as well, as financial services are sold through arm's length delivery such as the mail, telephone, and personal computer.

Of course, it is arguable that financial innovation may be greater (not less) in heavily regulated financial systems in order to get around the regulatory structures and capture the resulting efficiency gains. Commercial banking products such as "loan notes" in the United States and "paperless commercial paper" in Switzerland can be viewed in these terms. However, regulation- or tax-induced innovation may be highly location-specific or idiosyncratic, and less broadly applicable than innovations spawned under free market conditions and triggered by such systematic factors as interest rate or exchange rate volatility.

It is against the backdrop of financial innovation, most especially in the United States and the United Kingdom, that international financial markets have evolved during the 1980s—innovations affecting the linkages between those markets and between the ultimate sources of funds and the ultimate users of funds domestically and internationally. Global financial markets for foreign exchange, debt, and even equity have developed various degrees of "seamlessness" that expand the debate on activity constraints for financial institutions far beyond domestic considerations.

This is well recognized in countries like the United Kingdom—for example, during the debates on the 1986 Financial Services Act—where the global competitive performance of national financial institutions and markets are of paramount importance. Even in countries like Canada, Australia, France, and Germany, discussions of financial reforms are invariably set against the need to jostle for advantage in the highly competitive global financial marketplace. Nor is Japan unmindful of these issues as regulatory reforms have gained momentum there [Walter and Hiraki 1993].

The United States is virtually alone as a nation where these discussions have traditionally relegated international competitive consequences to a subordinate position. Instead, the United States—from a policy perspective—must in the future recognize that the marketplace for financial services is already global, with respect to a large number of national financial institutions, and is getting more so for others (and for a broad range of specific financial services). An optimal domestic regulatory structure must therefore be designed with a view to actual and prospective financial globalization. Alternatively, there would have to be different regulatory structures for domestic and internationally active firms—a practical impossibility. Moreover, few people understand how a careful balancing of efficiency, stability, and competitiveness is possible when the bureaucratic and turf battles imbedded in the existing regulator structure

(Figures 1–1 and 1–2) are considered, especially when compounded by the state-level regulation of both the banking and the insurance industries.

An Outline of the Book

This book examines the case for and against a shift to some form of universal banking in the United States, using improved stability and international competitiveness as the benchmark criteria as to what constitutes the national interest. Universal banking is taken to refer to the ability of one firm or organization to provide a full range of financial services, including the products of commercial banks, investment banks, and insurance companies. The shift to universal banking would therefore remove many of the activity limits currently placed on U.S. banks. Questions related to the exact structure of the universal banking organization and to the institutions regulating universal banks are also examined in the book. Some attention is paid as well to questions of equity ownership links between banking and commerce, although that important issue is not a major focus of this volume [Walter 1993; Saunders 1994].

The book is organized into eight chapters. Chapter 2 examines issues related to international competitiveness. It provides a survey of indicators of competitive performance of financial institutions based in the United States and in other countries, as well as a discussion of the major factors that can affect relative competitive performance. On the whole, the evidence presents a somewhat mixed picture, although a number of important indicators suggest the competitive performance of U.S. banks has slipped relative to that of banks home-based in other countries.

Chapter 3 presents a new analysis of growth rates and cost functions of the world's largest banks. The focus is on cost functions, because they can provide information on existence of scale and cost-based scope economies for large banks. The analysis finds significant evidence of economies of super-scale for large banks, but that the economies of scale are not reflected in higher comparative growth rates. Furthermore, strong evidence exists to suggest the existence of supply-related diseconomies of scope between lending and fee-earning banking activities.

Chapter 4 contains descriptions of "universal banking" as it currently exists in three countries—Germany, Switzerland, and the United Kingdom. This discussion includes the types of banking institutions that exist in each of these countries, the domestic financial markets, the regulatory framework, and political issues related to universal banking. It also includes a discussion of liberalization efforts occurring in Europe as the European Community moves towards greater financial integration.

Chapter 5 of this book continues the analysis of the effects of activity limits on U.S. banks—and the implications of shifting to permitting universal banks—by examining issues of stability and risk. Specifically, this chapter examines the potential insolvency risk exposure of newly created U.S. universal banks. The current regulations and limitations on activities

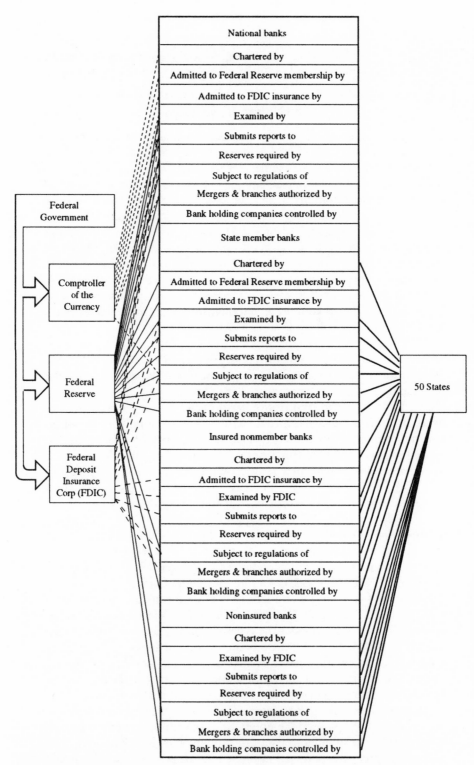

Figure 1-1 U.S. Banking Regulation. (*Source:* Federal Reserve Board, 1990)

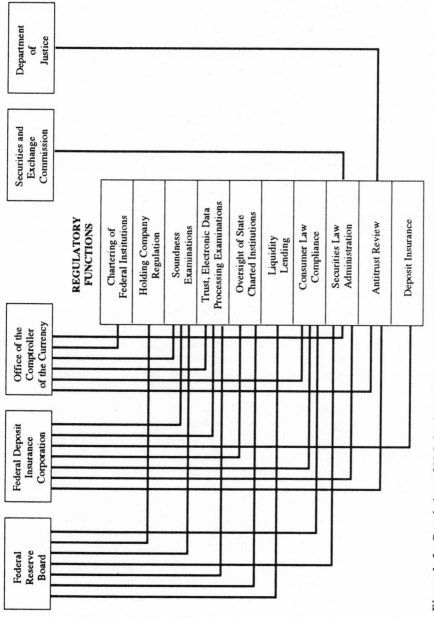

Figure 1-2 Regulation of U.S. banks and securities markets. (*Source: Report of the Task Group on Regulation of Financial Services.* Washington, D.C.: Group of Thirty, 1989)

by banks in three areas of financial services—securities, property–casualty insurance, and life insurance—are described and the types of risks inherent in these activities are discussed. This discussion also notes the similarities to standard banking products and activities of some of the products and decision-making processes involved in these "nonbank" financial product areas.

Chapter 6 evaluates the riskiness of combining banking, securities, and insurance activities using available data. This evaluation is accomplished through stock return-risk simulations by combining banks in various ways with securities, property–casualty insurance, and life insurance firms, including the simulation of actual mergers between existing firms. The results show some risk-reducing potential, especially for combinations of bank and insurance activities.

Chapter 7 assesses the federal safety net in a universal banking context. The current U.S. federal safety net—deposit insurance, the discount window, and guarantees of funds on wire transfer networks—is described and compared to the safety nets in universal banking countries, especially the United Kingdom and Germany. The current problems of the U.S. safety net are discussed, with the conclusion that reform of the safety net is vital, regardless of whether or not the United States decides to shift to a universal banking model. We argue that desirable reforms include a credible bank-closure rule based on the market value of capital (or net worth), premiums for deposit insurance that encourage appropriate risk-managing behavior, and elimination or modification of "too big to fail" guarantees in order to discipline large depositors—some of which were addressed in the FDIC Improvement Act of 1991. These reforms are evaluated with respect to universal banking, in order to show that a shift to universal banking need not increase the contingent exposure of taxpayers through the federal safety net.

Chapter 8 presents a summary of the major results and conclusions of the previous chapters of the book. It also discusses the implications for U.S. public policy. We find that the economic case for a shift to universal banking is sound and that such a shift is indeed in the national interest. In particular, it can improve the international competitiveness of U.S. financial institutions, and we point to studies that suggest such a shift can enhance the static and dynamic efficiency of the financial services sector in serving the needs of consumers/users in the United States. Furthermore, these benefits can be achieved without increasing the risks to financial system stability—indeed, diversification of activities can actually serve to *lower* the risks faced by financial institutions. Universal banks may or may not inherit the earth—there are plenty of reasons why they may not—but the playing field ought to be structured so as to let the market decide. This can be accomplished at acceptable risk to the financial system.

2

Measures of Competitive Performance in Global Financial Markets

What is the evidence regarding loss of competitiveness, if any, and how defensible is it—both with respect to the performance of U.S. financial firms internationally and of foreign-based financial firms in the United States. In this chapter we survey various measures of relative competitive performance widely used in the financial services industry, and make an assessment of how U.S. financial institutions stack up against these competitive benchmarks when compared with those based in countries with fewer activity constraints. How have U.S. financial firms fared in this environment? We consider as well the implications of any competitive shortfalls in the U.S. financial services industry for national economic performance, more broadly defined. This is important because the financial services sector produces both *final* services (used by consumers) and *intermediate* services (used by producers in generating further output).

Efficiency shortfalls in providing financial services are important because competitive distortions, whether domestic or international, cause an erosion of consumer welfare (*consumer surplus*). Efficiency shortfalls in intermediate services are important because they erode competitive capacity and shareholder returns (*producer surplus*) in industries that use financial services—which essentially comprise all other firms in the national economy. Competitive conditions in the steel industry, for example, have obvious implications for steel-using sectors like automobiles. A financial sector that is "overregulated" can thus cause simultaneous damage to economic efficiency, growth, income distribution, and the international competitiveness of the economic system as a whole. Consequently, in addition to the standard microeconomic indicators, competitive performance can also be defined in terms of the competitiveness of user industries and, indeed, the entire national economy.

Since financial institutions stand at the center of the capital allocation process, the competitiveness of the banking, securities, and insurance industries can be an enormous help or hindrance to the global competitive performance of a national economy such as the United States. A typical question in this regard is whether national economic restructuring via the corporate takeover market (as in the United States) or via universal bank holdings or control of equity positions in industrial and commercial firms (as in Germany) ultimately leads to superior competitive performance in global markets [Walter 1993].

Stylized Process of Financial Intermediation

A useful way to begin the discussion of competitive performance in financial intermediation, at both the firm level and the level of financial institutions, is to examine the nature of the conduits through which the financial assets of ultimate savers flow through to the liabilities of the ultimate users of finance, both within and between national economies. This involves alternative and competing modes of financial intermediation, or "contracting" between counterparties in financial transactions.

A convenient "model" that can be used to guide thinking on financial contracting and the role of financial institutions and markets can be summarized in Figure 2–1. The diagram depicts the financial process (flow of funds) among the different sectors of the economy in terms of the underlying environmental and regulatory determinants or drivers (discussed earlier) as well as the generic advantages needed to profit from the three primary intersectoral linkages:

1. Savings/commercial banking and other traditional forms of intermediated finance;
2. Investment banking and securitized intermediation; and
3. Various financial direct-connect mechanisms between borrowers and lenders.

Ultimate *sources* of surplus funds arise in the household sector (deferred consumption or savings), the corporate sector (retained earnings or business savings), and the government sector (budgetary surpluses).

Under the first or "classic" model of financial intermediation, savings (or funds sources) are held in the form of deposits or alternative types of liability claims issued by commercial banks, savings organizations, insurance companies, or other forms of financial institutions entitled to finance themselves by placing their liabilities directly with the general public. Financial institutions then use these funds flows (liabilities) to purchase domestic and international assets issued by nonfinancial institution agents such as firms and governments.

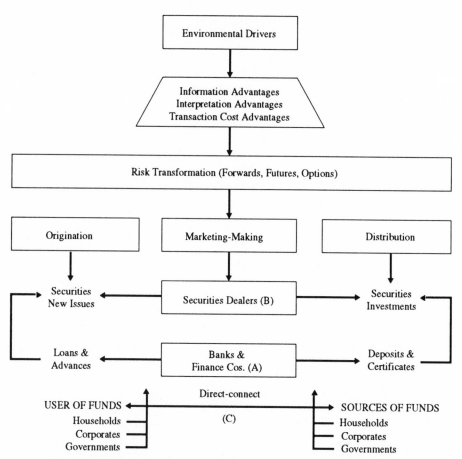

Figure 2–1 Financial flows.

Under the second model of funds flows, savings may be allocated directly to the purchase of securities publicly issued and sold by various governmental and private sector organizations in the domestic and international financial markets.

Under the third alternative, savings surpluses may be allocated directly to borrowers through various forms of private placement and other direct-sale mechanisms.

Ultimate *users* of funds comprise the same three segments of the economy: the household or consumer sector, the business sector, and the government sector.

Consumers may finance purchases by means of personal loans from banks or by loans secured by purchased assets (hire-purchase or installment loans). These may appear on the asset side of the balance sheets of credit institutions on a revolving basis, for the duration of the respective loan contracts, or they may be sold off into the financial market in the form of securities backed by consumer credit receivables.

Corporations may borrow from banks in the form of unsecured or asset-backed straight or revolving credit facilities and/or may sell debt obligations (e.g., commercial paper, receivables financing, fixed-income securities of various types), or equities directly into the financial market.

Governments may likewise borrow from credit institutions (sovereign borrowing) or issue securities directly.

With the exception of consumers, other borrowers such as corporations and governments also have the possibility of privately issuing and placing their obligations with institutional investors, thereby circumventing both credit institutions and the public debt and equity markets. Even consumer debt can be repackaged as asset-backed securities and sold to privately investors.

Alternative Modes of Financial Contracting

In the first mode of financial contracting, depositors buy the "secondary" financial claims or liabilities issued by credit institutions, and benefit from liquidity, convenience, and safety through the ability of financial institutions to diversify risk and improve credit quality through professional asset management, and monitoring of their holdings of primary financial claims (debt and equity). Savers can choose among a set of standardized contracts and receive payments services and interest that may or may not be subject to varying degrees of government regulation.

In the second mode, investors may select their own portfolios of financial assets directly from among the publicly issued debt and equity instruments on offer. This may provide a broader range of options than standardized bank contracts, and permit the large investors to tailor portfolios more closely to their objectives while still achieving acceptable liquidity through rapid execution of trades—aided by linkages with banks and other financial institutions that are part of the domestic payments mechanism. Small investors may choose to have their portfolios professionally managed, for a fee, through various types of mutual funds.

In the third mode, investors buy large blocks of privately issued securities. In doing so, they often face a liquidity penalty—due to the absence or limited availability of a liquid secondary market—for which they are rewarded by a higher yield. Recent institutional and regulatory developments have added to the liquidity of some direct-placement markets.

Value to ultimate savers and investors, inherent in the financial processes described earlier, comes in the form of a combination of yield, safety, and liquidity. Value to ultimate users of funds comes in the form of a combination of financing cost, transactions cost, flexibility, and liquidity. This value can be enhanced through credit backstops, guarantees and derivative instruments such as forward rate agreements, caps, collars, futures, and options. Furthermore, markets can be linked functionally and geographically, both domestically and internationally.

Functional linkages permit bank receivables, for example, to be repackaged and sold to nonbank securities investors. Privately placed securities, once seasoned, may be able to be sold in public markets.

Geographic linkages make it possible for savers and issuers to gain incremental benefits in foreign and offshore markets, thereby enhancing liquidity and yield or reducing transaction costs.

If permitted by financial regulation, various kinds of financial firms emerge to perform the roles identified in Figure 2–1—commercial banks, savings banks, postal savings institutions, savings cooperatives, credit unions, securities firms (full-service firms and various kinds of specialists), mutual funds, insurance companies, finance companies, finance subsidiaries of industrial companies, and various others. Members of each strategic group compete with each other, as well as with members of other strategic groups. Assuming it is allowed to do so, each organization elects to operate in one or more of the three financial-process modes identified in Figure 2–1, according to its own competitive advantages (i.e., its relative efficiency in the relevant financial production mode compared to that of other firms).

Financial System Benchmarks

The structure of the financial intermediation process can be calibrated against a set of normative benchmarks that would appear to describe optimum, performance-oriented financial systems which are at once *efficient*, *creative* (in terms of generating innovative financial products and processes), *globally competitive*, and *stable*. The first three of these benchmarks can be discussed in terms of Figure 2–2.

Static efficiency is modeled in the diagram as the all-in, weighted average spread (differential) between rates of return provided to ultimate savers and the cost of funds to users. This "gap," or intermediation spread, depicts the overall cost of a financial process or mode. In particular, it reflects the direct costs of producing financial services (operating and administrative costs, cost of capital, etc.). It also reflects losses incurred in the financial process, as well as any monopoly profits earned and liquidity premia. Financial processes that are considered "statically inefficient" are usually characterized by high "spreads" due to high overhead costs, high losses, barriers to entry, and the like.

Dynamic efficiency is characterized by high rates of financial product and process innovation through time. As noted earlier:

> *Product* innovations usually involve creation of new financial instruments (e.g., caps, futures, options, swaps) along with the ability to replicate certain instruments by bundling existing ones (synthetic securities) or to highlight a new financial attribute by rebundling existing instruments.
>
> *Process* innovations include contract design (e.g., cash settlement futures contracts), methods of settlement and trading, tech-

niques for efficient margin calculation, new approaches to contract pricing, passive or index-based portfolio investment techniques, and a range of others.

Successful product and process innovation broadens the menu of financial services available to ultimate borrowers and/or ultimate savers.

A final benchmark related to financial system stability, by which we mean the absence of *negative externalities*—costs imposed on society at large (the general public) that are attributable to either systemic failure or bailouts of individual institutions dictated by the political process. There are clearly trade-offs between stability (which is often addressed via regulation) and efficiency, so that the task is to find a socially optimum balance in a globally competitive environment. Financial systems that are statically or dynamically inefficient impose a burden on producers as well as consumers and may encourage them to shift transactions abroad or promote incursions by more efficient financial channels.

Statically and dynamically efficient financial systems are those which minimize the "spread" depicted in Figure 2–2 and at the same time produce a constant stream of innovations that successfully address ever-

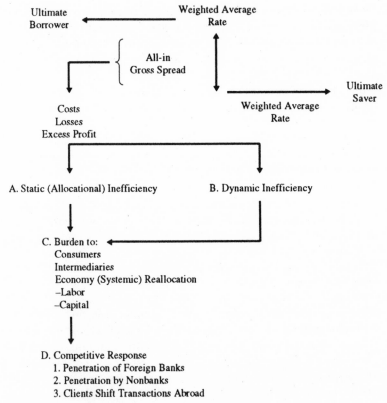

Figure 2–2 Efficiency in financial intermediation.

changing needs in the financial marketplace. Indeed, one can argue that the most advanced financial systems approach a theoretical, "complete" optimum where there are sufficient financial instruments and markets which, individually and in combination, span the entire state-space of risk and return outcomes. Financial systems that are deemed *inefficient* or *incomplete* are characterized by a limited range of financial services and obsolescent financial processes.

Both static and dynamic efficiency are of obvious importance from the standpoint of national and global resource allocation, not only within the financial services industry itself but also as it effects users of financial services. That is, since financial services can be viewed as "inputs" to the overall production process of a nation, the level of national output and income—as well as its rate of economic growth—are directly affected by the efficiency characteristics of the financial services sector.

A "retarded" financial services industry, in this sense, can represent a major impediment to a nation's overall real economic performance. Such retardation represents a burden on the final consumers of financial services and potentially reduces the level of private and social welfare. It also represents a burden on producers, by raising their cost structures and eroding their competitive performance in domestic and global markets. As such, a retarded financial services industry distorts the pattern of resource allocation in the national economy. Financial system inefficiencies can be traced to a number of factors:

1. Regulations that prevent financial firms from complete access to alternative sources of funding or the full range of borrowers and issuers;
2. Taxation imposed at various stages of the financial intermediation process, including securities transfer taxes, transactions taxes, etc.;
3. Lack of competition that reduces incentives to cut intermediation costs and promote innovation; and
4. Lack of market discipline imposed on owners and managers of financial intermediaries, leading to poor risk management, agency problems, and increased costs.
5. Existence of major information imperfections among contracting parties.

National financial systems that are statically and/or dynamically inefficient tend to be disintermediated. Borrowers or issuers in a position to do so seek foreign markets or offshore markets that offer lower costs or a more suitable range of products. Investors likewise seek markets abroad that offer higher rates of return or improved opportunities to construct more efficient portfolios. Such systems can be termed "uncompetitive" or "unattractive" as venues for financial intermediation in the context of global markets—although individual institutions may be able for a time to cross-subsidize foreign activities from abnormal profits earned at home.

Strategic Positioning and Competitive Performance

In the delivery of financial services, it is useful to visualize a market structure that combines three principal dimensions in the delivery of financial services in terms of the clients served (C), the geographic arenas where business is done (A), and the products supplied (P) [Walter 1988]. Figure 2–3 depicts these dimensions in the form of a matrix of C × A × P cells. Individual cell characteristics can be analyzed in terms of conventional competitive structure criteria.

The inherent attractiveness of each cell to suppliers of financial services clearly depends on the size of the prospective risk-adjusted returns that can be extracted from it. The durability of returns generated will depend on the ability of new players to enter the cell and the development of substitute products over time. Largely as a result of technological change and financial deregulation, competitors confront expanded potential access to each dimension of the C-A-P opportunity set.

Financial institutions will want to allocate available resources to those C-A-P cells in Figure 2–3 promising to generate the highest risk-adjusted returns. In order to do this, they will also have to allocate capital, costs, returns, and risks appropriately across cells. Beyond this, however, the economics of supplying financial services internationally is jointly subject to economies of scale and economies of scope.

The existence of both types of economies have strategic implications for players in the industry [see Clark 1988]. Economies of scale suggest an

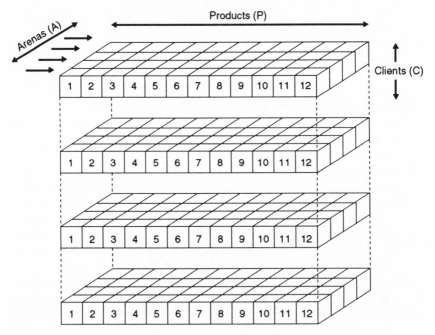

Figure 2–3   The Client-Arena-Product (C-A-P) Matrix.

emphasis on *deepening* the activities of individual firms within a cell, or across cells in the product dimension. Economies of scope suggest an emphasis on *broadening* activities across cells, that is, a player can produce a given level of output in a given cell more cheaply or market it more effectively than institutions that are less active across multiple cells. This depends importantly on the benefits and costs of linking cells together in a coherent fashion.

Regulation has an important influence in terms of: (1) accessibility of geographical arenas; (2) accessibility of individual client groups by players originating in different sectors of the financial services business; and (3) substitutability among financial products in meeting personal, corporate, or government financial needs.

Financial intermediaries are obviously sensitive to incremental competition in C-A-P cells depicted in Figure 2–3, especially where economic entry barriers are limited. Market penetration by competitors can erode indigenous players' returns and raises protectionist motivations. Given the economic interests involved, banks and other financial institutions are in an excellent position to convert them into political power in order to achieve protection against potential rivals. They are often exceedingly well connected politically, and their lobbying power motivated by protectionist drives can be awesome [Walter 1988].

Competitive distortions in the financial services industry take the form of entry barriers and operating restrictions. In terms of Figure 2–3, *entry barriers* restrict the movement of financial services firms in the lateral "arenas" dimension of the matrix. A firm that is locked out of a particular national market faces a restricted lateral opportunity set that excludes the relevant tranche of "client" and "product" cells.

Once having gained access to a particular arena, *operating restrictions* may constrain either the depth of service a financial institution can supply to a particular cell (e.g., lending limits, staffing limits, restrictions on physical location) or in the feasible set of cells within the tranche (e.g., limits on services banks or securities firms are allowed to supply and the client groups they are allowed to serve). Operating restrictions in turn can be subclassified in terms of whether they place limits on the kinds of financial services that may be sold locally (Type A) or the specific client-groups that may be served (Type B). Operating limits may severely reduce profitability associated with the arena concerned, while creating significant excess returns for the protected industry. Regulators may also tolerate a certain amount of anticompetitive, cartel-like behavior on the part of domestic financial institutions.

Economies of scope and scale may be significantly constrained by entry and operating restrictions in a particular market, indicating the importance of the impact of competitive distortions on horizontal integration in the financial services industry.

Under universal banking structures the entire C-A-P matrix is available to financial institutions in terms of their competitive positioning and execution, providing the potential—absent anticompetitive behavior—for maximum static and dynamic efficiency in the financial system. Limits on entry by "fit and proper" players, whether domestic or foreign-based—as well as limits on the business that may be done and the clients that may be served—carry a significant potential for eroding the domestic and international performance of financial institutions and of the national economy as a whole.

The key issue is how regulatory barriers affecting the lines of business banks or other financial intermediaries may pursue affect the static and dynamic efficiency characteristics enumerated in the previous section of this chapter. One might argue, for example, that strict line-of-business limits prevent monopolization of the market and stimulate creative ways of competing, assuring vibrant rivalry among firms both within and between financial intermediation channels. One might also argue that such limits inhibit competition and innovation as firms are prevented from fully bringing to bear their competitive strengths against protected rivals and fully utilizing available economies of scale and scope.

Indicators of Competitive Performance

It should be noted that international comparisons of financial institutions are fraught with statistical and other problems. However, a study by the Federal Reserve Bank of New York [Spindler, Howe, and Dedyo 1990] attempted to assess the performance of 51 banks and securities firms based in various countries (the United States, Canada, France, Germany, Japan, Switzerland, and the United Kingdom) that were internationally active during the second half of the 1980s (see Table 2–1). The performance measures used include firm size (total assets and total revenue, in real terms); profitability (return on assets [ROA] and return on equity [ROE]); productivity (ratio of total revenue to total non-interest expense); and capitalization (as measured by the ratio of shareholder equity to total assets, and the ratio of market capitalization to reported earnings).

In terms of size, U.S. *banks* fell consistently throughout the period, especially against their Japanese competitors. Roughly the same pattern emerged with respect to revenue growth. (Although a significant component of this "size effect" is attributable to the decline in the value of the dollar against the yen and other major currencies over the period.) They performed slightly below the sample mean on ROA, well below their Swiss, British, and Japanese counterparts. The same was true of ROE in comparison with Japanese and French banks. In terms of productivity, U.S. banks fell into the middle of the range. On capitalization, U.S. banks were high in the rankings on the first measure cited above, but well behind Japanese, German, and Swiss banks on the second.

With respect to *securities firms*, the Big-Four Japanese securities companies outstripped their U.S. competitors on size and growth during this period. The same is true with respect to their ROA and ROE, mainly

Table 2-1 Performance Summary of Sample Banks and Securities Firms by Country Group

Overall Performance	Banks							Securities Firms	
	U.S.	Canada	France	Germany	Japan	Switzerland	U.K.	U.S.	Japan
Firm Size									
Total assets	1 of top 10	0 of top 10	2 of top 10	0 of top 10	6 of top 10	0 of top 10	1 of top 10	Comparable	
Real asset growth	1.8% (6)	1.1% (7)	2.0% (5)	5.5% (2)	12.1% (1)	3.6% (3)	2.5% (4)	8.3%	42.2%
Total revenue	3 of top 10	0 of top 10	2 of top 10	1 of top 10	1 of top 10	0 of top 10	3 of top 10	Comparable	
Real revenue growth	7.1% (2)	7.1% (3)	4.5% (6)	4.5% (5)	20.3% (1)	3.3% (7)	5.5% (4)	15.6%	20.3%
Profitability									
Real return on assets	0.22% (5)	0.21% (6)	0.20% (7)	0.24% (4)	0.29% (3)	0.32% (2)	0.34% (1)	0.39%	2.06%
Real return on equity	3.8% (7)	4.2% (6)	9.3% (2)	6.8% (3)	12.3% (1)	5.3% (5)	6.7% (4)	11.4%	21.1%
Productivity									
Total revenue/ Noninterest expense	1.52 (3)	1.74 (2)	1.48 (5)	1.45 (6)	1.91 (1)	1.37 (7)	1.52 (4)	1.20	2.14
Capitalization									
Shareholder's equity ratio	5.2% (3)	5.1% (4)	2.4% (7)	3.5% (5)	2.8% (6)	6.1% (1)	5.9% (2)	3.3%	9.5%
Price-earnings multiple	8 (4)	8 (5)	No Data	19 (3)	51 (1)	22 (2)	6 (6)	9	21

Source: Spindler, Howye, and Dedyo, 1990.

Note: Figures represent country averages for the sample period, except for the shareholders' equity ratio country averages, which are as of fiscal year-end 1988; Ordinal ranking among the seven national groupings of banks appears in parentheses where appropriate; Average price-earnings multiples of the U.S., Canadian, and U.K. bank group as are calculated from their 1985 and 1986 results only.

based on strong domestic performance, as well as on productivity and capitalization criteria.

The study's findings are summarized in Table 2-1. It illustrates some of the measures used to assess relative competitive performance in the global financial services industry, as well as some of the pitfalls of these measures. There are major problems with international comparability of accounting and disclosure standards, exchange rate appreciation/deprection, inflation rates, comparative stock market performance, extraordinary gains and losses as well as identifying quantitative measures that serve as the "best" proxies for performance.

In addition to being notoriously difficult to measure internationally, such indicators may not involve in fact "clean" outcomes of competitive activity on a level playing field; rather, they may reflect barriers to market-access and competition either benefiting or damaging particular players as well as differences among competitive structures of individual markets. Consequently, assessing performance in the financial services sector involves building a mosaic of performance indicators and using a good deal of caution and judgment in interpreting them.

Comparative Market Shares

One way to define competitiveness at the industry level is in terms of market shares, domestically and internationally. This is relatively easy to do in industries such as steel or automobiles that offer comparatively homogeneous goods and services. But such a definition is extraordinarily difficult to apply to financial services. Nor may it be particularly reflective of profitability, which depends as well on a variety of market structure and other cost factors such as scale and scope economies. On the other hand, market share is a commonly used indicator of the *outcome* of the competitive process itself. In free markets, those firms that have the lowest cost structure or highest product quality generally gain market share against those with a higher cost structure or lower product quality.

The financial services industry sells perhaps 50 more or less distinct services to perhaps 20 more or less distinct client groups. They range from credit card loans to lower middle income households all the way to swap-driven repackaged synthetic securities engineered for the largest multinational companies. Some of these services are highly internationalized, indeed globalized, while others are individually sold or mass-marketed domestically. For some, market share data are reasonably available; for others, there are no available market share data whatsoever. Some are also contaminated by exchange rate changes over the periods of time that data are available. In addition, all time series data that do not reduce to relative market shares should be adjusted by an appropriate price deflator to correct for general inflation.

Table 2–2 shows the size of U.S. banks' international assets in December 1984 and 1991 and their share of world banking assets in both years

Table 2–2 International Bank Assets by Nationality of Bank

Parent Country of Bank	December 1984		December 1991	
	Amount ($ Billions)	Share of Total Assets (%)	Amount ($ Billions)	Share of Total Assets (%)
U.S.	595.5	26.4	711.6	11.6
Japan	517.9	23.0	1,931.5	31.4
France	200.7	8.9	542.6	8.8
U.K.	168.9	7.5	260.2	4.2
Germany	143.2	6.4	636.6	10.4
Italy	90.6	4.0	348.8	5.7
Switzerland	82.9	3.7	—	—
Other	450.7	20.1	1,715.5	27.9
Total	$2,250.4	100.0%	$6,146.8	100.0%

Source: Bank for International Settlements, *Annual Reports,* various issues.

Note: International bank assets are defined to include claims in foreign and domestic currencies of bank offices on nonlocal customers and claims in foreign currencies on local residents.

compared with those of banks based in Japan and a number of European countries. The data show that U.S. banks slipped dramatically in asset shares, both in total and among the largest such institutions, for much of the period virtually a mirror image of the gains achieved by Japanese institutions. In addition to the aforementioned measurement and interpretation problems, asset-based market share comparisons of performance include significant amounts of interbank activity, another reason why they must be viewed with caution. (Moreover, as discussed earlier, the U.S. dollar has fallen almost systematically against the yen over most of this period.)

Size Rankings

As will be discussed, size has often been considered useful in international comparisons of financial services firms. Assets and capital are often used in size comparisons of banks, capital in size comparisons among securities firms, and either assets or premium flows in size comparisons among insurance companies.

Table 2–3 indicates the international size rankings at the end of 1991 (and 1990), along with deposits, loans, profits, and stockholders' equity. The shift among the 10 largest banks in the world can be seen in Table 2–4, which reports the size information over a 20-year time span. Table 2–5 gives the size rankings in terms of capital for 1980 and 1991, respectively.

Table 2–6 presents the 1991 (and 1990) size rankings for nonbank financial firms using the same criteria as in Table 2–3. Note that U.S. financial firms fare considerably better than they do in the banking industry. Table 2–7 arrays the largest insurance companies alone by 1991 (and 1990) assets,

Table 2–3 The World's Top 50 Banks

1991	1990	Companies Ranked by Assets		Assets[a] $ Millions	Assets % Change from 1990	Deposits[b] $ Millions	Deposits Rank	Loans[c] $ Millions	Loans Rank	Profits $ Millions	Profits Rank	Profits % Change from 1990	Stock-Holders' Equity $ Millions	Stock-Holders' Equity Rank
1	1	Dai Ichi Kangyo Bank[d]	Japan	475,831.4	3.7	374,631.7	1	280,889.8	2	624.3	24	(3.3)	14,942.7	3
2	2	Sumitomo Bank[d]	Japan	464,113.7	4.0	367,266.7	2	270,624.3	3	874.5	9	(14.3)	16,925.8	2
3	3	Fuji Bank[d]	Japan	455,357.6	4.2	352,896.8	5	259,733.0	5	690.7	20	(3.0)	14,703.3	4
4	5	Sakura Bank [d,e]	Japan	448,291.0	2.9	360,389.1	3	289,577.5	1	603.9	27	(0.4)	12,770.7	9
5	4	Sanwa Bank[d]	Japan	445,027.2	1.9	357,150.9	4	268,514.2	4	800.5	14	0.3	14,550.3	5
6	6	Mitsubishi Bank[d]	Japan	432,092.9	2.1	349,294.6	6	253,198.3	6	462.7	38	(27.4)	13,292.3	6
7	7	Industrial Bank of Japan[d]	Japan	333,321.5	4.0	254,553.6	9	193,074.2	11	438.1	40	(5.8)	10,375.0	13
8	14	Norinchukin Bank[d,f]	Japan	311,033.9	23.1	261,530.4	8	130,412.3	22	304.0	50	(6.7)	2,049.9	89
9	8	Crédit Agricole	France	306,316.4	0.5	211,639.0	13	237,293.5	7	874.6[g]	8	1.4	17,551.6	1
10	10	Crédit Lyonnais[G]	France	305,450.4	6.5	125,088.4	35	149,792.9	17	560.7	30	(17.6)	13,062.0	8
11	12	Deutsche Bank[g]	Germany	295,446.8	10.5	265,328.0	7	235,406.9	8	834.5	12	31.7	12,450.9	10
12	9	Banque Nationale de Paris[G]	France	275,079.7	(5.6)	132,682.6	34	154,285.1	15	606.8[*]	25	104.4	10,330.3	15
13	11	Tokai Bank[d]	Japan	270,974.7	0.5	211,663.6	12	160,622.7	12	382.0	43	23.7	8,224.7	22
14	16	Mitsubishi Trust & Banking[d]	Japan	261,561.5	5.6	221,252.2	10	123,065.2	25	217.1	61	(35.7)	6,067.9	38
15	13	Barclays Bank	Britain	257,709.5	(0.9)	210,188.1	14	199,639.6	10	(169.8)	98	(116.1)	10,710.8	12
16	20	Long-Term Credit Bank of Japan[d]	Japan	255,663.4	10.8	209,476.6	15	156,189.1	13	471.4	37	79.9	8,246.3	21

17	15	Bank of Tokyo[d]	Japan	247,187.9	(2.0)	149,707.3	25	124,612.3	24	301.5	51	(13.2)	7,441.1	26
18	18	ABN Amro Holding	Netherlands	242,374.2	4.1	188,964.7	18	140,546.0	21	821.4	13	12.9	8,961.8	19
19	19	Sumitomo Trust & Banking[d]	Japan	234,917.1	1.0	214,111.5	11	105,888.4	31	227.9	60	(38.0)	5,847.2	41
20	21	Société Générale[d]	France	234,070.5	6.6	177,321.3	21	111,182.9	28	597.4	28	21.5	7,015.2	29
21	17	National Westminster Bank	Britain	231,510.9	(0.9)	200,583.8	17	200,876.8	9	127.3*	79	(80.8)	10,345.1	14
22	30	Bank of China[G]	China	229,385.3	39.8	147,372.9	26	101,392.2	32	1,816.1	2	39.4	NA	
23	44	Kyowa Saitama Bank[d,h]	Japan	227,270.7	89.1	184,936.1	19	152,754.1	16	283.3	54	17.7	7,879.9	24
24	23	Mitsui Trust & Banking[d]	Japan	226,658.4	7.3	201,675.0	16	99,732.0	33	191.3	68	(26.3)	4,854.9	47
25	22	Citicorp[d]	U.S.	216,922.0	(0.0)	146,475.0	27	147,636.0	19	(457.0)	99	(199.8)	9,489.0	17
26	25	Cie Financière de Paribas	France	199,150.9	7.5	38,967.5	93	87,173.4	43	(32.6)	96	(107.0)	11,035.2	11
27	24	Dresdner Bank[d]	Germany	193,976.7	2.5	176,281.8	22	154,325.1	14	381.0	44	(31.8)	7,231.2	28
28	26	Union Bank of Switzerland	Switzerland	183,100.3	(0.1)	152,285.7	24	148,123.4	18	847.9	11	31.4	13,073.1	7
29	28	Yasuda Trust & Banking[d]	Japan	181,347.6	2.8	164,445.5	23	89,327.4	38	160.7	72	(14.1)	3,864.6	62
30	41	Istit. Banc. San Paolo di Torino	Italy	178,218.9	33.5	136,555.6	32	107,730.6	30	605.6	26	(3.9)	5,964.4	40
31	29	Groupe des Caisses d'Épargne	France	172,473.5	(0.7)	177,478.3	20	71,222.3	54	443.3	39	(14.0)	9,566.9	16
32	32	Hongkong & Shanghai Banking	Hong Kong	160,513.6	8.1	142,370.4	28	73,693.1	52	1,097.0	6	176.0	9,015.8	18

continued

Table 2–3 (Continued)

1991	1990	Companies Ranked by Assets		Assets[a]		Deposits[b]		Loans[c]		Profits			Stock-Holders' Equity	
				$ Millions	% Change from 1990	$ Millions	Rank	$ Millions	Rank	$ Millions	Rank	% Change from 1990	$ Millions	Rank
33	45	Rabobank	Netherlands	158,268.7	32.4	73,596.9	62	84,102.0	44	541.2	33	1.5	7,573.3	25
34	34	Toyo Trust & Banking[d]	Japan	153,531.5	7.9	134,896.7	33	66,363.5	58	115.6	82	(28.0)	3,302.1	73
35	31	Swiss Bank Corp.	Switzerland	151,891.4	0.5	106,423.4	39	141,190.8	20	719.4	16	21.9	8,748.7	20
36	40	Westdeutsche Landesbank[g]	Germany	151,516.2	10.5	138,675.8	30	115,051.6	27	137.3	78	271.7	2,240.1	88
37	56	Monte Dei Paschi di Siena	Italy	150,426.8	48.1	83,422.8	56	62,239.2	62	268.1	56	(23.5)	4,928.4	46
38	33	Commerzbank[g]	Germany	149,112.5	3.4	138,852.4	29	119,732.3	26	327.0	48	(4.7)	5,740.0	43
39	37	Bayerische Vereinsbank[g]	Germany	149,101.6	8.4	138,361.2	31	127,384.7	23	147.1*	75	(26.8)	3,807.3	64
40	79	Banco di Napoli[G]	Italy	146,991.0	100.0	66,320.8	66	55,340.8	69	143.0	76	8.1	3,853.2	63
41	43	Diawa Bank[d]	Japan	139,877.8	7.8	108,622.9	38	81,154.2	46	236.3	58	(9.5)	4,602.4	50
42	80	Chemical Banking Corp[j]	U.S.	138,930.0	90.3	92,950.0	48	80,962.0	47	154.0	74	(47.1)	7,281.0	27
43	42	Nippon Credit Bank[d]	Japan	136,736.5	4.1	119,401.6	36	88,542.1	39	308.6	49	98.9	4,161.9	56
44	39	Deutsche Genossenschraftsbank[g]	Germany	135,312.9	(1.4)	93,619.1	46	91,822.4	36	169.4†	71	13.0	2,701.5	85

45	36	Banca Nazionale del Lavoro^G	Italy	130,584.1	(5.2)	101,971.8	42	96,232.8	35	66.1*	90	(40.0)	6,453.9	32
46	58	Bank Melli Iran^j	Iran	130,093.6	32.0	87,750.7	50	44,281.0	84	30.0	94	257.0	556.7	99
47	47	Bayerische Hypobank^g	Germany	127,040.8	9.0	117,218.6	37	109,134.7	29	212.7	63	12.6	3,914.0	61
48	49	Bayerische Landesbank^g	Germany	121,818.4	7.2	102,228.1	41	90,235.0	37	176.1	70	61.9	2,863.9	81
49	51	Royal Bank of Canada^k	Canada	117,855.7	9.3	93,519.5	47	87,573.0	42	855.2	10	3.4	6,911.5	30
50	53	Shoko Chukin Bank^G,d,f	Japan	116,437.6	12.9	20,026.8	100	88,478.9	40	208.2	64	7.8	3,052.1	77
		Total		15,574,718.9		11,729,487.1		9,530,422.5		40,488.4			579,322.5	

Source: Reprinted, with permission, from *Fortune*, 24 August 1992.

Notes:

NA = Not available.

• = Not on previous year's list.

GGovernment owned.

*Reflects an extraordinary credit of at least 10%.

†Reflects an extraordinary charge of at least 10%.

aAs of 31 December 1991, unless otherwise noted. All companies on the list must have more than 80% of their assets in commercial banking institutions. Daiwa, Mitsubishi Trust, Mitsui Trust, Sumitomo Trust, Toyo Trust, and Yasuda Trust include holdings of major trusts in their assets.

bFigures for German banks include their own bonds; so do figures for Bank of Tokyo, Industrial Bank of Japan, Long-Term Credit Bank of Japan, Norinchukin Bank, and Shoko Chukin Bank.

cFigures include lease financing and call loans and are net of loan-loss reserves.

dFigures are for fiscal year ended 31 March 1992.

eName changed from Mitsui Taiyo Kobe Bank, April 1992.

fFigures are unconsolidated.

gFigures exclude some subsidiaries more than 50% owned.

hFormed by merger in April 1991 of Kyowa Bank and Saitama Bank (1990 Global Service ranks: B-51 and B-49).

iFigures reflect merger with Manufacturers Hanover, December 1991.

jFigures are for fiscal year ended 31 March 1991.

29

Table 2–4 World Bank Ranking by Total Assets Less Contra Accounts

Rank	1970	1975	1980	1985	1991
1	Bank of America	Bank of America	Crédit Agricole	Citicorp	Sumitomo
2	Citicorp	Citicorp	Bank of America	Dai Ichi Kangyo	Dai Ichi Kangyo
3	Chase	Chase	Citicorp	Fuji	Fuji
4	Barclays	Banque Nationale de Paris	Banque Nationale de Paris	Bank of America	Sanwa
5	Manufacturers Hanover	Barclays	Deutsche	Mitsubishi	Crédit Agricole
6	JP Morgan	Crédit Lyonnais	Crédit Lyonnais	Sumitomo	Sakura
7	National Westminster	Deutsche	Société Générale	Banque Nationale de Paris	Union Bank of Switzerland
8	Western Bancorp	National Westminster	Dresdner	Sanwa	Mitsubishi
9	Banca Nationale del Lavoro	Dai Ichi Kangyo	Barclays	Crédit Agricole	Barclays
10	Chemical	Société Générale	Dai Ichi Kangyo	Crédit Lyonnais	Deutsche
Total assets ($ billions)	151	377	882	1,087	3,594

Source: The Banker, July 1992.
Note: In the 1950s, Midland was the largest bank in the world. Deutsche Bank was largest in 1960.

Table 2–5 Biggest Banks, By Capital

Rank	1980	$ Billions	Rank	1991	$ Billions
1	Crédit Agricole	6.2	1	Sumitomo	16.9
2	National Westminster	5.1	2	Dai Ichi Kangyo	16.0
3	Barclays	4.8	3	Fuji	15.2
4	Bank of America	3.9	4	Sanwa	14.8
5	Citicorp	3.9	5	Crédit Agricole	14.7
6	Banco do Brasil	3.6	6	Sakura	13.5
7	Lloyds	3.3	7	Union Bank of Switzerland	13.1
8	Midland	3.2	8	Mitsubishi	13.0
9	Paribas	3.0	9	Barclays	11.6
10	Algemene Spaar-en Lijfrenteras	3.0	10	Deutsche	11.3

Source: The Banker

again reflecting a more favorable positioning of U.S. firms than in the case of banks. This presumably has to do with the source of insurance premium flows, which continues to be high in the United States—although representing a declining share of global premium flows during the 1980s.

Profitability and Market Capitalization Rankings

Another way competitiveness can be defined is in terms of profitability. More competitive firms are presumably more (or at least no less) profitable than less competitive ones, either because they have superior products, lower costs, higher productivity, or all three. However, high profits could also be the result of the domestic industry being protected from international competition or from competition at home. For example, foreign banks find it possible to acquire U.S. banks, but the latter would find it difficult if not impossible to acquire a major U.K., Japanese, or German player for political/regulatory reasons. Profitability figures reflect as well international differences in reserve requirements, taxes, interest on reserves, and other factors. Table 2–8 ranks banks by pre-tax profits for the years from 1980, 1985, and 1991.

Profitability as a measure of competitiveness is also difficult to apply in the financial services industry partly for competitive confidentiality reasons, disclosure of information, and measurement difficulties. Profitability data are rarely available at the industry level on a consistent international basis. Figure 2–4 and Table 2–9 nevertheless compare U.S. rates of return on equity and assets with published data for bank composites in Europe, Japan, Australia, and Hong Kong during the 1980s, with Table 2–10 showing the world's top 10 banks in 1991 in terms of a "real profitability" index.

Note that U.S. ROAs and ROEs do not compare unfavorably with those of other composites throughout the decade of the 1980s. As pointed out earlier, however, return on assets and equity are highly suspect as

Table 2–6 The 25 Largest Diversified Financial Companies

1991	1990	Companies Ranked by Assets		Assets $ Millions	Assets % Change from 1990	Revenues $ Millions	Revenues Rank	Revenues % Change from 1990	Profits $ Millions	Profits Rank	Profits % Change from 1990	Stock-Holders' Equity $ Millions	Stock-Holders' Equity Rank
1	•	ING Group	Netherlands	173,908.7	—	24,652.4	5	—	841.7	5	—	8,092.4	5
2	1	Cie de Suez	France	154,481.2	(1.9)	33,225.5	1	(5.0)	680.2	10	(0.2)	9,348.8	3
3	3	Fed. Natl. Mortgage Assn.	U.S.	147,072.0	10.5	13,585.0	15	7.7	1,363.0	3	16.2	5,547.0	18
4	2	American Express	U.S.	146,411.0	6.3	25,763.0	4	5.9	789.0	7	335.9	7,465.0	7
5	4	GANᴳ	France	120,292.4	3.1	20,510.0	6	16.9	411.6	24	(4.9)	4,170.4	23
6	6	Allianz Holding	Germany	118,726.9	20.9	29,389.4	2	25.0	632.1	12	(11.7)	7,013.0	10
7	7	Union des Assurances de Parisᴳ	France	107,505.7	10.1	27,545.4	3	5.8	667.8	11	(13.8)	6,717.0	12
8	5	Salomon	U.S.	97,402.0	(11.4)	9,175.0	24	2.6	507.0	14	67.3	3,315.0	28
9	8	Aetna Life & Casualty	U.S.	91,987.6	3.0	19,195.6	8	(1.2)	505.2	15	(17.7)	7,384.5	8
10	9	Merrill Lynch	U.S.	86,259.3	26.6	12,362.8	17	10.3	696.1	9	262.8	3,818.1	26
11	11	American International Group	U.S.	69,389.5	19.3	15,833.9	11	0.8	1,553.0	2	7.7	11,463.5	2
12	10	Cigna	U.S.	66,737.0	4.8	18,750.0	9	2.2	449.0	22	36.1	5,863.0	14
13	14	Morgan Stanley Group	U.S.	63,709.1	19.0	6,785.1	28	15.6	475.1	20	75.7	2,993.4	32
14	29	Assurances Générales de Franceᴳ	France	60,287.6	63.4	11,012.4	20	13.0	477.0	19	(3.9)	3,962.5	25

15	12	Nomura Securities[c]	Japan	57,791.9	3.5	4,797.5	32	(29.4)	217.4	32	(72.1)	13,476.7	1
16	17	Orient[c,d]	Japan	55,077.3	17.3	3,556.3	38	19.2	55.9	43	(22.7)	1,950.4	35
17	18	Nippon Shinpan[c]	Japan	54,605.4	16.4	2,871.9	43	20.8	27.5	45	(37.1)	1,536.1	41
18	15	ITT	U.S.	53,867.0	9.8	20,421.0	7	(0.9)	817.0	6	(14.7)	9,173.0	4
19	13	Travelers Corp.	U.S.	52,709.0	(4.8)	11,377.0	18	(6.4)	318.0	27	—	4,590.0	20
20	16	BAT Industries	Britain	51,641.5	7.2	16,652.4	10	7.2	728.6	8	(51.0)	5,577.5	17
21	20	Zurich Insurance	Switzer-land	49,130.6	10.7	13,646.3	13	0.1	301.1	28	8.3	5,063.8	19
22	27	Assicurazioni Generali	Italy	47,547.8	27.6	14,231.2	12	14.6	454.9	21	16.5	7,289.3	9
23	21	Trygg-Hansa SPP	Sweden	47,344.7	7.5	6,898.3	26	4.5	2,398.7	1	44.9	1,528.9	42
24	24	Federal Home Loan Mortgage	U.S.	46,860.0	15.5	4,219.0	36	6.4	555.0	13	34.1	2,566.0	33
25	23	Student Loan Marketing Assn.	U.S.	45,320.1	10.2	3,257.4	39	(10.0)	345.1	26	14.7	1,149.8	45
	Total			2,858,983.3		508,176.5			20,720.5				

Source: Reprinted, with permission, from *Fortune*, 24 August 1992.

Notes:

NA = not available.

• = not on previous year's list.

G = government owned.

[a]Assets as of 31 December 1991, unless otherwise noted. Assets of consolidated subsidiaries are included. Holding companies engaged in commercial banking, savings, or life insurance are listed here only when assets of those businesses represent less than 80% of the company's total. All U.S. companies on the list must have a widely held and actively traded stock.

[b]Total revenues during the year, including any consolidated or nonfinancial revenues from manufacturing, retailing, etc., and revenues from discontinued operations when published. All companies on the list must have derived more than 50% of their revenues from financial businesses.

[c]Figures are for fiscal year ended 31 March 1992.

[d]Figures are unconsolidated.

Table 2-7 The 25 Largest Life Insurance Companies

1991	1990	Companies Ranked by Assets		Assets[a]		Life Insurance in Force[b]		Premium and Annuity Income[c]		Net Investment Income		Net Income[d]			
				$ Millions	% Change from 1990	$ Millions	Rank	$ Millions	Rank	$ Millions	Rank	$ Millions	Mutual Rank	Stock Rank	% Change from 1990
1	1	Nippon Life*,e	Japan	222,018.2	13.8	2,711,085.7	1	39,968.6	1	10,009.0	1	4,948.6	1		(20.1)
2	2	Dai Ichi Mutual Life*,e	Japan	155,121.7	13.7	1,898,890.5	2	28,863.0	2	7,117.3	4	3,531.9	5		(15.6)
3	3	Prudential of America*	U.S.	148,417.6	11.2	820,708.7	8	24,861.9	4	8,977.9	2	1,386.7	12		590.6
4	4	Sumitomo Life*,e	Japan	135,624.1	15.2	1,790,776.2	3	25,521.7	3	6,051.5	5	2,694.3	8		(20.5)
5	5	Metropolitan Life*	U.S.	110,799.5	7.3	948,020.9	5	19,458.4	5	7,584.5	3	237.0	23		(34.1)
6	6	Meiji Mutual Life*,e	Japan	93,477.1	16.3	1,242,936.7	4	18,154.3	6	3,868.0	9	2,022.6	9		(15.1)
7	8	Prudential	Britain	72,402.7	15.6	NA		10,643.6	11	4,380.2	7	153.8		9	260.6
8	7	Asahi Mutual Life*,e	Japan	71,919.2	14.7	835,895.4	7	13,621.6	8	3,767.8	10	1,734.2	10		(14.8)
9	10	Mitsui Mutual Life*,e	Japan	58,526.2	16.2	744,750.4	9	12,110.4	9	2,483.0	22	1,165.4	13		(22.4)
10	12	Teachers Insurance & Annuity	U.S.	55,575.8	11.4	29,804.4	46	3,233.6	40	4,706.6	6	331.6		3	(13.8)
11	13	Allianz	Germany	53,428.7	7.2	137,727.9	28	5,850.5	26	3,296.8	14	56.7		12	13.2
12	9	Aetna Life	U.S.	52,355.0	0.0	311,108.9	16	8,045.3	14	3,409.1	12	310.3		4	(27.4)
13	15	Yasuda Mutual Life*,e	Japan	50,947.9	16.2	847,070.4	6	11,036.8	10	2,613.8	17	1,408.2	11		(9.4)
14	11	Equitable Life Assurance[g]	U.S.	50,352.8	0.1	308,211.5	17	3,452.5	39	2,451.0	23	75.5	29		0.0

		Company	Country											
15	14	Australian Mutual Provident*	Australia	49,756.8	8.6	129,109.1	29	6,373.1	21	3,036.4	16	3,241.3	6	4.3
16	18	Standard Life*	Britain	45,623.3	22.7	36,722.1	41	5,873.2	25	2,499.7	21	4,246.8	3	7.6
17	16	New York Life*	U.S.	42,749.5	7.2	311,532.2	15	7,646.1	15	3,299.1	13	221.3	24	1.1
18	19	Chiyoda Mutual Life*,c	Japan	42,291.8	15.4	422,974.4	12	7,226.2	19	2,350.9	27	837.8	15	(9.1)
19	17	Connecticut General Life	U.S.	41,692.3	11.5	421,375.7	13	4,724.0	30	2,403.1	24	453.5	2	85.4
20	20	Taiyo Mutual Life*,c	Japan	39,092.7	13.5	147,938.1	25	8,937.8	12	2,213.4	29	515.7	17	(13.4)
21	21	Toho Mutual Life*,c	Japan	38,508.5	14.0	267,036.7	18	8,563.7	13	1,191.0	41	411.8	19	(33.5)
22	22	John Hancock Mutual Life*	U.S.	36,220.2	7.3	246,162.0	20	5,947.0	24	2,601.7	18	209.0	25	1.4
23	26	Legal & General	Britain	36,172.4	22.0	NA		3,716.0	37	3,762.5	11	36.1	14	(76.7)
24	24	Northwestern Mutual Life*	U.S.	35,743.8	13.9	251,128.8	19	4,678.2	31	2,536.9	20	538.5	16	275.0
25	23	Travelers	U.S.	35,662.7	8.0	214,870.8	22	7,626.0	16	2,577.0	19	191.7	6	23.3
		Totals		2,372,375.2		18,464,063.2		414,830.2		138,573.9		48,572.8		

Source: Reprinted, with permission, from *Fortune,* 24 August 1992.

Note: Date for all U.S. companies are calculated on the statutory accounting basis required by state insurance regulatory authorities.

NA = Not available

• = Not on previous year's list.

cGovernment owned.

*Indicates a mutual company.

aAs of 31 December 1991, unless otherwise noted.

bFace value of all life policies, including variable life insurance, as of fiscal year-end.

cIncludes premium income from life, accident, and health policies, annuities, and contributions to deposit administration funds.

dAfter dividends to policyholders and income taxes, excluding realized capital gains and losses. Figures in parentheses indicate a loss.

eFigures are for fiscal year ended 31 March 1992.

Table 2–8 World Bank Ranking by Pre-Tax Profits

Rank	1980[a]	1985[b]	1991
1	Barclays	Citicorp	Industrial & Comm'l Bank of China
2	National Westminster	Banco de Brasil	Deutsche
3	Bank of America	National Westminster	Sumitomo
4	Citicorp	Barclays	Bank America Corp
5	Midland	Ratidain Bank	Hongkong Bank Group
6	Deutsche	JP Morgan	Crédit Agricole
7	Lloyds	Royal Bank of Canada	Sanwa
8	Chase	Chase	Bank of China
9	Banque Nationale de Paris	Sumitomo	Banco Bilboa Vizcaya
10	Banco do Brasil	Deutsche	JP Morgan

Source: The Banker, July 1992.

[a]1980 excludes Japanese banks and Crédit Agricole.
[b]1985 excludes Crédit Agricole.

performance measures, if only due to accounting and disclosure differences (e.g., hidden "reserves" in German banks).

Recall the variegated picture presented in Table 2–1, which compares U.S. banks and securities firms across various performance criteria using a number of measures. Additional criteria also present a mixed picture. Table 2–11 ranks banks by market capitalization. It shows no U.S. banking institution in the world's top 25 as of mid-1991. The table also provides information from published sources on the market to book ratio, relative price/earnings (P/Es), book equity, net income in U.S. dollars, and profitability. Table 2–12 traces the equity to asset ratio—a key indicator

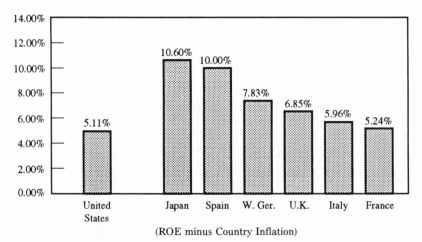

(ROE minus Country Inflation)

Figure 2–4 Rates of return in selected countries. Real return on equity (ROE), 1984–88. (Data: IBCA, Ltd. 1989)

Table 2-9 International Bank Composites—Returns on Assets and Equity, 1981–90

	1981	1982	1983	1984	1985	1986	1987	1988	1989	1990
	Net Income as a Percentage (%) of Average Earning Assets									
Australian Bank Composite	1.16	1.04	0.90	1.07	1.03	0.90	0.79	1.10	1.01	0.73
British Bank Composite	0.95	0.67	0.58	0.36	0.58	0.79	(0.17)	1.06	0.01	0.26
French Bank Composite	0.33	0.23	0.19	0.19	0.23	0.33	0.35	0.43	0.47	0.35
Hongkong and Shanghai Banking Corp.[a]	0.97	0.88	0.79	0.73	0.72	0.65	0.60	0.58	0.63	0.36
Japanese Bank Composite	0.27	0.24	0.28	0.25	0.27	0.29	0.33	0.37	0.28	0.22
Spanish Bank Composite	—	—	—	—	0.83	0.90	0.99	1.23	1.28	1.13
Swiss Bank Composite	0.42	0.42	0.45	0.57	0.62	0.62	0.56	0.54	0.57	0.44
U.S. Money Center Bank Composite	0.63	0.63	0.74	0.69	0.78	0.81	0.84[b]	1.16	0.74	0.36
West German Bank Composite[a]	0.13	0.15	0.26	0.26	0.34	0.33	0.27	0.33	0.35	0.30
	Net Income as a Percentage (%) of Average Equity									
Australian Bank Composite	18.9	18.4	16.6	18.6	16.7	14.6	12.6	11.7	13.1	10.0
British Bank Composite	17.2	13.1	11.3	7.9	13.4	16.6	(3.8)	18.0	0.1	4.7
French Bank Composite	14.1	10.7	9.5	9.5	11.5	13.3	10.9	13.0	14.1	9.4
Hongkong and Shanghai Banking Corp	17.5	15.9	14.4	12.9	12.8	12.7	12.0	12.7	10.9	6.7
Japanese Bank Composite	9.9	9.5	11.5	10.7	11.1	11.9	13.4	14.1	9.5	6.4
Spanish Bank Composite	—	—	—	—	14.7	16.0	17.4	21.7	21.5	17.4
Swiss Bank Composite	7.0	7.4	8.2	8.8	9.3	9.1	8.1	13.0	14.1	9.4
U.S. Money Center Bank Composite	14.2	13.7	14.1	12.8	13.9	13.7	15.9[b]	21.5	12.6	6.5
West German Bank Composite	4.3	4.9	8.7	8.6	10.5	14.6	7.5	9.3	9.3	8.2

Source: Salomon Brothers, Inc., *Bank Annual* (New York: Salomon Brothers, Inc., 1992).

[a]As a percentage of average total assets.
[b]Based on operating earnings.

Table 2-10   World's Top 10 Banks in Terms of Real
Profitability, 1991

Rank		Real Profitability Index [a]
1	Banco Popular Espanol, Spain	1,398
2	Banc One, U.S.	1,300
3	Banco Santander, Spain	1,254
4	Banco Bilbao Vizcaya, Spain	1,224
5	Bankers Trust New York, U.S.	1,223
6	Norwest, U.S.	1,218
7	Bank of China, China	1,217
8	JP Morgan, U.S.	1,216
9	Suntrust Banks, U.S.	1,215
10	Bank of Taiwan, Taiwan	1,196

Source: IBCA, Ltd., 1992

[a]Based on return on equity, adjusted for differing capital ratios, inflation,
and tax rates, global industry average = 1,029.

not only of bank safety and soundness, but also regulatory and bank ownership differences—for U.S. and foreign banking composites throughout
the 1980s. Here again, U.S. money center banks fall into the middle
range.

Performance of Financial Services Firms Outside Their Home Markets

International competitive performance as reflected (however imperfectly)
in aggregate indicators such as those presented earlier can be divided into
two aspects—how firms did in their own home market and how they fared
once they ventured into the home markets of others. Here we shall attempt to compare the performance of U.S. banks abroad and foreign
banks in the United States.

U.S. Banks Abroad

It is generally believed that the heyday of U.S. commercial banks' growth
internationally occurred in the 1970s, which coincided with foreign direct
investment (FDI) dominance of U.S.-based multinational corporations.
In response to the growth of U.S. firms' FDI, American banks followed
their customers into markets abroad. The international growth of U.S.
banks also coincided with the growth and development of the Eurocurren-
cy markets and the recycling of petrodollars into balance of payments
lending to less developed countries (LDCs) and project financings, where
American banks played a dominant role in loan syndications. As both of
these growth factors waned (especially as the LDC financing boom turned

into a crisis after the fall of 1982), overseas activities of U.S. banks changed as well. They now had to compete head-on against entrenched foreign banks—often favored by lower-cost capital and superior credit standing—for local business as well as that of their own multinational clients. While some banks retreated from international activities generally, others shifted away from commodity-type lending in response to the narrowing of interest spreads and the need to conserve capital, as well as in response to the migration of various corporate and institutional clients to the securities markets for funds. They often moved aggressively towards off-balance sheet business, fee-based services, and profits in foreign exchange and other traded markets, for example.

Figure 2–5 shows that the international earnings of U.S. banks were often positive and rising during the 1980s once the impact of LDC loan write-downs have been taken into account. Figure 2–6 indicates that international dollar assets of U.S. banks declined during the same period as interbank lending in the Euromarket dropped and local currency lending in foreign markets increased, presumably reflecting corresponding differences in spreads.

The international assets of U.S. banks are highly concentrated, both geographically and institutionally. Borrowers in Organization for Economic Cooperation and Development (OECD) countries account for about two-thirds of U.S. banks' international assets, with four money center banks accounting for roughly 55% and 10 banks accounting for over 75% at the end of 1991, according to the Federal Reserve Board.

Figure 2–7 shows that the international earnings of U.S. banks have increased significantly in terms of noninterest income, which has become

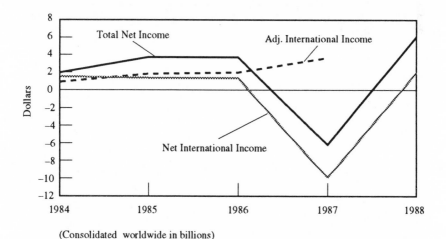

(Consolidated worldwide in billions)

Figure 2–5 Profitability during the 1980s of nine money center banks with large international business. (Consolidated worldwide in billions.) (*Source:* Federal Reserve Board. Testimony presented to the Subcommittee on Banking Competitiveness, House Banking Committee, U.S. Congress, March 1990)

Table 2–11 World Bank Ranking by Market Capitalization

	Companies		Assets $ Millions	Assets Change from 1990 %	Capital Equity $ Millions	Equity as % of Assets	Net Income $ Millions	Performance Change from 1990 %	Return on Equity %	Real Profitability	Market Value 5/31/92 $ Millions	Market to Book Ratio	P/E Ratio
1	Dai Ichi Kangyo Bank	Japan	446,881.4	-1.36	15,459.5	3.46	689.5	-7.57	4.52	1.014	34,677	2.3	53.0
2	Sumitomo Bank	Japan	428,226.6	-1.09	17,203.6	4.02	909.3	-19.31	5.39	1.025	37,119	2.2	32.8
3	Sakura Bank	Japan	421,455.0	-2.55	13,427.2	3.19	609.7	-5.92	4.75	1.015	29,047	2.3	45.9
4	Fuji Bank	Japan	420,059.5	-0.64	14,679.7	3.49	715.1	-9.61	4.92	1.018	33,991	2.3	47.0
5	Sanwa Bank	Japan	412,788.9	-3.12	14,470.5	3.51	805.4	-5.39	5.69	1.024	30,408	2.1	36.3
6	Mitsubishi Bank	Japan	401,327.8	-3.13	13,216.4	3.29	467.4	-31.23	3.58	1.006	39,839	3.0	54.5
7	Norinchukin Bank	Japan	307,741.8	16.49	1,905.2	0.62	304.9	-11.96	16.70	1.023	NT		
8	Crédit Agricole	France	307,203.5	2.40	15,042.1	4.90	986.5	6.64	7.02	1.042	NT		
9	Crédit Lyonnais	France	306,334.9	8.46	9,651.5	3.15	787.3	-10.61	8.57	1.044	4,109	0.6	6.5
10	Industrial Bank of Japan	Japan	303,214.9	-1.21	10,420.0	3.44	448.6	-10.38	4.36	1.012	34,045	3.2	74.1
11	Deutsche Bank	Germany	288,879.4	12.86	11,497.7	3.98	930.3	32.11	8.42	1.041	20,158	1.9	NA
12	Banque Nationale de Paris	France	275,876.3	-3.84	9,366.6	3.40	660.6	58.65	7.65	1.036	5,193	0.7	9.6
13	Tokai Bank	Japan	252,877.7	-4.31	8,170.1	3.23	384.6	16.40	4.79	1.015	14,590	1.8	36.5
14	Barclays	Britain	251,052.7	2.39	11,461.2	4.57	538.1	-30.84	4.50	1.000	10,979	1.1	24.7
15	ABN Amro Holding	Netherlands	242,685.9	5.55	9,344.0	3.85	912.1	12.07	10.02	1.047	6,466	0.8	8.6
16	Long-Term Credit Bank of Japan	Japan	241,007.9	6.00	8,817.4	3.40	475.7	69.44	5.94	1.026	14,607	1.8	29.6
17	Société Générale	France	234,748.3	8.56	6,860.4	2.92	711.6	25.63	11.16	1.059	7,544	1.3	12.1
18	National Westminster Bank	Britain	222,805.9	1.21	10,328.7	4.64	94.5	-75.47	0.88	0.959	10,498	1.0	NM
19	Bank of Tokyo	Japan	219,105.8	-7.22	7,733.5	3.53	332.0	-19.67	4.35	1.013	17,322	2.3	54.8
20	Citicorp	U.S.	212,922.0	-0.03	9,489.0	4.37	-457.0	NM	-4.50	0.915	6,449	0.7	NM
21	Kyowa Saitama Bank	Japan	212,940.9	-8.24	7,820.9	3.67	285.3	-25.10	3.69	1.008	13,147	3.2	44.4
22	Paribas	France	199,973.9	9.62	11,279.0	5.64	211.8	-73.16	2.06	0.982	NT		

23	Mitsubishi Trust & Banking	Japan	194,243.9	−3.09	6,417.8	3.30	264.2	−14.81	4.18	1.011	9,896	1.5	36.1
24	Dresdner Bank	Germany	189,444.5	3.92	6,500.6	3.43	430.0	−29.23	6.67	1.021	7,717	1.3	NA
25	Union Bank of Switzerland	Switzerland	181,905.6	6.59	13,266.0	7.29	911.8	35.08	6.99	1.048	12,257	1.0	14.5
26	Sumitomo Trust & Banking	Japan	178,325.9	−0.44	6,304.9	3.54	243.1	−29.48	3.91	1.010	9,050	1.4	35.9
27	Istit. Banc. San Paolo di Torino	Italy	178,078.7	38.38	6,890.4	3.87	773.7	8.11	12.88	1.062	5,857	1.6	13.1
28	Caisses d'Épargne	France	172,973.0	1.13	7,072.2	4.09	482.6	−10.87	7.17	1.039	NT		
29	Mitsui Trust & Banking	Japan	168,975.5	−0.86	5,238.2	3.10	186.7	−26.84	3.61	1.006	8,102	1.5	41.7
30	Bank of China	China	162,987.4	33.85	9,837.1	6.04	1,533.4	35.25	17.32	1.217	NT		
31	HSBC Holdings	Hong Kong	160,354.9	7.82	10,405.8	6.49	1,321.1	85.74	13.27	1.074	10,052	1.4	13.7
32	Swiss Bank Corp.	Switzerland	152,484.8	8.50	9,579.3	6.28	796.0	29.83	8.65	1.062	6,391	0.8	9.3
33	Bayerische Vereinsbank	Germany	147,306.3	9.80	3,848.5	2.61	242.5	2.08	6.85	1.016	4,925	1.6	NA
34	Westdeutsche Landesbank	Germany	146,741.1	11.29	3,360.0	2.29	148.2	298.93	4.45	1.002	NT		
35	Commerzbank	Germany	146,661.1	5.01	4,493.5	3.06	360.9	−1.81	8.21	1.030	4,161	1.0	NA
36	Daiwa Bank	Japan	142,289.0	1.96	4,564.5	3.21	237.9	−14.82	5.31	1.020	10,631	2.3	36.6
37	Chemical Banking	U.S.	138,930.0	1.97	7,281.0	5.24	154.0	−65.00	2.02	0.984	8,761	1.5	NM
38	DG Bank	Germany	135,670.2	3.30	3,470.3	2.56	195.3	0.00	5.81	1.010	NT		
39	Nippon Credit Bank	Japan	134,098.6	−1.24	4,137.7	3.09	313.1	84.89	7.79	1.037	9,236	2.3	53.6
40	Yasuda Trust & Banking	Japan	130,472.0	−5.03	4,158.8	3.19	174.6	−12.78	4.26	1.011	7,399	1.7	35.6
41	Rabobank	Netherlands	126,900.7	7.50	7,612.8	6.00	594.0	4.31	8.12	1.048	NT		
42	Hypo-Bank	Germany	125,539.8	10.29	3,155.7	2.51	238.1	15.19	7.61	1.022	4,732	1.7	NA
43	Banca Nazionale del Lavoro	Italy	122,929.4	−4.45	5,580.7	4.54	73.8	−24.78	1.55	0.959	NT		
44	Shoko Chukin Bank	Japan	115,999.2	6.78	3,026.7	2.61	208.5	1.47	7.25	1.028	NT		
45	Bank America	U.S.	115,509.0	4.32	8,063.0	6.98	1,123.7	0.78	15.78	1.190	15,578	2.3	9.6
46	Credit Suisse†	Switzerland	114,116.6	4.07	6,689.0	5.86	689.8	70.31	10.68	1.084	5,855	1.1	8.8
47	Bayerische Landesbank	Germany	111,635.3	10.24	2,830.9	2.54	192.5	66.04	7.77	1.020	NT		
48	Royal Bank of Canada (10)	Canada	111,445.4	8.28	6,977.4	6.26	889.9	2.62	14.28	1.136	5,984	1.2	8.2
49	Nationsbank	U.S.	110,319.0	−2.19	6,518.0	5.91	201.9	−66.06	3.06	0.998	11,034	1.8	61.2
50	Toyo Trust & Banking	Japan	110,236.4	−1.45	3,534.1	3.21	136.2	−16.59	3.91	1.009	5,555	1.5	32.7

Source: Reprinted, with permission, from *Business Week*, 6 July 1992.

Note: Japanese data are for fiscal year ended 31 March 1992. Data for all other banks are for fiscal year ended 31 December 1991, unless otherwise designated. †Stock market date are for CS Holding. NA = not available; NM = not meaningful; NT = not traded; P/E = price/earnings.

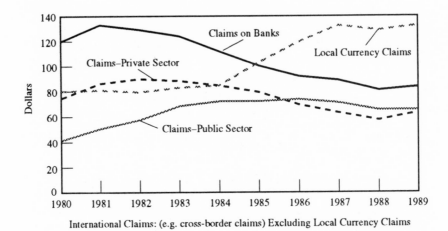

International Claims: (e.g. cross-border claims) Excluding Local Currency Claims

(Consolidated worldwide in billions/data covers 22 banks)

Figure 2–6 Composition of foreign assets of U.S. banks. (*Source:* Federal Reserve Board. Testimony presented to the Subcommittee on Banking Competitiveness, House Banking Committee, U.S. Congress, March 1990)

as important as net interest income. This reflects the growth of transactions-related fees, positioning-related profits in traded markets, spreads in swaps, and other derivative instruments, advisory fees, and guarantee fees—all of which may reflect U.S. banks' comparative advantage in services that require specialized technologies and investments in human capital and know-how.

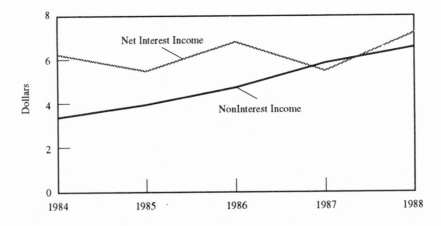

(Consolidated worldwide in billions/data covers 22 banks)

Figure 2–7 Growth in international income. (*Source:* Federal Reserve Board. Testimony presented to the Subcommittee on Banking Competitiveness, House Banking Committee, U.S. Congress, March 1990)

Table 2-12 International Bank Composites—Equity as a Percentage (%) of Year-End Total Assets, 1981–90

	1981	1982	1983	1984	1985	1986	1987	1988	1989	1990	Tier 1 Capital	Total Capital
Australian Bank Composite	5.7	5.0	5.1	5.7	5.9	5.6	5.8	7.1	6.8	6.7	6.6	10.2
British Bank Composite	5.3	5.0	5.1	4.0	4.5	5.1	5.4	5.9	5.0	4.8	6.3	9.7
French Bank Composite	2.2	2.0	1.9	1.8	2.1	2.7	2.8	2.8	2.9	3.3	5.9	9.1
Hongkong and Shanghai Banking Corp.	5.8	5.3	5.6	5.8	5.5	4.9	4.4	4.6	5.8	5.2	6.5	—
Japanese Bank Composite	2.4	2.3	2.3	2.2	2.4	2.3	2.4	2.8	3.0	3.2	4.8	8.5
Spanish Bank Composite	—	—	—	4.9	5.1	5.3	5.1	6.0	6.4	6.1	10.4	12.5
Swiss Bank Composite	5.8	5.7	5.5	5.5	6.0	6.0	6.1	6.2	6.8	6.6	—	10.4
U.S. Money Center Bank Composite	3.6	3.9	4.5	4.7	4.9	5.2	4.4	5.4	5.0	5.1	5.0	8.9
West German Bank Composite	3.0	2.9	3.0	3.0	3.2	3.5	3.5	3.5	3.9	3.7	6.4	9.8

Source: Salomon Brothers, Inc., Bank Annual (New York: Salomon Brothers, Inc., 1992).

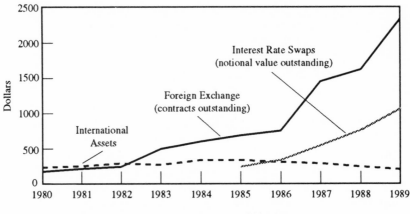

(Consolidated worldwide in billions/data covers 22 banks)

Figure 2-8 Comparison of foreign exchange and swap volume against international assets. (*Source:* Federal Reserve Board. Testimony presented to the Subcommittee on Banking Competitiveness, House Banking Committee, U.S. Congress, March 1990)

Indeed, derivatives business has assumed both large volumes and rapid growth during the 1980s and early 1990s. The volume of foreign exchange transactions and swaps are shown against the static picture of international assets in Figure 2–8, indicating the aforementioned emphasis on trading and positioning activities, especially in the latter part of the 1980s. Outstanding derivatives contracts in 1991 are depicted in Figure 2–9, both exchange-traded and over-the-counter. Exchange-traded derivatives comprise interest rate and currency options and futures, where interest-rate derivatives assume the largest share. The largest markets in exchange-traded derivatives are the Chicago Board of Trade and the Chicago Mercantile Exchange in futures and the Chicago Board Options Exchange in options contracts. The U.S. dollar dominance of these markets, illustrated in Table 2–13, has assured a number of American financial institutions a leadership position in swaps. As that table also shows, the bulk of swaps volume comprises interest rate swaps. Table 2–14 shows the rapid growth of the swaps business during the period 1985–90 and estimates for 1991–95. Note in Table 2–15 the U.S. dominance of the options business as well, suggesting strong competitive positioning on the part of American firms.

Unfortunately, there are no comparable data to indicate the record of activity by U.S.-based securities firms and insurance companies abroad. Available evidence based on staffing levels, transaction league tables reflecting underwriting of new issues in the Eurobond market, fee-generating advisory roles in international merger and acquisition activities, international investment management, and brokerage activities involving international secondary market transactions, however, suggest that the late

1980s represented an international boom period for securities firms much as the earlier decade had been for commercial banks [Walter and Smith 1989]. Much of this international growth may be ascribed to superior financial technologies developed in the United States and adapted to specific foreign environments. On the other hand, with few exceptions such as American International Group (AIG), the growth in the international activities of U.S. insurance companies (other than in the reinsurance market) have been minimal.

Table 2–16, for example, shows the relative 1991 positions of U.S. commercial and investment banks in five different activities in international financial markets—arranging international loans, lead managing international bond issues, lead managing international equity issues, lead managing international medium-term notes (MTNs), and lead advising

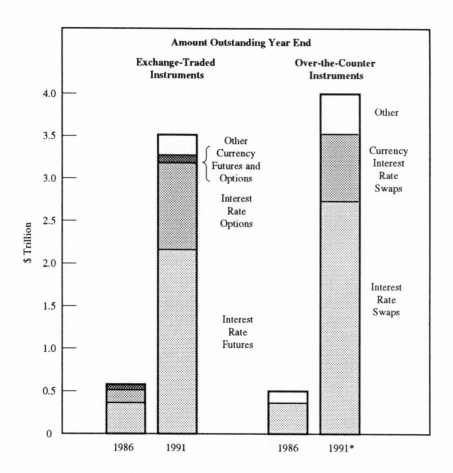

* End June Estimate

Figure 2–9 Exchange traded and over-the-counter derivatives outstanding, end-1991. (*Data:* BIS, 1985 or 1986)

Table 2-13 Interest Rate and Currency Swaps Volume

Survey Period (yr)	Survey Responses (N)	% Change	Total Interest Rate Swaps Total Notional Principal $ Equiv. ($ Millions)	% Change	Total Currency Swaps Total Notional Principal $ Equiv./2 ($ Millions)	% Change	U.S. Dollar Interest Rate Swaps Principal ($ Millions)	% Change	U.S. Dollar Currency Swaps Principal ($ Millions)/2	% Change
1987	49		682,888		182,807		541,517		81,303	
1988	57	16.3	1,010,203	47.9	316,821	73.3	728,166	34.5	134,739	65.7
1989	64	12.3	1,539,320	52.4	434,849	37.3	1,011,199	38.9	177,083	31.4
1990	63	1.6	2,311,544	50.2	577,535	32.8	1,272,653	25.9	214,178	20.9
%			(80)		(20)		(55)		(37)	

Data: International Swap Dealers Association (ISDA).

Table 2–14 Growth of Swap Activity,
1985–95 (est.)

	Swaps	
	Outstanding ($ Billions)	Completed During Year ($ Billions)
1985		82
1986		249
1987	866	388
1988	1,327	568
1989	1,973	834
1990	2,889	1,264
1991E[a]	3,200	1,416
1992E		
1993E		
1994E		
1995E	5,200	2,228
Compound Annual Growth	(1987–90)	(1985–90)
19xx–1990	49.4%	50.1%
1990–1995E	12.5%	12.0%

Data: International Swap Dealers Association (ISDA).

[a]E = estimate.

Table 2–15 Gross Turnover in Options, 1990

Country	Average Daily Dollar Volume ($ Billions)	Percentage of Global Turnover in Options (%)	Options Activity as a Percentage of Local Turnover (%)
U.S.	11.1	50.2	6.1
Japan	4.2	19.0	2.9
U.K.	3.0	13.6	1.2
France	2.0	9.1	6.3
Switzerland	1.0	4.5	1.5
Others	0.8	3.6	—
Total	22.1	100.0	2.4
			(Global average)

Data: Salomon Brothers, Inc.

international mergers and acquisitions (M&As). Counting Credit Suisse-First Boston as Swiss-American, the entire top bracket of firms are American-based, with the first non-American firm being Barclays. Indeed, 13 of the top 20 firms were U.S.-based. The top 20 had a 67% share of the total market for these activities, and U.S.-based firms, in turn, had 76% of the share captured by the top 20 firms combined.

Table 2–16 International Wholesale Banking and Investment Banking, 1991 ($ Billions)

	Intl Loans Arranged[a]	Intl Bonds Lead Managed[b]	Intl Equity Issues Lead Managed[c]	Intl MTNs Lead Managed[d]	Intl M&A Lead Advisor[c]	Total	Share of Top 20 (%)	Share of Market (%)
CS-First Boston	25.4	23.0	1.9	16.7	31.9	98.9	10.31	6.89
Goldman Sachs	—	14.5	4.6	6.8	61.1	87.0	9.06	6.06
Citicorp	70.1	0.6	—	12.3	—	83.0	8.65	5.78
JP Morgan	47.2	7.6	—	—	17.5	72.3	7.54	5.04
Merrill Lynch	—	12.3	1.0	19.1	34.3	66.7	6.95	4.65
Chemical Bank[f]	63.9	—	—	—	—	63.9	6.66	4.45
Morgan Stanley	—	12.2	0.7	4.5	44.0	61.4	6.40	4.28
Barclays Bank Grp	32.9	3.0	0.4	—	6.8	43.1	4.49	3.00
SG Warburg	4.5	7.3	2.6	—	28.0	42.4	4.42	2.95
Salomon Bros	—	8.0	0.9	2.1	29.6	40.6	4.23	2.83
Shearson Lehman	—	2.0	1.1	2.8	31.9	37.8	3.94	2.63
Deutsche Bank	12.5	15.6	0.2	1.3	7.4	37.0	3.86	2.58
First of Chicago	32.7	—	—	—	—	32.7	3.41	2.28

Union Bank of Switzerland	19.0	12.2	—	—	—	31.2	3.25	2.17
Bank of America	28.7	—	—	—	—	28.7	2.99	2.00
Nomura Securities	—	25.9	0.5	0.7	—	27.1	2.82	1.89
Crédit Lyonnais	20.6	6.8	0.1	—	—	27.5	2.87	1.92
Swiss Bank Corp.	14.8	12.1	—	—	—	26.9	2.80	1.87
Bankers Trust	21.1	2.1	—	2.5	—	25.7	2.68	1.79
Chase Manhattan	22.0	0.6	—	—	3.0	25.6	2.67	1.78
Total top 20	415.4	165.8	14.0	68.8	295.5	959.4	100.00	67.00
Industry totals	727.0	299.8	15.5	77.7	311.5	1431.5		
Top 20 as % of total	57.1%	55.3%	90.3%	88.5%	94.9%	67.0%		

aIFR *International Financing Review*, 4 January 1992. Top lead managers loans and Euro-note programs, arrangers only.
bIFR *International Financing Review*, 4 January 1992. Top 60 lead managers only Eurobonds and international issues.
cIFR *International Financing Review*, 4 January 1992. Top 20 lead managers only international equity issues.
dInvestment Dealers Digest, 20 January 1992. Top 15 agents. World-Wide MTMs full credit to lead agents only.
eMergers and Acquisitions Magazine, Securities Data Corp. (top 25) lead agents.
fChemical Bank plus Manufacturers Hanover totals.
M&A = mergers and acquisitions; MTN = medium-term notes.

Foreign-Based Banks' U.S. Activities

Foreign penetration in the United States in terms of bank assets has been impressive, as shown in Figure 2–10, attaining about 23% of total U.S. bank assets by the end of 1991 (including subsidiaries). The principal vehicles have been branches and agencies, as opposed to separately incorporated subsidiaries. The largest share (50% of the foreign banks' share) is accounted for by Japanese banks, with assets of almost $430 billion at year-end 1991. Indeed, if all of the assets and liabilities of the branches, agencies, and subsidiaries of Japanese banks were consolidated into individual pro forma balance sheets at the end of the 1980s, six Japanese banks would be among the top 30 U.S. bank holding companies and several would be within striking distance of the top 10 [Corrigan 1990].

Foreign banks from an array of countries are active in U.S. interbank and business lending, attaining a 45% market share by 1991 as indicated

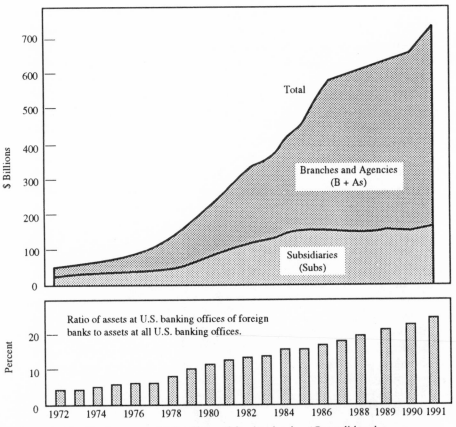

Figure 2–10   Total assets at U.S. offices of foreign banks. (Consolidated worldwide in billions.) (*Source:* Federal Reserve Board)

in Table 2–17. Much of this was booked at offshore offices. Trade finance, project financing, credit guarantees and backstops, private banking as well as securities business comprise their range of activities. Fifteen foreign banks—including all the principal German and Swiss universals—were grandfathered under the 1978 International Banking Act and have both banking and securities affiliates in the United States. Few, however, have exploited their grandfathered status with a great deal of success, presumably because of thin placing power among U.S. investors in relation to the "bulge bracket" domestic investment banks.

As has been true of other investment banking markets as well, becoming a major player in a local capital market abroad in competition against concentrated indigenous firms is extraordinarily difficult. Table 2–18 illustrates that concentration and the difficulties foreign-based firms face in breaking into the top bracket of the league tables. The table covers U.S. underwriting of debt and equity instruments, U.S. private placement of securities with institutional investors, global M&A advisory services, arrangement of international loans to U.S. companies and U.S. affiliates of foreign companies, and arranging of MTN programs. Note that the top 20 firms have nearly a 72% share of all firms engaged in these activities, with foreign-based firms accounting for zero market share among the top 20—unless First Boston is assigned the role of foreign-controlled firm.

Many foreign banks and securities firms base their activities on dealings with companies from their home countries that are active in the United States—resulting in a large international share in their U.S. business profile, in part because some (mainly Japanese financial firms) are constrained at home from doing some of the kinds of business they can do in the United States. For example, the Big Four Japanese securities firms have developed a significant presence in the New York fixed-income market during the 1980s, propelled by their superior ability to sell American bonds to Japanese investors and portfolio managers. None, however, made significant inroads in underwriting new issues in the American market, M&A advisory work, secondary market trading, or investment management for American clients. Foreign securities firms have funded themselves mostly in the U.S. bank market, representing about 80% of their liabilities.

In the insurance sector, apart from the general international character of commercial risk insurance and the reinsurance market, foreign activity appears so far to be limited to individual acquisitions of U.S. insurance companies. The largest among these was the acquisition in 1988 of the Farmers Group of insurance companies by BAT Industries of the United Kingdom, which added to its insurance and financial services holdings comprising Eagle Star Insurance and Allied Dunbar PLC, and acquisition of a significant stake (up to 49%) in Equitable Life (the fourth largest U.S. mutual insurer) by France's AXA Group, forced to demutualize in order to shore-up its depleted capital. Given the troubled financial state of several major U.S. insurance companies, it may be only a matter of time before

Table 2-17 Foreign Bank Share of U.S. Commercial and Industrial Loan Market ($ Billions, Except as Noted)

	1983	1984	1985	1986	1987	1988	1989	1990	1991-I	1991-II	1991-III	1991-IV
Commercial and industrial loans to U.S. addressees	467	512	556	623	654	712	765	803	797	786	782	777
Loans by U.S.-owned banks	381	402	419	454	445	464	481	477	466	453	440	428
Onshore	364	382	401	439	431	446	460	454	443	430	417	407
Offshore	17	20	18	15	15	18	21	22	23	23	23	22
Loans by foreign-owned banks[a]	86	110	137	169	209	248	284	327	332	333	342	348
Onshore	66	78	92	109	130	153	168	179	185	186	191	196
Estimated offshore[b]	20	31	45	60	79	95	116	148	146	148	151	152
Memo: Foreign Share (%)	18	21	25	27	32	35	37	41	42	42	44	45
Onshore	14	15	17	18	20	21	22	22	23	24	24	25
Offshore	4	6	8	10	12	13	15	18	18	19	19	20

Sources: Bank for International Settlements; Federal Financial Institutions Examination Council, Reports of Condition; Federal Reserve Form 2951; *Federal Reserve Bulletin,* Statistical Table 4.3; Federal Reserve Bank of New York staff estimates.

Note: Banks in the United States include all banking institutions that file Reports of Condition with the Federal Financial Institutions Examinations Council. Numbers may not add due to rounding.

aIncludes branches, agencies, and subsidiaries with at least 10% foreign ownership.

bThese figures are estimated in two steps. We calculate the commercial and industrial proportion of total claims on nonbanks of branches and agencies of foreign banks in the United States. Then, assuming that the offshore proportion is the same, we apply this fraction, 60%, to the offshore claims on U.S. nonbanks of foreign banks. Also, 1991-I Bahamian and 1991-I and 1991-II Cayman Islands' figures for lending are carried over from end-1990.

Table 2-18 U.S. Firms Wholesale Banking and Investment Banking, 1991 ($ Billions)

	U.S. Under-Writing[a]	U.S. Private Placements[b]	Global M&A Advisory[c]	Intl Loans Arranged[d]	MTNs Lead Mgd[e]	Total	Share of Top 20 (%)	Share of Market (%)
Merrill Lynch	100.9	8.2	21.5	—	67.7	198.3	15.2	10.9
Goldman Sachs	71.2	13.0	36.0	—	25.2	145.4	11.1	8.0
First Boston	58.4	9.4	26.8	25.4	19.1	139.1	10.6	7.6
Lehman Bros	69.1	5.6	21.1	—	15.6	111.4	8.5	6.1
Morgan Stanley	48.8	7.2	27.2	—	20.3	103.5	7.9	5.7
Salomon Bros.	46.3	8.1	21.8	—	11.9	88.1	6.7	4.8
Citicorp	4.7	5.5	2.2	70.1	—	82.5	6.3	4.5
JP Morgan	9.7	6.3	10.7	47.2	1.5	75.4	5.8	4.1
Chemical Bank[f]	—	5.8	—	63.9	—	69.7	5.3	3.8
Kidder Peabody	50.9	4.6	2.6	—	1.2	59.3	4.5	3.3
Bear Sterns	33.9	2.2	—	—	1.7	37.8	2.9	2.1
Bank of America	—	1.5	—	28.7	3.0	33.2	2.5	1.8
Chase Securities	3.3	4.1	2.4	22.0	—	31.8	2.4	1.7
Bankers Trust	—	2.8	2.3	21.1	0.6	26.8	2.0	1.4

Table 2-18 U.S. Firms Wholesale Banking and Investment Banking, 1991 ($ Billions) (Continued)

	U.S. Under-Writing[a]	U.S. Private Placements[b]	Global M&A Advisory[c]	Intl Loans Arranged[d]	MTNs Lead Mgd[e]	Total	Share of Top 20 (%)	Share of Market (%)
Lazard Houses	—	—	21.0	—	—	21.0	1.7	1.2
Donaldson, Lufkin	11.5	1.8	6.2	—	—	19.5	1.5	1.1
Prudential Securities	17.2	0.2	1.5	—	0.3	19.2	1.5	1.1
Paine Webber	11.1	3.0	3.9	—	0.3	18.3	1.4	1.0
Smith Barney	6.2	1.4	5.8	—	—	13.4	1.1	0.8
North Carolina National Bank	—	—	—	12.5	—	12.5	1.0	0.7
Total Top 20	543.2	90.7	213.0	290.9	168.4	1306.2	100.00	71.8
Industry Totals	588.9	110.4	218.7	727.0	174.3	1819.3		
Top 20 as % of total	92.2%	82.2%	97.4%	40.0%	96.6%	71.8%		

aSecurities Data Corp. Full credit to lead manager (top 25).

bInvestment Dealers Digest, 9 March 1992. Top 20 (full credit to lead manager).

cSecurities Data Corp. Top 25 U.S. targets only.

dIFR International Financing Review, 4 January 1992. Top 50 lead managers.
All loans and nifs, arrangers only.

eInvestment Dealers Digest, 20 January 1992, Top 15 agents, domestic programs (full credit to lead agent).

fChemical Bank plus Manufacturers Hanover totals.

M&A = mergers and acquisitions; MTNs = medium-term notes.

other European insurers, such as Allianz Versicherungs AG of Germany, make major acquisitions.

The U.S. banking industry and, to the extent evidence is available, the securities and insurance industries thus present a mixed picture with regard to conventional market share and related indicators vis-à-vis foreign-based banks. The key issue is whether and how these indicators would change if the U.S. lifted domestic geographic and activity-based limits, thereby permitting the development of truly universal financial institutions at home.

Determinants of Competitive Performance

An array of factors seem to explain the competitive performance results discussed earlier, and will determine the fate of U.S.-based financial firms in terms of their ability to compete globally with players headquartered in other countries and subject to different economic and regulatory conditions. Some of these are imbedded in the economic environment; others are managerial and strategy-oriented. Still others can be traced to the regulatory overlay. Table 2–19 gives a national summary of 15 factors that may affect the international competitive performance of financial services firms. The major factors are discussed in this section, and the last among them is the focus of the balance of this chapter.

Funding Access and Related Issues

Given relatively thin U.S. and U.K. savings rates compared to those in continental Europe and Japan, American and British financial institutions that are active internationally may carry an inherent competitive disadvantage in tapping into the savings end of the international flow of funds spectrum sketched out in Figure 2–1. Table 2–20 indicates the size of the differences in savings rates across the principal OECD countries for 1990. Figure 2–11 indicates differences in investment rates for West Germany, Japan, and the United States during the entire period 1980–91 (1991 includes East Germany).

Large U.S. banks that are active internationally may have to rely relatively more heavily on funding themselves in costly wholesale markets as opposed to cheaper retail deposits. While they have always been good at wholesale funding and institutional placement of securities, this pattern differs from the (usually larger) wholesale-to-retail margins available to foreign players (universal and commercial banks, insurance companies, and retail-oriented securities firms). Moreover, short-term financial markets such as the federal funds market do not exist or are very limited in a number of foreign countries such as Japan, Switzerland, and Germany, thereby giving banks based in those countries an advantage in tapping savings as against disintermediated channels such as money market mutual funds. Additionally, there are significant differences in the *composition* of

Table 2-19 Elements of Competitive Positioning:
Mid-1993 Ad Hoc Assessment

Competitive Determinant	U.S.	Europe	Japan
Capitalization	Adequate	Very good	Adequate
Book	Good	Good	Adequate
Market	Poor	Very good	Good
Credit standing	Poor	Very good	Adequate
Funding access	Adequate	Very good	Good
Wholesale	Good	Good	Good
Retail	Uneven[a]	Excellent	Excellent
Placing power	Adequate	Excellent	Good
Wholesale	Very good	Very good	Very good
Retail	Uneven[a]	Excellent	Good
Borrower access	Excellent	Very good	Very good
Wholesale	Excellent	Good	Good
Retail	Excellent	Good	Good
Scale economies	Good	Good	Good
Scope economies	Poor	Excellent	Poor
Financial technologies	Excellent	Adequate	Adequate
Product	Excellent	Poor	Poor
Process	Excellent	Good	Good
Human resources	Adequate	Adequate	Adequate
Professional	Excellent	Good	Poor
Support	Adequate	Very good	Excellent
Staying power	Poor	Excellent	Good
Cross-subsidization ability	Poor	Very good	Good
Organizational structures	Good	Good	Adequate
Cost structures	Good	Good	Adequate
Risk management	Very good	Adequate	Adequate
Home-country regulation	Poor	Excellent	Adequate

[a]Depends on type of firms due to Glass-Steagall, Bank Holding Company, McFadden Acts, and related constraints.

savings across countries that may affect their allocation, for example, an American or British preference for equities as against a German preference for bank deposits or government bonds.

On the other hand, given a continued strong U.S. spending and anti-savings bias, U.S. institutions may have an advantage in retail lending and origination of asset-backed securities, agency securities, and the like that can be of interest to investors in Europe and Japan as well as to domestic investors. The flow of financial resources into household consumption or investment in the form of mortgage debt provides U.S. institutions with the ability to originate transactions that have the potential to become securitized and sold to investors both nationally and internationally. Table 2–21 provides a cross-country comparison of household debt, indicating these differences over the past 30 years. It shows significant differences among the countries indicated, but some degree of convergence that may influence this factor in the years ahead. Table 2–22 shows the kinds of asset-backed securities that have emerged from this environment, and their timing.

Global flows of funds rooted in saving and spending patterns may thus give U.S. financial institutions an inherent retail comparative advantage at the *borrower* end of the spectrum and foreign-based institutions an advantage at the *savings* end of the spectrum. A key competitive question, then, is whether U.S. institutions can more easily get close to the savers abroad, or whether foreign-based institutions can more easily get close to the users of credit in the United States.

Economies of Scale and Scope

Size conveys certain competitive advantages on both the funding and asset sides of bank activities. For example, large size is linked to the ability to undertake major transactions and the ability to fund cheaply in the wholesale and retail markets. It may also be linked to portfolio diversification and perceived credit quality issues.

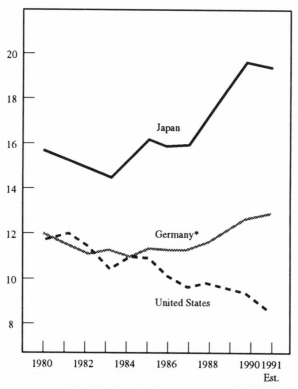

* West Germany except 1991

Figure 2–11 Business fixed investment as percent of gross national product (GNP). (*Source: International Financial Statistics.*)

Table 2-20 Gross National Savings, 1990

	Canada (Can $ Billions)	France (FF Billions)	Germany (DM Billions)	Italy (L Trillions)	Japan (¥ Trillions)	U.K. (£ Billions)	U.S. ($ Billions)
GDP	671.58	6,482.10	2,403.40	1,306.80	425.74	549.92	5,423.40
Private consumption	398.71	3,888.70	1,297.70	812.06	244.21	349.42	3,657.30
Government consumption (& Investment)	131.83	1,186.40	443.20	229.70	38.84	109.50	1,098.10
Government investment (add back, if applicable)	—	—	—	—	—	—	
National savings	141.04	1,407.00	662.50	265.04	142.69	91.00	668.00
Savings rate (%)	21.0	21.7	27.6	20.3	33.5	16.5	12.3

Source: IMF, International Financial Statistics. Washington, D.C.: IMF, February 1992.

GDP = gross domestic product.

Table 2–21 Household Debt as a
Share of Gross National Product
(GNP)

Country	Year	Household Debt/GNP (%)
U.S.	1963	5.86
	1970	2.57
	1980	4.03
	1989	5.56
Germany	1963	0.81
	1970	0.62
	1980	0.80
	1985	0.67
Japan	1963	4.65
	1970	6.12
	1980	5.70
	1990	7.28
U.K.	1963	4.07[a]
	1971	4.62[a]
	1980	4.61[a]
	1990	8.65[a]

Data: Organization for Economic Cooperation
and Development.

[a]Household debt as a share of gross domestic
product.

Table 2–22 Securitized Asset
Classes

1970	Mortgages
1985	Autos
	Boats
	Equipment leases
1986	Recreational vehicles
	Light trucks
1987	Credit cards
	Comsumer loans
	Trucks
	Trade receivables
1988	Affiliate notes
	Insurance policy loans
	Hospital receivables
1989	Home equity loans
	Time shares
	Junk bonds
1990+	Middle market commercial and industrial loans
	Developing country debt

It is important to note that asset size is severely limited as a measure of the kinds of competitiveness variables that are supposed to be linked to firm size, and it is difficult to avoid comparing apples and oranges. Nevertheless, these measures are commonly used both in industry and political circles; they are presented here in that context.

Assuming it is correctly measured, institutional size may also be linked to the ability to achieve economies of scale in financial activities. Empirical evidence from the U.S. banking experience has generally suggested that economies of scale in producing financial services flattens out at size levels well below some of the larger international competitors that exist today [Clark 1988]. Nor does there appear to be much evidence that U.S. financial institutions with international aspirations suffer significantly from scale deficiency. Recent evidence, on the other hand, suggests that "economies of super-scale" may well be achieved in the case of very large financial institutions (see Chapter 3).

On the negative side, size brings with it the potential for complexity and inertia that can be a serious disadvantage in dynamic financial markets. Figures 2–12 and 2–13 show average bank assets and their growth, respectively, for major countries.

Residual domestic banking and securities activity constraints and market penetration barriers, especially with respect to the insurance industry, limit the development of true U.S.-based universals. If scope and cross-selling (as well as super-scale) benefits are indeed significant, this may represent a competitive disadvantage of U.S. banks with respect to the European and Japanese financial institutions. The issue is discussed in detail, conceptually and empirically, in Chapter 3, which presents some new evidence on this topic.

Capitalization

The Bank for International Settlements (BIS) risk-based capital standards will do much to level the international playing field with respect to book capital among banks—although there remains the problem of "hidden reserves," varying capital adequacy standards between banks, securities firms, and insurance companies (discussed in more detail later) and their competitive impact in cases where the different strategic groups meet. In 1992, the top four banks in France had risk-based BIS capital ratios ranging from 8.7% to 9.0%, while two of Germany's top three banks had levels of 8.1% and 10.7%. Japan's top seven banks had ratios ranging from 7.9% to 8.8%, and three of the U.K.'s clearing banks had between 8.7% and 9.7%. In the United States, four major banks had ratios ranging from 9.1% to 10.8%, and only Citicorp—with a capital ratio of 7.5% in 1992—appeared to be struggling to reach the required level.

Nevertheless, for most of the 1980s U.S. institutions were seriously

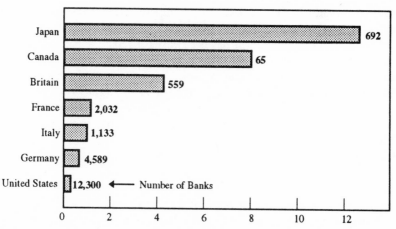

Figure 2–12 Average assets per bank, $Billions, end-1990. (*Data:* Bank of America)

disadvantaged by poor market capitalization. This meant that foreign-based financial institutions could undertake transactions and make strategic moves more easily and quickly than were often possible for their U.S. competitors. High P/E ratios for foreign banks also served as useful protection against unwanted takeover bids.

In addition to the aforementioned consideration, high P/E ratios are significant for at least two other reasons: (1) high P/E ratio banks find it easier and cheaper to raise capital in the marketplace in order to undertake expansion and grasp strategic opportunities such as acquisitions without creating unacceptable earnings dilution; and (2) high P/E ratios permit

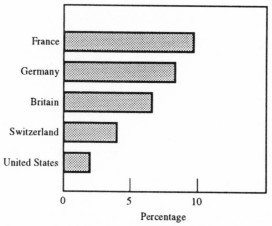

Figure 2–13 Banks' assets average annual increase, 1987–91. (*Data:* Thomson BankWatch)

sharper pricing in transactions that compete with banks having lower ratios as well as the ability to tolerate lower returns on assets. So, for example, in the recent past it has been easy for Japanese banks to expand by acquisition in the United States but virtually unthinkable for U.S. banks to do so in Japan. Simultaneously, American banks have had to cede to their Japanese competitors a variety of low-margin businesses, both domestically and internationally. However, the declines in Japanse share prices (and property values) in the early 1990s has gone a long way towards eradicating this P/E effect.

Credit Standing

With the progressive downrating of U.S. bank holding companies and securities firms, a premier credit standing has become a designation reserved for an array of nonfinancial corporations and non-U.S. financial institutions. Figure 2–14 illustrates this erosion with respect to U.S. commercial banks over the 1980–88 period. It represents an obvious competitive millstone for U.S. banks in terms of funding costs, one that is increasingly used as a competitive marketing weapon by nonfinancial institutions

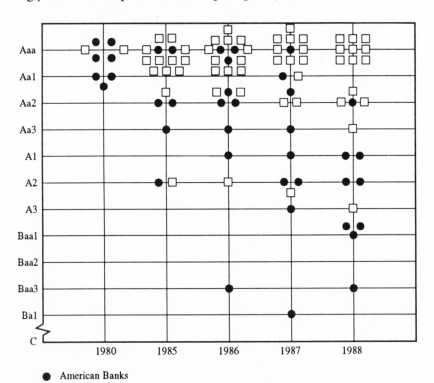

● American Banks
□ Foreign Banks

Figure 2–14 Moody's Long-Term Bond Ratings, 1980–88 (*Source:* Moody's Investor Service)

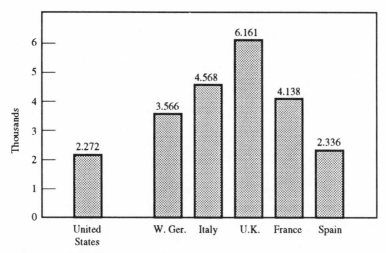

Figure 2–15 United States and European bank assets per employee, 1992. (*Data:* Salomon Bros., Inc.)

as well. The question here is how quickly U.S. institutions can digest the mistakes of the past (e.g., LDC exposures, impaired real estate loans, highly leveraged transaction loans) without taking on any new ones in order to reclaim credit standing that is on a par with the best of their foreign competitors.

Human Resources and Productivity

Productivity in banking is notoriously difficult to assess, although assets per employee may be as good a proxy as any. Figure 2–15 indicates the differences against this standard between U.S. banks and those of European countries that have universal banking systems. The relatively low productivity levels attained by U.S. banks may be partially attributable to the domestic regulatory environment, particularly interstate banking and branching restrictions that prevent optimal use of labor in transactions processing, information collection and dissemination, and various other banking functions.

In terms of human resource quality, U.S. financial institutions continue to be relatively attractive to some of the best and brightest professionals domestically and internationally—helped by a relatively "open" and "inclusive" culture as compared with German or Japanese competitors, for example. This competitive advantage may be more durable than some others.

The pace of change and an increasing knowledge content of financial innovations (and risk control) will place far higher demands on those performing on the front lines. The banking, securities sales and trading, corporate finance, and financial advisory skills required will continue to place a heavy responsibility on the banks and securities firms for recruitment, training at the cutting edge of financial technologies, and management development and succession planning. Critical will be the development of true "decathlon players" in the various sales forces. Equally important, there must be a highly performance-oriented attitude ingrained in the people on the front lines—including an open, global view, a strong competitive ethic, lateral thinking, and a willingness to accept new ideas.

Operating Costs and Risk Management

Although evidence is scarce, U.S. financial institutions appear to have relatively good control over their cost structures given the regulatory constraints under which they operate. Excess costs due to overmanning and inflated expenses seem to have been driven out of many financial institutions in both commercial and investment banking. Similarly, most U.S. institutions have a better handle on position-risk (as opposed to credit-risk) management than their international competitors, in part due to their arguably greater past exposure to financial volatility and better understanding of risk management techniques. Indeed, according to one observer, the one undoubted advantage in global finance retained by the large U.S. commercial banks consists of ". . . computer-aided risk management systems, developed in the past decade and which allow the banks to adjust their basic market positions for superior returns on equity while minimizing risk. European banks trail five to seven years behind in this technology" [Koenig 1990].

The first of these two dimensions may be a relatively durable advantage, since social legislation makes it more difficult to adapt employment-related costs to changing markets in many environments abroad, especially in the European Community (EC), than in the United States. The second is probably a temporary advantage, as foreign-based institutions eventually catch up with U.S. risk management techniques.

Financial Innovation

U.S. financial institutions continue to turn in world-class performances with respect to financial innovation on the product side, ranging from new forms of securitization and financial repackaging to embedded options and futures. The same is true with respect to process technologies, including state-of-the-art applications in information- and transactions-processing. This has been driven largely by the extremely competitive character of the U.S. domestic financial services industry. However, the half-life of excess returns attributable to many financial technologies (especially product innovations) is short, and may be getting shorter, so that sustained competitive advantage depends on a continued stream of innovations. While the innovations themselves (e.g., foreign exchange and interest rate futures) become a permanent aspect of the financial landscape if they have enduring value, the ability to extract excess returns on the part of the innovating firm evaporates as soon as the product becomes a commodity and the market becomes highly competitive.

Staying Power

U.S. financial institutions have earned a reputation in some international markets and with some groups of clients as "fair weather bankers" with relatively little tolerance for even temporarily adverse market conditions or financial problems of clients. Especially in Europe and Japan, they appear to be regarded as excessively transactions as opposed to relationship-oriented, taking the relatively short-term view that they can abandon markets or clients in tough times and later regain easy access through competitive products and pricing when things improve. Credit lines are valuable options to borrowers, and implied lines are even more valuable. Banks that cannot make credible commitments that doing business with them carries positive implication regarding future lines may suffer losses of market share in some international environments. This attribute may be linked to short-term versus long-term profit maximization behavior on the part of financial firms based in different national environments.

Organizational Structure and Adaptability

Organizationally, the adaptability of U.S. financial institutions to changing competitive conditions appears to be relatively good, conditioned by the need to adapt actively at home. Adaptability is nevertheless quite uneven among individual institutions, although such differences have made themselves felt fairly quickly in the relative standing of individual institutions. This ability will become more valuable in the future. Aspects of organizational structures have to be reexamined periodically, so that they can be bent to operational necessity more quickly when opportunities arise.

Adaptability may be one of the most underrated qualities in terms of competitive performance in the financial markets of the 1990s. To be a significant force in the securities industry in particular, management must become accustomed to the fact that this will always be an inherently unstable business, with profit opportunities appearing and disappearing across the principal business segments. It is also an industry prone to tensions between the origination, trading, and distribution functions. Each of these characteristics will place a premium on senior management vision, continuity, and diplomacy. Even greater potential tensions reside in universal wholesale banking.

Impact of Geographic, Client, and Activity Limits

The critical question from the perspective of this study is whether restrictions imposed by regulatory authorities on market access by firms in the financial services industry may have a significant impact on international competitive performance. First, barriers imposed on foreign-based firms restricting entry to national financial markets will clearly have a bearing on their global performance, as will restrictions on access to particular clients, regions, and products. But beyond this, domestic regulatory requirements such as capital ratios, deposit insurance, and taxation may also affect their ability to compete internationally—as well as domestic geographic and activity limits that prevent them from reaping the benefits of scale and scope economies and risk diversification.

The legal and regulatory constraints on banking organizations cover restrictions on branching, scope of permissible activities, organizational structure, capital requirements, deposit insurance, reserve requirements, processes for merger approval, bank ownership consumer protection laws, and restrictions on foreign banks (see Annex 8–1).

The United States is alone among major competitor countries in applying significant geographic restrictions. The same is true (together with Japan) in restricting banks or their subsidiaries from securities underwriting and (together with Japan, Italy and, recently changed, Canada) insurance. Germany alone has unrestricted bank powers in holding investments in industrial companies, subject to an EC-wide own-funds limitation. Germany is also alone in not imposing restrictions or approval processes in nonbank holdings of bank stocks. On the other hand, the regulatory capital convergence under the BIS risk-based standards is readily apparent. The picture is more heterogeneous with respect to the acceptable organizational forms, with the exception of frequent prohibitions of bank organization as sole proprietorships.

Bank mergers are generally subject to regulatory and/or antitrust review, and virtually all countries have consumer protection laws that bear on banks. Essentially all subscribe to "reciprocal national treatment" regarding the operation of foreign banks—although Japan has variously been accused of de facto violations of this market-access standard.

From the point of view of choosing the optimal competitiveness characteristics for U.S. banking organizations in terms of the data in Table 2–18, it is clear that Germany provides the greatest latitude and the United States the least. Japan is as restrictive as the United States in some respects (notably the separation of banking, securities business, and insurance), but it seems likely that the Japanese *keiretsu* form of corporate cross-holdings provides some of the same kinds of competitive advantages that may be open to German-style universals. Japan explicitly *prohibits* the holding company form of organization for a financial institution, and therefore one bank holding companies do not represent a viable type of structure in that country.

The linkage between corporate structure and competitive performance in financial services has been actively debated. For example, Herring and Santomero [1990] review the three basic types of structures that cover multiproduct financial services firms:

1. The fully integrated financial conglomerate is the German-Swiss model or "true universal." The same corporate entity may legally supply all types of financial services, but may also create separate subsidiaries or affiliates when warranted by market conditions. Management has complete freedom to structure the organization to achieve maximum competitive advantage, which may involve the creation of separate legal or functional entities, fire walls, or other forms of fragmentation. Under this arrangement, the optimum delivery system from the standpoint of competitiveness dictates the form of the organization.

2. The bank subsidiary structure is the British model or "financial universal." The core of the organization is a bank and a broad range of nonbanking financial activities is carried out through legally separate subsidiaries of that bank.

3. The bank holding company model is the "American model." A holding company owns both banking and nonbanking subsidiaries that are legally separate, insofar as nonbanking activities are permitted by law.

In terms of international competitive performance, financial institutions that are subject to different organizational forms as a result of legal or regulatory barriers may suffer against those institutions that are freely able to choose the optimal organizational form. The fact that regulatory environments that are totally unrestricted as to the organizational form of financial services firms are home to true universal banks suggests (assuming competitive markets) that structure-related sources of institutional competitiveness do in fact exist.

Limitations on bank activities can also affect risk and hence the cost of capital to banks in at least two ways—by limiting product diversification and by limiting geographic diversification. In both cases, but particularly the latter, there is evidence that the cost-of-capital aspect of competitiveness may be affected and that large universal banks may in this way obtain a competitive advantage. Failure rates among both banks and S&Ls in the United States appear to have been significantly higher in states that have imposed geographic limits on their operations than in states that did not.

Nor does it appear that the introduction of universal banking necessarily leads to monopolization of the market. In an econometric study of Canadian banking during the 1965–89 period, for example, Shaffer [1990] finds evidence that the degree of competition is exceedingly high and that the market has shown no discernible signs of monopolization, even after the structural changes of the early 1980s that further increased Canadian banking concentration. This is consistent with findings in another study by Nathan and Neave [1989], which rejects the hypothesis of monopoly power for Canadian banks, as well as for trust companies and mortgage companies.

And, there is evidence to suggest that the competitiveness of bond markets is significantly greater in the presence of commercial and universal banks than in their absence. A study of the Eurobond market in the mid-1980s, for example, concludes that by using the Eurobond affiliate of a commercial or universal bank as an underwriter, a borrower would have cut all-in issuing costs by 17.5 basis points and reduced total borrowing costs by 16.5 basis points [Macey, Marr, and Young 1987].

Conclusion

This chapter has attempted to pull together a broad range of criteria and performance data that are purported to describe the "competitiveness" of financial institutions in the international environment. It should be clear that each of these is partial in nature and must be interpreted cautiously. This is in part attributable to informational shortcomings and in part to the unique character of the financial services industry. Nevertheless, there is enough inferential evidence to suggest that the permissible institutional form does in fact make a difference. Removal of U.S. restrictions on the search for optimum institutional forms in an environment of intense international competition may well influence the competitive performance of domestic financial services firms.

3

Economies of Scale and Scope Among the World's Largest Banks

Do economies of scale and scope exist in financial services? This question lies at the heart of strategic and regulatory discussions about optimal firm size in the banking sector. From a public policy perspective, geographic restrictions and barriers between banking, securities, and insurance have prevailed in the United States, but are either less onerous or entirely absent in most of the other OECD countries. If economies of scale and scope are indeed important determinants of competitive performance, then the traditional U.S. interstate branching and functional limits may have had a significant adverse impact on U.S. banks' attempts to compete against their foreign-based rivals.

In this chapter, we consider economies of scale and scope in the financial services sector in the context of the distinction between universal banking and functionally separated banking. We sketch out an analytical framework, review the literature, and present two sets of empirical tests on data taken from the world's 200 largest banks during the 1980s. We find statistically significant evidence, among these 200 very large banks, that some enjoyed overall economies of scale, but that these economies of scale were not reflected in higher comparative growth rates. We also find strong evidence of supply-related diseconomies of scope between lending and fee-earning banking activities. These findings may be important as explanations for the competitive performance of individual banks, as well as for regulatory reforms.

In an information- and distribution-intensive industry with substantial fixed costs, such as financial services, there is ample potential for scale economies—as well as for diseconomies attributable to administrative overhead, agency problems, and other cost factors. Similarly, there is ample potential for economies and diseconomies of scope, which may arise either through supply- or demand-side linkages.

Individually or in combination, economies (diseconomies) of scale and scope may be passed along to the buyer in the form of lower (higher) prices resulting in a gain (loss) of market share or absorbed by the supplier to increase (decrease) profitability. If all other factors are held constant, firms enjoying either supply- or demand-side economies of scale or scope should enjoy faster rates of growth than those that do not. Moreover, supply-side scale and scope economies should be directly observable in cost functions of service suppliers.

Studies of scale and scope economies in financial services are numerous, and it is not our purpose to attempt a survey of the literature here. Although somewhat dated, Jeffrey Clark [1988] provides a good, short, comprehensive introduction to this vast field. As of the time of his writing, the consensus of empirical research was that significant supply economies of scale were exhausted at a relatively small asset size (i.e., less than $100 million in total deposits) and that no overall scope economies were available. Using the Federal Reserve System's Financial Cost Analysis data base, favored by many empiricists because of its homogeneity and breadth, but shunned by others because of its focus on smaller U.S. commercial banks, Gropper [1991] updates Clark's summary by finding strong economies of scale for banks with below $50 million in assets throughout the years under study (1979–86), with economies of scale becoming significant for banks up to $200 million in assets after 1982. By avoiding smaller institutions, recent studies find scale economies in evidence for banks with assets up to $6 billion [Noulas, Ray, and Miller 1990]. The identification of scope economies continues to be highly dependent on the definition of products. In studies with results complementary to ours, Mester [1992], looking at U.S. banks and Nathan and Neave [1989], looking at Canadian banks, identify strong diseconomies of scope between traditional and non-traditional banking activities. In this chapter we shall examine an international sample of banks in the light of differences between universal and separated banking systems.

As has been amply recognized by past researchers, tests of scale and scope are as problematic as they are numerous, even at the domestic level.[1] Test specifications, functional forms, uniqueness of optima, and even the standard assumption that firms exhibit cost-minimizing behavior,[2] all pre-

---

[1]We are unaware of any other study attempting to perform tests of scale and scope on an international data set, with the exception of Tschoegl [1983], who looked only at scale. See also Berger, Hunter, and Timme [1993].

[2]The cost-minimizing behavior of firms is an assumption long questioned in the organi-

sent conceptual difficulties. The limited availability and conformity of data become especially acute when the sample includes institutions under different regulatory regimes. Conclusions of any study regarding empirically observed economies of scale and/or scope in a given sample of financial institutions do not necessarily have general applicability. With these caveats in mind, we test whether economies of scale and scope exist among the world's largest banks indirectly, through growth rate tests, and directly, through the estimation of cost functions.

Growth Rate Tests

Comparisons of the growth rates of banks form one group of simply specified, indirect tests of economies of scale and scope. According to the "Law of Proportionate Effect",[3] proportional growth rates of firms should appear in the data as if randomly and independently drawn from the same sample. As Tschoegl [1983]—the only other researcher who has used growth rate tests in examining banking—notes, the law is an extreme proposition, but may not be far off the mark in turbulent environments. As he did, we identified whether systematic violations to the law exist. Tschoegl concluded that proportionate growth did indeed hold for banks in the 1970s. We repeated his tests a decade later in order to determine whether a systematic pattern or higher or lower growth is observed for banks conditional on their activities.

In addition to measures of firm size, we selected three scope-related ratios: (1) total noninterest income to total revenue, (2) total deposits to total loans, and (3) total loans to total assets. The traditional commercial bank, as compared to a diversified financial institution, would tend to have lower noninterest income to total revenue, fund its loan portfolio more from deposits than from other kinds of liabilities, and maintain a higher percentage of its total assets in loans. If any or all of these measures prove to be a significant predictor of growth rates, one could infer that, in the period under study, there was a worldwide bias based on activity structure.

The difficulty with this test is that one cannot ascribe the discovered differences in growth rates to any specific demand, market structure, or supply factors. The one fully justifiable economic conclusion is that if

---

zational behavior literature [see Cyert and March 1963]. Berger and Humphrey [1990], recognizing the problem of inefficiencies in banking and use of cost functions, apply linear programming to identify, by quartile of efficiency, the efficient production frontier for each quartile. They thereby derive what they term to be a "thick frontier" cost function. A somewhat more restrictive approach to modeling inefficiency is Aigner, Knox, and Schmidt's [1977] model that posits that the error term is made up of two disturbances—a normal and a seminormal—with the latter being interpreted as a failure to optimize. We attempted to fit the model with our data using a translog function, but failed to attain convergence.

[3]Gibrat [1957].

different (or indeed any non-zero) growth rates are exhibited, the firms under study must not be in long-term (size) equilibrium. Without a knowledge of the path towards equilibrium, conclusions as to whether different growth rates rise from scale and/or scope economies are unjustified.[4] Nevertheless, the tests give the analyst valuable insight into the development of the structure of the banking industry.

The basic growth rate test conducted here is to determine whether the first four coefficients in the expression

$$\ln S_{t+1} = \alpha + \beta_1 NTR + \beta_2 DPL + \beta_3 LA + \beta_4 \ln S_t + \epsilon_{t+1} \quad (1)$$

are significantly different from zero, and whether the last coefficient (β_4) is significantly different from 1, where S_t is the measure of bank size (we use both book assets and capital); NTR is the log of the ratio of a banks noninterest income to total revenue, DPL is the log of the ratio of total deposits to total loans, and LA is the log of the ratio of total loans to assets, and ϵ_{t+1} is a normally distributed, zero-mean error term. The growth rate is a sum of α plus βs 1 through 3 times their respective coefficients, while β_4 is the elasticity of growth with respect to size.

In order to determine whether any further explanatory power is added by inclusion of βs 1 through 3, we conducted a standard likelihood ratio test, where failure to reject the null would lead to the substitution of the expression:

$$\ln S_{t+1} = \alpha + \beta_4 \ln S_t + \epsilon_{t+1} \quad (2)$$

in place of expression (1).

In each case, we ran two statistical models suited to panel data with a sample of banks in each country over a series of years—with and without the explanatory ratios. As we discuss later, we used a fixed effects model, where α is decomposed into country and temporal constants, and a random effects model, where ϵ_{t+1} is decomposed into country and temporal error terms.

Cost Function Tests

The translog function is somewhat of an academic standard for testing supply economies of scope and scale. Derived from the maximized production function subject to input price constraints, it can be written as:

$$\begin{aligned} \ln(TC) = \alpha_0 &+ \Sigma_i \beta_{1i} \ln(P_i) + \Sigma_k \beta_{2k} \ln(x_k) \\ &+ (1/2)\Sigma_i \Sigma_j \beta_{3ij} \ln(P_i)\ln(P_j) + (1/2)\Sigma_k \Sigma_l \beta_{4kl} \ln(x_k)\ln(x_l) \\ &+ \Sigma_i \Sigma_k \beta_{5ik} \ln(P_i)\ln(x_k) + \epsilon. \end{aligned} \quad (3)$$

---

[4]For example, if the largest firms had reached and were determined to remain at their optimal size, while smaller firms were pursuing restricted dividend payout and enhanced capital raising policies to attain that size, the analysis would reveal a bias to growth among smaller firms. The same effect would be visible if diseconomies of scale gave smaller firms a

Here, TC is the total cost; the products P are indexed i and j (from 1 to N) and the unit factor costs x are indexed k and l (from 1 to M); the βs are the parameters to be estimated, and ε is an error term. Logarithms are used since total cost is the product of number of units of output and input cost per unit, but sums are easier to estimate econometrically.[5]

In our estimation of (3), the dependent variable is total operating costs of the bank.[6] We use two input factor costs—wages and interest (denoted w and r)—and two outputs—loans and noninterest income (denoted l and n). With regard to the inputs, we have not separated, because of lack of conformable data, the cost of physical capital from the interest rate.[7] Moreover, our wages and interest rates are national, not bank-specific.[8] In a departure from previous studies and in order to achieve conformability across countries and time, we used constant dollars and real rates of interest rather than nominal figures. Our choice of loans as an output (we were only able to use a single, all-inclusive category of loans because of restrictions of data availability) is in accord with the intermediation approach to banking whereby banks are viewed as inter-mediating liabilities in the creation of income earning assets.[9] But we wish also to emphasize the provision of fee-earning services as the second major activity of large internationally active banks.

---

structural cost advantage and if all firms, disregarding optimal size, pursued common divi-dend payout policies.

[5]An estimation problem occurs if one of the banks in the sample has zero output of a particular product. One way of solving that problem is to drop such banks from the sample. An alternate method, made readily accessible by the availability of non-linear routines in available econometric software, is the Box-Cox transformation [see Kellner and Mathewson 1983; Lawrence 1989; Mester 1990] $g(x)$ to all outputs x such that $g(x) = (x^a - 1)/a$, where a is held constant across all outputs. We have avoided that technique due to the lack of economic interpretation that we can give to the additional parameter a, except in the case where $a = 1$ or $a = 0$ (the levels and logs case, respectively). The a is typically estimated to be nearly zero—which implies that the relationship is "nearly logarithmic." Any large negative impact to total costs then typically accrues to the zero output. This implies a gain which, given that the dependent variable is typically operating costs, is not really available to the firms in question.

[6]This differs in some respects from other studies [see, e.g., Hunter and Timme 1991; Mester 1990; and Schaffer and David 1991], which include interest expenses as well as operating expenses in total costs. Our reason for not so including was twofold: (1) with the prevalence of liability management among the largest banks in the world, the cost of funds for loan funding is largely outside the control of banks in question and (2) the inclusion of such a term in total costs would tend to swamp the noninterest cost items of particular interest to us in the comparison of fee-earning with lending activities.

[7]We doubt, however, that this seriously affects our results, since measured capital prices are very noisy due to imperfect measurement of capital vintage and depreciation. As Sherrill Shaffer has noted to us, the cost share of physical capital is very low in banking (as low as 2–5% for Canadian banks and 5% in 1989 for U.S. banks in aggregate).

[8]Concentration of banks within money centers in each of the countries in the study justifies this assumption, while the large number of countries represented (16) allows suffi-cient international variation to permit meaningful estimation.

[9]See Klein [1972].

In the U.S. tradition, commercial banks mainly accept deposits and make loans while investment banks mainly engage in fee-earning activities such as securities underwriting and corporate finance, market making, and other trading-related activities. Most of the world's leading banks outside the United States and Japan (and, increasingly, large banks in the United States) engage actively in both kinds of activities. Our simple characterization of bank output into two products allows a rough analysis of the complementarities of commercial and investment banking. We further divided the sample according to regulatory structure, calling those banks from countries with a high degree of integration of banking and securities activities *universal banks* and banks from countries with a low degree of such integration *separated banks*.[10]

The number of parameters to be estimated in (3) was reduced by imposing the money-neutrality, cost-share restriction: If the prices of all of the inputs are doubled, the price of the output should also double. Mathematically, this requires that the sum of the elasticities of total cost with respect to factor prices equal 1, that is,

$$\delta\ln(TC)/\delta\ln(w) + \delta\ln(TC)/\delta\ln(r) = 1. \qquad (4)$$

By alternately setting the factor levels at 1 (so their logs are 0), one can see that equation (4) implies the following linear restrictions:

$$\beta_w + \beta_r = 1; \qquad (5)$$

$$\beta_{ww} + \beta_{wr} = 0; \qquad (6)$$

$$\beta_{wr} + \beta_{rr} = 0; \qquad (7)$$

$$\beta_{lw} + \beta_{lr} = 0, \text{ and} \qquad (8)$$

$$\beta_{nw} + \beta_{nr} = 0. \qquad (9)$$

By substituting these restrictions directly into (3), the following model to be estimated is derived:

$$
\begin{aligned}
\ln(TC) = {} & \alpha + \beta_w \left[\ln(w) - \ln(r)\right] + \beta_l \ln(l) + \beta_n \ln(n) \qquad (10) \\
& + \beta_{ww} \left[\tfrac{1}{2}\ln^2(w) - \ln(w)\ln(r) + \tfrac{1}{2}\ln^2(r)\right] \\
& + \beta_{ll} \left[\tfrac{1}{2}\ln^2(l)\right] + \beta_{nn} \left[\tfrac{1}{2}\ln^2(n)\right] + \beta_{nl} \left[\ln(n)\ln(l)\right] \\
& + \beta_{lr} \left[\ln(l)\ln(r) - \ln(l)\ln(w)\right] \\
& + \beta_{nr} \left[\ln(n)\ln(r) - \ln(n)\ln(w)\right] + \epsilon_{ijt} + u_j + w_t \,.
\end{aligned}
$$

Subscripts i (i = 1, . . .), j (j = 1, . . . , 16) and t (t = 1, . . . , 6) for the i th bank in the j th country in the t th year have been omitted in all variables

[10]We used Cumming and Sweet [1987–88] to identify those countries that had a high degree of integration of banking and securities services as of the mid-1980s. Such countries were France, Germany, Italy, Netherlands, Switzerland, and Belgium. The United States and Japan were identified as having a low degree of integration. Since Cumming and Sweet classified Canada, Sweden, and the United Kingdom as recently (i.e., mid- to late-1980s) allowing high integration, we classified them for our years under study as separated. Not included in their study were Australia, which we classified as separated, and Austria, Finland, Denmark, and Spain, which we classified as universal.

except for the error terms to emphasize that we are estimating a random effects model (see below).[11]

The random effects model only is used to estimate economies of scale and scope, since we are estimating the model as if the production function across banks worldwide is roughly the same. Consequently, we are not interested only in measuring how the differences from the mean in each country interact internationally, but also how the different means themselves come about.

Further simplification is achieved upon estimation because the factor prices used as independent variables are common within countries. Thus, the coefficients of B_w and B_{ww} (the difference between two country-specific factor prices) are perfectly correlated with the u_j error term. Hence, the β_w and β_{ww} terms are dropped from the estimation. This raises no econometric difficulty with respect to the tests of interest in this study since their coefficients do not enter into the calculation of economies of scale and scope.

An important issue concerns the existence of a time-invariant, smooth[12] cost function in a world where market, regulatory, and technological changes frequently bombard firms. Lawrence [1989] rigorously tests the translog function for banks against other model specifications, and shows that the estimated functions are not stable through time. Hunter and Timme [1991] identify this intertemporal instability as technological change, concluding that such change lowered real costs of U.S. commercial banking by 1% per year over the period 1980–86. We proceed with our analysis on the premise that, notwithstanding variation, cost functions over relatively short periods of time are close enough to make the approximation valid, and we model them explicitly in the error term of the random effects model (see later).

The translog is chosen because of its generality [Clark 1988]. For each output or input it fits at most one maximum (or minimum) point.[13] Considering that, as discussed earlier, at least two optimum points—one for large banks and one for small banks—seem to have been identified for U.S. commercial banks, such a function is at best only a local approximation. The translog estimates the *total cost* (not average cost) function. The standard rendition is a cubic function with a concave lower range and a convex upper range. This gives rise to the conventional U-shaped average cost and marginal cost curves, with the optimum occurring where the marginal cost curve intersects the average cost curve from below—$\delta TC/\delta y$

---

[11]The model was estimated by the method of maximizing the likelihood function using William Greene's Limdep software.

[12]In the financial services industry, where quantum changes in investment are often the only way to achieve desired levels of output using current technology, this assumption is easily violated.

[13]This is true in a second order expansion such as the one we are estimating. Problems with the proliferation of parameters in higher order expansions have led to the avoidance of such expressions unless the higher order terms are needed for their economic content [as in Hunter and Timme 1991].

= TC/y—which is the same point as that on the *total* cost curve at which the elasticity is unity—that is, $E_{tc} = (\delta TC/\delta y)/(TC/y) = 1$. Using the translog, we are estimating a cubic function with a quadratic. Hence, we have a strong theoretical reason for believing that *any* extrapolation of the function beyond its sample average values will be erroneous.

Ray scale economies are in evidence if the sum of elasticities of total cost with respect to outputs are less than 1:

$$E_{tc} = \delta\ln(TC)/\delta\ln(l) + \delta\ln(TC)/\delta\ln(n) = E_{tcl} + E_{tcn} ; \qquad (11)$$

$$E_{tcl} = \beta_1 + \beta_{ll}\ln(l) + \beta_{lr}[\ln(r) - \ln(w)] + \beta_{nl}\ln(n); \text{ and} \qquad (12)$$

$$E_{tcn} = \beta_n + \beta_{nn}\ln(n) + \beta_{nr}[\ln(r) - \ln(w)] + \beta_{nl}\ln(l) . \qquad (13)$$

To determine whether these elasticities differ significantly from unity, a Wald test was conducted using the test statistic

$$W = [1 - E_{tc}]^2 /[R_{tc}' \text{ VARB } R_{tc}] \sim X^2_{df=1} , \qquad (14)$$

where R_{tc} is the restriction vector implied by the null hypothesis that $E_{tc} = 1$ and VARB is the MLE of the variance covariance matrix. The actual restriction vector is

$$R_{tc} = [1,1, \textit{LOANS, NII, LOANS+NII, RENT} - \textit{WAGE, RENT} - \textit{WAGE}, 0], \qquad (15)$$

where *LOANS, NII, RENT*, and *WAGE* are the means of the logs of the sample values and the ordering of the terms in the variance covariance matrix is defined by the variable ordering [LOANS, NII, BLL, BNN, BNL, BLR, BNR, ONE].

Second derivative tests for loans are conducted as follows:

$$\delta^2 TC/\delta l^2 = TC/l^2 [\delta^2\ln(TC)/\delta\ln^2(l) + E_{tcl} (E_{tcl} - 1)]. \qquad (16)$$

Since the expression TC/l^2 (and similar terms for noninterest income and the loans/noninterest income cross-product) does not change the sign, and since it appears squared in both the numerator and denominator of the significance tests, it is dropped for simplicity. For loans, the restriction is

$$R_{ll} = \delta[.]/\delta\Theta , \qquad (17)$$

where [.] refers to the term in square brackets in (16) and Θ refers to the vector of 8 coefficient parameters estimated. Explicitly the vector is

$$R_{ll} = [0, 0, 1, 0, 0, 0, 0, 0]+(1 - 2Ecl)R_{tcl} , \qquad (18)$$

where $R_{tcl} = [1, 0, \textit{LOANS}, 0, \textit{NII}, \textit{RENT} - \textit{WAGE}, 0, 0]$.

The second derivative tests with respect to noninterest income are defined analogously.

Pairwise scope economies are found in the second derivative of total costs with respect to the cross-product.

The test for economies of scope is similar to the second derivative test for the curvature of the total cost function. Specifically, we wish to detect whether the expression $\delta^2 TC/\delta n \delta l$ is greater than or less than zero. The second cross-derivative is

$$\delta^2 TC/\delta n \delta l = [TC/nl]\{\delta^2 \ln(TC)/\delta \ln(n)\delta \ln(l) + E_{tcn}E_{tcl}\}. \quad (19)$$

The Random Effects Model

As noted earlier, in performing both the growth rate tests and the cost function tests, we make use of the random effects model. An econometric difficulty related to the panel data used is that relatively few years' data are spread over relatively few banks per country. Clearly, whatever pooling of the data is used, some explicit recognition of country and period effects should be made. Two choices are readily available: (1) account for country and period effects in a decomposition of the constant term through a matrix of dummy variables and (2) account for them through separately estimating country- and time-specific error terms. The fixed effects model takes the first route:

$$y_{ijt} = \alpha + \alpha_j + \alpha_t + \beta x_{ijt} + \epsilon_{ijt}, \quad (20)$$

where the ij th observation is explained by a general constant α, an α_j term that is constant across all observations in a specific group, an α_t term that is a constant across all observations in a specific year, a linear combination of a matrix of explanatory factors $x_{i,j,t}$, a parameter vector β, and a stochastic error term $\epsilon_{i,j,t}$ that hits every observation. In this case, the constants would represent country and temporal effects, and each observation would be the state of a bank at a certain point in time.

If the value of these constants is of interest—as they may well be in growth rate tests—their calculation is highly desirable. The fixed effects model's noncountry-specific and nontime-specific coefficients, however, are calculated on data (both the dependent and the independent variables) that has had its country and time means subtracted. If the comparison of absolute differences between identified groups is of interest, the use of the fixed effects model defeats that purpose.[14]

In using the random effects model, however, it is necessary to assume that the country and temporal effects are random and normally distributed. If one makes these assumptions (without doing too much violence to the facts), the result is the random effects model:

$$y_{ijt} = \alpha + \beta x_{ijt} + \epsilon_{ijt} + u_j + w_t. \quad (21)$$

In contrast to the fixed effects model, the random effects model has a single intercept but three independent error terms: One that is specific to each country constant across banks from the same country (u_j), a second

---

[14]See Greene [1990, 482] and the following for a comparative discussion of the fixed and random effects models.

that is specific to all banks worldwide across a given year (w_t), and a third that affects each bank in each year in each country separately ($\epsilon_{i,j,t}$).

A bonus from the use of the random effects model is an increase in degrees of freedom, which may permit more precise estimation. The critical assumption—and the econometric price paid for the augmented degrees of freedom—is that the two error terms are uncorrelated.[15]

Data

To perform our empirical tests, we used bank financial statement data from the Worldscope data base, which takes figures from banks' published annual reports and categorizes entries under standard terms across countries. The data cover 1982–87 for the growth rate tests and 1981–86 for the cost function tests. They relate to, respectively, 143 and 133 of the largest 200 banks in the world (in terms of assets as of year-end 1985) as of year-end 1988[16] for the growth rate tests and the cost function test. Exclusion of banks from the study was due to lack of data. An exception concerned three Korean banks. Although the relevant data were available, they were excluded because they represented the only developing country banks in the reduced sample and, as such, represented serious outliers.[17]

Fundamental incompatibilities in accounting practices and data unavailability make comparison of most detailed entries in the data base across countries futile. Consequently, we were confined to aggregate entries in the panel analysis. In order to avoid the impact of exchange rate swings that characterized the 1980s, each currency was deflated to a 1980-base value domestic wholesale price index and translated into millions of U.S. dollars at the 1980 daily average exchange rate. This technique, of course, itself introduces some errors, the most obvious involving Canada in 1982. The Canadian wholesale price collapse in 1982 led to that year's

---

[15]Specification tests were performed that generally confirmed the reasonableness of this assumption. The Breusch and Pagan [1980] Lagrange Multiplier statistic tests the null hypothesis that $\sigma_u^2 = 0$. Hence, it is a test of whether any panel effect exists, whether best explained with a fixed effects or a random effects model. It is distributed as a chi-square with one degree of freedom. Hence the null hypothesis is rejected at the 1% level of confidence if the statistic exceeds 6.63. As expected, all of the Lagrange multiplier statistics in both the cost function and growth rate tests exceed this critical value by large margins. Hausmann's chi-square statistic uses the fact that, under the null hypothesis that the random effects model is true, both fixed effects OLS and random effects GLS are consistent, while under the alternate $E[u_i \, u_j] = 0$, and therefore random effects GLS is inconsistent. A large value of the Hausmann chi-square statistic would lead to a rejection of the random effects model in favor of the fixed effects model. The critical value for the 1% confidence bound is 18.84, for the 5% bound 14.07, and for the 10% bound 12.02. On the total sample in the cost function tests, we are unable to reject the null hypothesis that the random effects model is appropriate with any reasonable degree of confidence. Hence, we feel justified in using the random effects model only in the estimation of the cost functions.

[16]Rankings as reported in *Institutional Investor*, June 1989.

[17]Inclusion of the Korean banks did not substantially affect the results.

"deflated" financial figures ballooning in a manner that logically reflects neither real growth nor real rises in labor costs. We consider, however, that such introduced errors are less systematic than those related to exchange rate movements.[18]

Wage data were obtained from the *United Nations Monthly Bulletin of Statistics* or from the United Nations' *Yearbook of Labour Statistics*. Where the wage series did not extend for the full 6 years, trends were extrapolated using the index numbers reported in the International Monetary Fund's (IMF) *International Financial Statistics*, which also served as the source of raw interest rates (period average money market or commercial paper rates) converted into the real interest rate using the IMF domestic whole-sale price indexes.

Results

Growth Rate Tests

The results of the growth rate tests are reported in Table 3–1. Positive growth rates characterized the period under study. Our results reject the Law of Proportionate Effect during the 1980s, representing a departure from Tschoegl's conclusions (1983). There is strong evidence that the larger the bank, the less rapid was its growth in the period under study. The elasticity of growth with respect to size was found to be less than one in all cases. Moreover, it was significantly less than one for asset growth in both the random effects model and the fixed effects model. Having netted out national growth rates (fully in the fixed effects model and partially in the random effects model), we are unable to attribute this growth rate effect simply to the relative ascendence of formerly smaller European and Japanese banks and the relative decline in the position of U.S. banks. It is possible that diseconomies of scale are involved in this pattern.

The explanatory power of the ratios was poor. We were unable to reject statistically the hypothesis that our ratios taken together added no explanatory power to growth.[19] Across all models, a higher ratio of nonin-terest income to total income did contribute to higher growth, but the ratio's coefficient was only significant (at the 10% level) with respect to capital growth in the fixed effects model. For asset growth in the fixed effects model, the coefficient of the deposits to loans ratio was positive and significant, suggesting the importance of funding loans with a large depos-it base for relative asset growth across all countries and years. With regard to the other ratios, however, we were unable to interpret satisfactorily the signs of coefficients due to lack of statistical significance.

---

[18]We estimated separately the models without the Canadian data and found that the results were not substantially altered.

[19]The null hypothesis of no explanatory power in the likelihood ratio test could only be rejected at the 20% level.

Table 3–1   Growth Rate Tests

Size Elasticity of Growth

	Assets	Capital
Fixed effects model		
with ratios	< 1[a]	—[b]
without ratios	< 1	—
Random effects model		
with ratios	< 1	—
without ratios	< 1	—

Effects of the Ratios on Growth Rates

	Assets	Capital
Fixed effects model		
Noninterest income/total revenue	+	+[d]
Deposits/loans	+[c]	+
Loans/assets	+	−
Random effects model		
Noninterest income/total revenue	+	+
Deposits/loans	+	−
Loans/assets	−	−

[a]"< 1" indicates that the elasticity is significantly less than 1 at the 5% level of significance.
[b]"—" indicates that, although the estimated coefficient was < 1, it was not significantly so.
[c]significance at the 10% level.
[d]significance at the 5% level.
All other signs not significant.

Cost Function Tests

The results of the cost function analysis are summarized in Table 3–2. With regard to economies of scale, a striking reversal is revealed. Although the total sample taken together shows significant economies of scale, diseconomies are revealed in that the subsample of banks with loans of less than $10 billion (1980 dollars) of loans and again in banks with more than $25 billion of loans.

A second surprising point is the degree to which this pattern is "driven" by the banks that were characterized by a separated rather than a universal banking structure. For the universal banks, although none of the coefficients were significant at the 5% level, scale economies appear to predominate among those with loans of less than $10 billion (1980 dollars) as well as for the middle-range banks. However, as for the separated banks, diseconomies appear to be the rule for banks with loans in excess of $25 billion.

Scope diseconomies between interest-earning and noninterest-earning

Table 3–2   Cost Function Tests

	Scale	Scope
Total sample	Parameter Estimate[a]	
All banks	0.96099[c]	0.30471[c]
Loans < $10b[b]	1.04892[d]	0.24868[c]
$10b < loans < $25b	0.83937[d]	0.28351[d]
$25b < loans	1.13394[d]	0.60001[c]
Universal banks		
All universal banks	1.01167	0.53999[c]
Loans < $10b	0.65236	0.33759
$10b < loans < $25b	0.88804	0.15044
$25b < loans	1.26736	0.73900[c]
Separated banks		
All separated banks	0.93757[c]	0.22494[c]
Loans < $10b	1.04881[c]	0.11858[e]
$10b < loans < $25b	0.82402[d]	0.33696
$25b < loans	1.14511[d]	0.04456

[a]Parameter estimated is the elasticity of total cost with respect to output. Elasticities less than one imply economies of scale, whereas elasticities greater than one imply diseconomies of scale.
[b]b = billion.
[c]Statistically significant at the 0.01 percent level.
[d]Statistically significant at the 0.05 percent level.
[e]Statistically significant at the 0.10 percent level.

financial services appears to be the rule. For the total sample, diseconomies prevail significantly in every bank size category. There does, however, appear to be a subtle distinction between the universal and the separated banks. Whereas for the universal banks, diseconomies of scope for the largest banks appear with a high degree of significance, for the large separated banks, there is no evidence that diseconomies of scope exist at all. One possible reason is that the largest universal banks, unfettered by regulation, have diversified to the point where supply-side scope economies associated with further diversification have disappeared.

Our findings thus confirm recent conclusions in the literature that, although economies of scale appear to be dissipated at very small bank sizes if the focus of study is smaller banks, "economies of super-scale"[20] are available to larger banks, particularly at the mean of the world's largest, but not the very largest (the five super-sized). We can reconcile these seemingly contradictory results by citing evidence of multiple optima. When our sample is divided into three roughly equal groups based on loan amounts, we find that the group having the smallest loan balances among the world's largest banks (loans less than $10 billion in 1980 dollars) show diseconomies of scale; the middle third ($10–25 billion) show economies of

[20]The term is coined by Schaffer and David [1991].

scale, and the final group (above $25 billion) show diseconomies of scale. Assuming multiple optima do exist, the tests conducted on small banks and reported in the literature might have detected small-bank local optima. If so, they would interpret secondary optima away from the mean as mere "noise."

Of the studies investigating economies and diseconomies of *scope*, cited earlier, very few failed to find any economies of scope. This result is important—given the coarse nature of product definition—with multiproduct firms being represented by only two, three, or at most four outputs. If both economies and diseconomies are observed at this level of aggregation, one could surmise that more precise definitions of products could reveal more dramatic economies and diseconomies of scope. This inference is strengthened when one considers that model specification problems are sure to occur with increased aggregation. In particular, our findings lend support to the conclusion that scope (cost) diseconomies between fee-earning and interest-earning activities are important.

Conclusion

This examination of the data suggests that, using the historical evidence of the 1980s, very large banks have grown more slowly than the smallest among the big banks in the world. Also, positive supply-side economies of scale appear to exist only in the middle range of the big banks in the world, with diseconomies of scope being the rule for very largest banks. Some tentative explanations may be made regarding such apparently paradoxical findings.

In most national markets for financial services, suppliers have shown a tendency towards oligopoly but are prevented from developing into monopolies.[21] Internationally, there are relatively few cases where foreign-based financial institutions have made significant inroads into domestic markets. This suggests that gains to scale may be fully utilized in domestic markets, but may be prevented from being utilized in international markets. By looking only at the large banks across many countries, we may have detected this lack of full utilization of potential economies of scale. If this conjecture is true, considerable consolidation of banking worldwide may follow international liberalization of markets for financial services.

With regard to diseconomies of scope, the 1981–86 period was one during which institutions wishing to diversify away from purely commercial banking activities incurred considerable costs in expanding the range of their activities. If this diversification effort involved significant sunk costs (expensed during the period under study on the accounting statements) to effect future penetration of fee-earning service markets, then we might expect to see some of the particularly strong conclusions in this

---

[21]Nathan and Neave [1989] demonstrate that Canadian banks behave competitively, despite the oligopolistic structure of the banking industry there.

study regarding diseconomies scope, between lending and noninterest-related activities, reversed in future periods. If the banks' investment in staff, training, and systems bear returns in future periods commensurate with these expenditures—and if those banks that offer nontraditional banking services unprofitably retreat from the field—neutrality or possibly positive cost economies of scope will replace the observed diseconomies in future empirical studies.

The distinction between supply-related economies of scope (which we attempted to measure here) and revenue- or demand-related economies of scope (which we did not measure) also merits repeating. It is reasonable to conclude that some demand-related scope economies (and scale economies) are realizable. Interestingly, a recent study on U.S. data [Berger, Hancock, and Humphrey 1993] looked at inefficiencies across banks in different size classes and found that most inefficiencies are from deficient output revenues (rather than input costs) and that larger banks were more efficient than smaller banks in revenue efficiency. Hence, if there are zero supply diseconomies of scope (as there appear to be for the large functionally separated banks included here) the existence of demand-related economies of scope and scale would tend to make a case for greater service integration, especially if revenue-related economies were the most important as appears to be the case in the United States.

4

The Nature of Universal
Banking

Universal banking can be defined as the conduct of a range of financial services comprising deposit-taking and lending, trading of financial instruments and foreign exchange (and their derivatives), underwriting of new debt and equity issues, brokerage, investment management, and insurance. As depicted in Figure 4–1, universal banking can take a number of forms, ranging from the "true" universal bank and the German model—subject to few restrictions as to what business banking and securities can be done and how it can be done but requiring separate subsidiaries for certain other activities—to the U.K. model involving the conduct of a relatively broad range of financial activities through separate affiliates of the bank, and the U.S. model, which generally requires a holding company structure and separately capitalized subsidiaries.

Functional universality along these lines is generally (but not necessarily) coupled to permitted territorial spreads across domains covered by the relevant regulatory authorities. It may also be coupled to factors such as different accounting and legal regimes for various financial services activities. A further consideration is whether banks or their parent companies may hold or control significant equity stakes in industrial companies, on the one hand, or in nonbank financial services firms on the other. The first concerns broad-gauge issues of corporate control, while the second is limited to issues concerning the choice of organizational form in the delivery of financial services.

The two principal countries subject to major constraints on universal banking activities, the United States and Japan, have had and continue to

(a)   FULL INTEGRATION

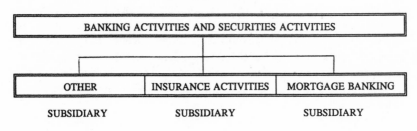

(b)   GERMAN VARIANT

(c)   U.K. VARIANT

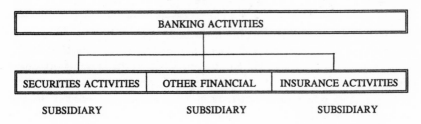

(d) U.S. VARIANT

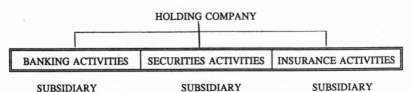

Figure 4–1   Universal bank organization structures.

have elements of universal banking in their systems. Historically, for example, the United States has had long experience with universal banking. U.S. commercial banks provided investment banking services directly from 1812 to nearly the turn of the century, and thereafter through securities affiliates until 1933. Japanese banks did as well. Today banks in Japan may hold up to 5% of their assets (10% prior to 1987) in the equity of industrial companies—about equal to the 4.9% limitation for U.S. bank holding companies—in addition to equity holdings in affiliated insurance companies. About 30% of the equity of industrial companies is held by banks in this manner, frequently within *keiretsu* cross-holding structures [Pozdena 1989].

It is useful to recall that, prior to World War II, Japan had no separation between banking and securities activities, and banks monopolized the underwriting of corporate as well as government securities under a cartel arrangement initially established in 1911—although distribution, brokerage, and related functions were carried out by securities firms. Equity underwriting and bond trading were done by the securities firms, mainly because banks were wary of the perceived risks involved. Acceptance of proposals by the General Headquarters of the Occupation to introduce Article 65 of the Securities and Exchange Law of 1947 was based on the view that underwriting even of bonds was excessively risky for banks. However, Article 65 did not place limits on bank holdings of either debt or equity securities for investment purposes.

An apparent further purpose of Japan's Article 65 was to prevent monopolization of the securities industry by favoring nonbank securities houses. This was later reinforced by "administrative guidance" from the Ministry of Finance to prevent banks from underwriting local and government-guaranteed bonds, in order to provide the securities firms with a monopoly that would help assure their survival.

In this chapter, we shall examine the properties of three sample universal banking systems—those of Germany, Switzerland, and the United Kingdom. They represent different approaches to the issue of organizational forms of financial institutions, and offer various competitive strengths and weaknesses that may appropriately be considered in any U.S. effort at legislative and regulatory change designed to introduce a version of universal banking to the national financial system.

Federal Republic of Germany

The term *universal bank* in Germany was originally applied to the major classification of financial institutions (in 1992 accounting for about 78% of the country's banking assets), whose members engaged in both commercial banking (deposit gathering and extending credit) and investment banking (securities underwriting and dealing, as well as investment management). The "universal" designation was used to distinguish them from "specialist" banks, which performed only one type of financial activity. The term does not imply that German universal banks are completely free to pursue all financial services activities. Aggregate assets held by these two major classes of banks and their sectors are given in Table 4–1, as of January 1992.

German Universal Banks

There are three broad classifications of German universal banks—commercial banks, savings banks, and cooperative banks.

Table 4–1 Size of Assets of German Banks by Type

Universal Banks	January 1992				1980	
	Assets (DM Millions)	% of Bank Assets	No. of Banks	% of Nos. of Banks	Assets (DM Millions)	% of Bank Assets
Commercial Banks						
Grossbanken[a]	524,340	9.40	4	.10	225,325	9.58
Regional and other commercial banks	786,086	14.15	197	4.50	249,550	10.61
Branches of foreign banks	74,079	1.33	60	1.39	44,520	1.89
Private banks	70,044	1.26	82	1.90	34,918	1.49
Total commercial bank	1,454,549	26.14	343	7.89	554,313	23.57
Savings Bank System						
Regional and giro institutions[b]	849,214	15.28	11	.26	382,512	16.27
Savings banks	1,154,456	20.78	736	17.12	518,959	22.07
Total savings bank system	2,003,670	36.06	747	17.38	901,471	38.34
Cooperative Bank System						
Regional institutes of credit cooperatives[c]	193,660	3.48	4	.10	100,745	4.28
Cooperative banks	633,869	11.41	3,152	73.40	256,872	10.92
Total cooperative bank system	827,529	14.89	3,156	73.50	357,617	15.20
Universal banks subtotal	4,285,748	77.14	4,197	98.92	1,813,401	77.12
Special Function Banks						
Mortgage Banks						
Private	491,723	8.85	28	.65	198,691	8.45
Public	131,756	2.37	7	.16	120,218	5.11
Total mortgage banks	623,479	11.22	35	.81	318,909	13.56
Other special function banks	646,157	11.63	17	.40	218,950	9.31
Special function Banks Subtotal	1,269,636	22.85	52	1.21	537,859	22.88
Total for all Banks	5,555,384	100.00	4,298	100.00	2,351,260	100.00

Source: Monthly Report of the Deutsche Bundesbank, November 1989 and March 1992.

[a]Grossbanken include Deutsche Bank, Commerzbank, Dresdner Bank and their Berlin subsidiaries.
[b]Regional giro institutions include Deutsche Gironzentrale.
[c]Regional institutes of credit cooperatives includes Deutsche Genossenshaftsbank.
Note: Totals may not add due to rounding.

Commercial Banks

German *Grossbanken* ("big banks") initially took shape in the early 1800s, during the country's initial period of industrialization, and they have remained a dominant force ever since, despite efforts by the Allies in the immediate postwar period to break them up as part of a policy to reduce the power of German industry and what were then regarded as its banking sector tools.

The *Grossbanken* today include Deutsche Bank (the country's largest, with assets of DM 449 billion at year-end 1991), Dresdner Bank (DM 295 billion), and Commerzbank (DM 227 billion). These are the institutions that are most often cited when the subject of German universal banking is raised.

The Big Three's activities span virtually the entire range of commercial and investment banking throughout the Federal Republic of Germany, now encompassing as well the former German Democratic Republic. Under German banking statutes, all activities can be carried out within the structure of the parent bank except for insurance, mortgage banking, building savings (*bauspar*) activities, and mutual funds, which require legally separate subsidiaries. Thus, although they are prevented from directly engaging in the large German mortgage-backed bond and insurance businesses, all have subsidiaries and/or holdings in financial service companies engaged in these restricted activities. The Big Three's major activities include retail deposit gathering, lending, investments, current accounts, discounting, brokerage, custody, and transactions services, as well as underwriting and distributing equity shares and fixed-income securities in which they both dominate domestically and have a strong presence in the Euromarkets.

Regional banks in Germany range in size from very large to quite small. They include two large Munich-based banks (just slightly smaller than Commerzbank)—Bayerische Vereinsbank and Bayerische Hypotheken und Wechsel-Bank—which are licensed to operate as mortgage banks in addition to the normal range of universal banking activities. With the exception of the Bank für Gemeinwirtschaft of Frankfurt, which has branches throughout the nation, however, the regional banks are geographically limited.

Foreign-based banks likewise carry out commercial and investment banking activities in Germany, competing with local institutions—except in securities underwriting, where foreign-based banks have been prohibited by law. Table 4–1 shows that their penetration is not very significant.

Private banks in Germany provide individual and middle-market financial services. Such banks are usually restricted as to customer, region, and types of activities they may undertake.

Savings Banks

Savings banks are arranged in a three-tier structure. The lowest level—the savings banks and their local branches—are universal only in the sense that they issue mortgage-backed securities and underwrite local government bonds, in addition to taking deposits and making commercial and individual loans, that is, they span the U.S. investment banking/commercial banking separation. Their aggregate size is significant—accounting for 55% of total German savings deposits—but each is restricted to a specific region and is prevented from making certain types of investments.

Savings deposits are guaranteed, either by the local government or by regional central giro institutes (*Gironzentralen*). Each savings bank is affiliated with one of the 12 regional giro institutes that holds its reserves and functions as its clearing bank. The largest central giro institute is also the fourth largest commercial bank in Germany, Westdeutsche Landesbank (WestLB) in Düsseldorf. Like the Big Three, WestLB has considerable Euromarket and foreign activities, including its 1989 involvement in the capital market activities of Standard Chartered Bank of the United Kingdom (which it later absorbed). All 12 giro institutions, in turn, maintain their reserves and clear their domestic and international transactions through Deutsche Girozentrale - Deutsche Kommunalbank, which has only one quarter the assets of its largest affiliated Gironzentralen.

Cooperative Banks

German cooperative banks were established as mutual societies to give support to their members rather than to earn profits for shareholders. Like the savings banks, they are organized into a three-tier structure, with each *urban cooperative bank* (*Volksbank*) and *rural cooperative bank* (*Raiffeisenbank*) affiliated with a *regional cooperative bank* (*genossenschaftliche Zentralbank*), each of which in turn is associated with a national clearing cooperative. Since the late 1970s, considerable consolidation of this structure has occurred. However, as Table 4–1 shows, it still retained about one-seventh of all banking assets in Germany as of 1990. The central clearing institution, the Deutsche Genossenschaftsbank (DG Bank), is the eighth largest bank in Germany, with substantial dealings in domestic securities, the Euromarkets, and national financial markets abroad.

Specialist Banks

German specialist banks, performing sector-, region-, and client-restricted financial services, account for the remaining 23% of German banking assets (see Table 4–1). This diverse group of institutions includes mortgage banks and building societies (active in the local government and mortgage-backed bond markets), installment credit institutions, security deposit banks, term and export credit banks, and the postal giro and postal savings banks.

Insurance

German banks are permitted to offer all types of insurance, but only through separately capitalized insurance subsidiaries of the parent banks, subject to federal insurance regulation both with respect to "fit and proper" criteria (including capital adequacy) and with respect to the conduct of business. However, only Deutsche Bank has opted to set up a wholly owned life insurance subsidiary in 1989, Deutsche Lebensversicherungs AG. It chose this particular activity because life insurance presumably has the highest cross-selling potential against other retail financial services, requires a tolerable level of capitalization, and contributes potential benefits on the liability side as well. In 1990, Deutsche Bank indicated that it had sold more than 64,000 life contracts with a value of over DM 3.7 billion in the first eight months after entering the business, although competitors suggested that this was more the result of novelty than proof that the *Allfinanz* concept works. Nor has there been any information made available concerning the proportion of those clients who were already customers of Deutsche Bank. In mid-1992 Deutsche Bank took a 30% stake in the Gerling Konzern, Germany's largest privately owned insurance group—mainly focusing on industrial business—as well as majority ownership of Deutscher Herold AG to build a sizable insurance presence in Germany.

The other major German banks have chosen to form strategic alliances with insurance companies, whereby the banks sell a range of insurance products while the insurance companies take on pension plans, mutual funds, and related financial services created by the banks. Such alliances must obviously be perceived as being in the interest of both parties. Among the banking–insurance alliances in Germany are the acquisition of Bank für Gemeinwirtschaft (formerly owned by labor unions) by the Aachener & Münchener insurance group and joint marketing ventures by Dresdner Bank with Allianz (Germany's largest insurer) in five states— with 22.3% of Dresdner owned by Allianz—and with three other insurers in the remainder of the Federal Republic. Deutsche Bank and Allianz-Dresdner are thus becoming serious *Allfinanz* rivals, complicated by 10% reciprocal shareholdings by Allianz and Deutsche Bank.

German banks have not chosen to underwrite personal property/ casualty lines (e.g., auto, homeowners) insurance, presumably because of a greater requirement for after sales service such as claims adjustment and lower benefits to the institution (especially in comparison to whole life insurance). Additionally, banks probably view the cross-selling potential with classic banking products, mutual funds, pension programs, and the like as more limited. This does not mean that such a move is excluded for the future, particularly if some of the after sales service aspects can be efficiently unbundled. The commercial insurance market in Germany, as elsewhere, is dominated by major domestic players, but at the same time it is highly international through the reinsurance market.

The German Industrial–Financial Alliance

There are three important attributes of the German financial service sector that must be understood in order to appreciate the unique German form of universal banking: (1) the *Hausbank* system, (2) bank ownership of nonbank stock, and (3) proxy voting of depository shares.

To a greater degree than in Switzerland and the United Kingdom, and to a far greater degree than in the United States (but similar to Japan), a long-standing alliance exists between the large banks and large German industrial corporations. This alliance has been strengthened by the evolution of universal banking relationships, whereby a corporation can access both capital market services (new issues of stocks and bonds, or merger and acquisitions transactions) and credit facilities from the same institution.

The Hausbank *System*

The *Hausbank* system has its basis in a business firm's reliance on one principal bank (its *Hausbank*) as its prime supplier of all forms of financing. The bank is deeply involved in company affairs and, in times of adversity, remains more committed to the continued well-being and survival of the company as a going concern than would a financial institution with a looser, "all debt" relationship. If the firm faces collapse, the *Hausbank* will often convert its debt into equity and take control, with a view to restructuring the firm or selling it to other investors. The archetype of the *Hausbank* arrangement is perhaps Deutsche Bank's relationship with Daimler-Benz AG, in which Deutsche holds a 28% equity stake.

German banks can gain *Hausbank* standing by providing all of the financing needs to start-up companies—subscribing seed capital, initiating public offerings of stock, underwriting bonds, and supplying working capital (with a rolling line of credit often constituting permanent financing) in return for the long-term loyalty of the client company—and/or by significant bank ownership or control of client company voting stock. It appears, however, that the mutual loyalties implied in the *Hausbank* system have been eroded to some extent in recent years among large industrial firms.

Bank Ownership of Nonbank Stock and Corporate Control

One result of the "German solution" to corporate financial distress has been to increase banks' holdings of nonbank shares. Table 4–2 shows the participations of the 10 largest privately owned banks in German nonbanking firms while Figure 4–2 shows the supervisory board representation of the three biggest German private banks and the Allianz Insurance Company in the top 100 German firms. Only an estimated 5% of the equity of the top 100 companies is owned by banks, although this greatly understates the influence of banks over industrial corporations, as discussed later. Also, each bank sits on less than 20 (of the top 100) supervisory boards. Table 4–3 shows major industrial shareholdings of Deutsche Bank AG.

Table 4–2   Participations of the 10 Largest German Banks in Nonbanking Firms

	(DM Millions) Nominal Capital		*No. of Firms*	
	1986	*1989*	*1986*	*1989*
All enterprises	1,748	1,676	89	101
Participations:				
from 10–25%	430	713	47	63
from 25–50%	1,277	919	33	29
over 50%	41	44	9	9
Enterprises listed on stock exchange	1,503	1,380	46	38
Participations:				
from 10–25%	287	536	19	23
from 25–50%	1,204	830	23	12
over 50%	12	14	4	3

Source: Steinherr and Huveneers, "Universal Banking," 30.

The Shareholder Trust Deposit System

In Germany, where share custody is a standard universal banking function, large portfolios of shares are often held by banks in trust for individuals and institutions. While the ultimate shareholders theoretically exercise the voting rights, in fact the voting rights of depository shares are typically exercised by the German banks through proxy voting (*Depotstimmrecht*), giving the banks a degree of control over industrial enterprises that is typically several times larger than their proportionate share ownership.

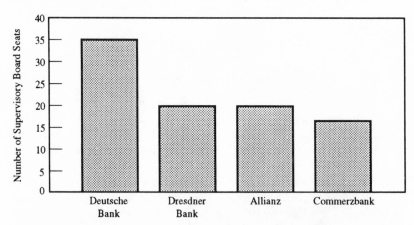

Figure 4–2   Supervisory board representation of the three biggest German private banks and the *Allianz* Insurance Company in the top 100 German firms, 1988. (*Source:* Eighth Report of the Germany Monopoly Commission, 1990)

German Financial Markets

Lending by commercial banks to German nonfinancial firms appears dominated by short-term credit facilities. The current account (with overdrafts) is the principal instrument for supplying essentially permanent working capital to enterprises, and thus is a ready substitute for term lending. Trade discounting of bills is also a prime source of credit, and these bills are eligible for rediscount at the Bundesbank.

Medium-term credits (6 months to 4 years) are often used for bridge financing. Long-term credits are usually in the form of promissory notes placed by commercial banks with insurance companies, regional giro institutions, savings banks, and regional banks.

Because the central banking authorities until 1991 opposed opening a commercial paper market for monetary policy reasons, the money market has remained almost entirely a market in deposits with the Bundesbank (see Figure 4–3). Little activity exists in the interbank treasury bill and government agency paper market. These markets themselves are small—total treasury discount paper in circulation was DM 9.2 billion in September 1989.

Table 4–3   Deutsche Bank's Major Industrial
Shareholdings

Company	Stake (%)	Value of Stake (DM Millions)
Daimler-Benz	28.24	8,579
Allianz	10.00	4,217
Munich Re	10.00	1,422
Karstadt	25.08	1,170
Holzmann	35.43	574
Heidelberger Zement	25.00[a]	480
Linde	10.00	463[b]
KHD	41.48	353[b]
Bergmann Elektrizitäts	36.46	352
Horten	25.00	263[b]
Metallgesellschaft	7.30[c]	254
Südzucker	23.05	213[b]
Hapag Lloyd	12.50	96[b]
Leonische Draht	21.50[a]	28[b]
Krauss Maffei	10.00	22[b]
Leifheit	10.00	18[b]
Phoenix	10.00	16[b]
Fuchs Petrolub	10.00	15[b]
Total		18,535

Source: Deutsche Bank Prospectus.

Note: Values correct at 30 November 30 1989.
[a]approximate;
[b]12 December 1988;
[c]Indirect.

The stock market in Germany is also poorly developed by industrial country standards. It is traditionally organized into eight regional exchanges—Frankfurt dominating (70% of volume in 1992), followed by Düsseldorf, with Hamburg, Munich, and Berlin vying for third place. All stock transactions up to a certain size must be carried out through one of the exchanges. Shares in circulation in the Federal Republic in September 1989 had a total nominal value of DM 129.3 billion. Total market capitalization at that time was about $268 billion, and monthly turnover $59 billion as compared with about $800 billion and $55 billion, respectively for the United Kingdom. Of almost 2,500 German joint stock companies in 1992, shares of only 660 were listed on the exchanges. Of these, a large proportion was not traded actively. The top 10 listed companies in April 1992 represented close to one-half of total market capitalization, as Figure 4–4 shows. The fragmented German equity markets have been thin and often inefficient, although the settlement system is the fastest in Europe (2 days). At the end of 1989, the German universal banks established a screen-based information system—*Ibis*—which posts the prices of the 14 blue-chip German companies that trade on the German options and futures exchange—the *Deutsche Terminbörse* (DTB)—which uses technology acquired from Switzerland.

The German bond markets are more active, including issues of the federal government, state and local governments, nonfinancial enterprises, commercial banks, and savings banks—that is, mortgage-backed bonds. As of October 1990, DM 1,412 billion in bonds were in circulation. Of these, DM 876 billion were bank bonds (covering obligations of mortgage, cooperative, private, and commercial banks), DM 533 billion were public bonds, DM 219 billion were foreign bonds, and only DM 2.7 billion were industrial company bonds.

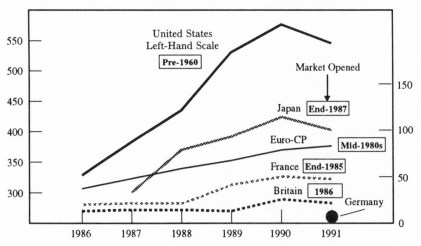

Figure 4–3 Growth of commercial paper volume, 1986–91. (*Data:* BIS, 1992)

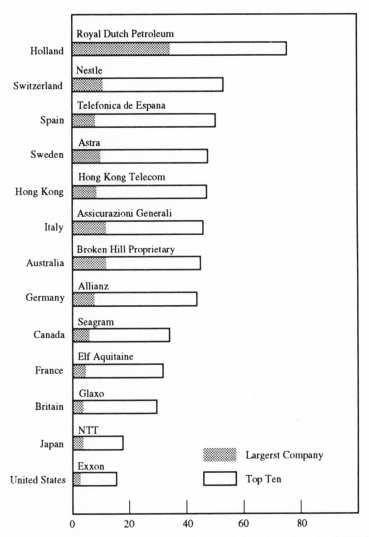

Figure 4–4 Ten biggest companies as percent of total market, April 1992. (*Data:* Morgan Stanley Capital International)

The Regulatory Environment

The *Bundesaufsichtsamt für das Kreditwesen*—the Federal Bank Supervisory Office (FBSO) in Berlin—supervises commercial banking activities in Germany in cooperation with the Deutsche Bundesbank in Frankfurt. The latter focuses on macroregulation and the conduct of monetary policy, while the former focuses on microregulation of financial institutions—unlike the joint responsibility of the Federal Reserve in the United States. The Bundesbank is charged with collecting and processing bank reports and making summary reports to the FBSO. The latter has the authority to conduct on-site examination of banks and to appoint or dismiss the auditors of the reporting banks' financial statements. The form and content of the auditors' reports is specified by the FBSO, which has the power to obtain supplementary information on demand. The FBSO issues banking licenses subject to banks conforming to "fit and proper" criteria covering capital adequacy, management competence, and a sound business plan. Although the FBSO has discretionary power to reject applications for banking licenses, it seldom does so.

The legal framework for supervision stems from the German Banking Act of 1961 as amended in 1984, which allows the universal banks to engage in all areas of activity except employee savings activities (where the employees themselves provide the bulk of the funds), building society activities (where the providers of funds acquire the right to take loans), mortgage and communal bond issuance (reserved for saving and cooperative banks), investment trust business, and insurance. As noted earlier, separate wholly owned subsidiaries, however, can undertake all of these activities.

The current prudential regulatory regime—traditionally comparatively lax and reliant on self-regulation—dates from 1974 when the Euromarkets were subjected to their first major crisis. This was the failure of Herstatt Bank in Germany, caused by losses in the foreign exchange market. Under the system now in force, aggregate credits outstanding to a single client in excess of 15% of capital must be reported to the Bundesbank. Exposure to a single client cannot exceed 50% of bank capital, and loans of more than DM 1 million must be reported to the Bundesbank on a quarterly basis. Net open foreign exchange positions must not exceed 30% of capital at each day's close of business, and total illiquid assets (land, buildings, equipment, and aggregate shares in other banks and nonbanking enterprises exceeding 10% of outstanding shares) may not exceed total capital. In addition, various ratios related to the maturity structure of assets and liabilities must be adhered to at all times, an attempt to assure that banks run a book that is relatively closely matched and constrained with respect to exposure to interest rate and liquidity risk. Loans and participations must not exceed 20 times capital (defined to include paid-in outstanding capital, recorded reserves, and retained earnings).

Mortgage lending, insurance, building and loan associations, and investment companies are subject to additional supervisory agencies. The savings bank system is subject to additional state laws. Leasing and factoring falls entirely outside FBSO jurisdiction.

German bank mergers must be approved by the FBSO and, if they are likely to lead to a reduction in competition, by the *Bundeskartellamt* (Federal Cartel Office). In practice, authorities have encouraged mergers during the 1980s in order to consolidate the fragmented savings bank and cooperative bank sectors.

Banks can access liquidity via the Bundesbank through rediscount of eligible paper, within certain limits and quotas. This is in the absence of a broad and deep federal funds market, such as exists in the United States, as a source of liquidity. For banks suffering temporary liquidity difficulties, the *Liquiditäts-Konsorialbank* (*Liko-Bank*), a joint venture between the Bundesbank and banks from all sectors, can also provide relief assuming it has satisfied itself as to the distressed bank's underlying solvency. The FBSO has the power to intervene in any German bank's activities in order to prevent insolvency, and a financial institution's bankruptcy can be filed only through the FBSO. Should a bank failure endanger the economy or the payments system, the federal government may intervene directly.

Deposit insurance is not a federal government function. Since 1966, the commercial banks have had a voluntary deposit insurance scheme funded by an annual fee of 0.03% of each participant bank's nonbank customer deposits. Coverage is for 100% of all nonbank deposits up to 30% of bank capital for any single depositor. The savings bank system, as noted earlier, has deposit guarantees extended by regional giro institutes, and a similar system exists for the cooperative banking system.

Financial Sector Restructuring, Politics and Banking

To an extent far greater than in the United States, the interests of German finance, industry, and government are perceived to be largely coincident. The need to separate capital from credit markets has never been perceived as a prerequisite to the maintenance of financial stability. In fact, the years when domestic banks have gained most in power have also been years of exceptional growth and stability for Germany. Moreover, to preserve the integrity of deposits, banks have been left largely to their own devices, with no apparent loss of perceived social welfare.

Nevertheless, three interrelated issues have tarnished the universal banks' public image in Germany: (1) Banks are perceived to possess excessive economic power, which they can potentially use for their own gain at the expense of the public interest; (2) Domestic capital markets are perceived to be relatively inefficient; and (3) German financial technology has been viewed as uncreative and poorly developed (e.g., the small number of automatic teller machines or ATMs per capita at the retail level, and a lack of sophisticated financial engineering at the wholesale level), especially in relation to the United Kingdom and the United States.

The idea that the *Hausbank*, bank equity shareholding, and proxy voting systems impart stability to industrial concerns is predicated on the theory that markets are shortsighted and dynamically inefficient, and that by placing a significant degree of corporate control in the domain of bankers, greater social welfare will be achieved over the long term. This view is supported to some degree by the argument that a strong benefit may arise in resolving information asymmetries when the bank is both an equity "insider" and a creditor "insider"—that is, the notion of an "internal capital market" that is more efficient than the external capital market

[Cable 1983]. Unconvinced tend to be politicians, the media, and members of the public, who see the banks profiting unfairly from their "insider" positions. One case in point concerns Deutsche Bank's "rescue" in late 1988 of Kloeckner & Co. by taking over all of the equity of the "failing" firm and restructuring it. Although perceived at the time as a *Hausbank* fulfilling its side of the loyalty bargain in times of corporate distress, Deutsche Bank stood to make large profits from a transaction well removed from the transparency of the capital market, while preventing others from participating in the transaction.

A second political case in point is Deutsche Bank's initiation and execution of the acquisition of Messerschmitt-Bölkow-Blohm (MBB) at the time Germany's largest aerospace firm, by Daimler-Benz in 1989. Apparently convinced of MBB's "fit" with the Daimler-Benz group, Deutsche Bank engineered and completed the acquisition, and the federal government gave its political approval over the strenuous objections of the Federal Cartel Office, evidently as a result of heavy political lobbying by the bank. Skeptics argued that the transaction (1) pulled Daimler Benz into the middle of the politically charged Airbus consortium; (2) created "synergies" of dubious value in the light of experience in aerospace by General Motors and Ford; and (3) established Europe's premier weapons supplier at a time of declining international tensions and rising concerns about the prospective European military role of a reunified German state—all coinciding with substantially greater competition in other parts of the Daimler-Benz portfolio, particularly motor vehicles. What has been viewed in this context as an industrial "blunder" of first magnitude could never have occurred, it is argued, under the transparent conditions of dominant "external" capital markets.

The conservative Christian Democratic party has strongly supported German-style universal banking as a basic contributor to German economic success, but nevertheless has focused some criticism on the big banks' rearguard actions in inhibiting the introduction of new financial instruments and markets, and the traditional role of Germany as "an industrial giant but a financial dwarf" [Delamide 1990]. The point has been made that the Bundesbank has been responsible to a significant degree for this state of affairs (e.g., by inhibiting the creation of money market mutual funds) ostensibly for monetary policy reasons—relating to the stability of the monetary demand function—but with strong approval of the German banks whose earnings such innovations could endanger.

The controversy surrounding the power of German banks thus involves four interrelated aspects: (1) direct share ownership by banks in industrial companies; (2) voting rights covering shares held in fiduciary accounts (*Auftragstimmrecht*); (3) board memberships (*Aufsichtsratsmandate*); and (4) tiering of influences through multiple bank–corporate relationships (*Kumulation*) [Krümmel 1980].

Overall, the German universal banks' direct ownership (as opposed to proxy control) of equity in industrial companies is not particularly large.

In 1976, it was about 1.3% of the outstanding shares, and by 1986 this had been reduced to 0.7% and by 1989 to 0.6%. In 1989, the total nominal value of the 10 largest universal banks' shareholdings amounted to DM 1.68 billion, as compared with the nominal share capital of BASF alone of DM 2.85 billion. Consequently, the EC's 10% cap on bank shareholdings in industrial companies may not be as important as is sometimes supposed.

The German universal banks have been prepared to discuss changes in their right to vote fiduciary shareholdings, but point out that they actually do attend shareholders meetings (unlike most shareholders) and vote in an informed manner, as against uninformed proxy voting that is frequently the case in the United States. In any case, they are prohibited from voting fiduciary shares in their own shareholders' meetings.

Membership on supervisory boards is by invitation of the firms themselves, and bank representatives are frequently called upon to provide advice on questions of financial management and capital markets. Under German law, advisory board members are required to act in the interests of the firm and its shareholders. In terms of the share of board memberships, the role of the universal banks is not large. Of 1,496 supervisory board seats among the 100 largest German industrial companies in 1988, 104 were occupied by representatives of the universal banks (114 in 1986) as compared with 729 seats occupied by employee representatives— including 187 by representatives of the labor unions [Roeller 1990]. Nevertheless, bank supervisory board memberships appear to be concentrated among the largest German firms, so that these figures may be consistent with a high degree of control in certain sectors or individual corporations. Banks also have large numbers of board memberships in companies below the top 100.

With respect to *Kumulation*, a 1979 Banking Commission report (*Studienkommission für Grundsatzfragen der Kreditwirtschaft*, or Gessler Commission) confirmed the results of an earlier 1976 investigation and found no evidence of excessive influence on the part of the universal banks that could be interpreted as inimical to the interests of shareholders, employees, suppliers, or the nation as a whole. The checks and balances implicit in market competition among some 4,000 financial institutions as well as insurance companies and other nonbanks, together with German banking and commercial law, were deemed sufficient safeguards. The three large German banks have a market share, in terms of transactions value, of only about 9%, and over half of the financial institutions are in the publicly owned sector.

The Gessler Commission did, however, point to information advantages obtained by banks in the course of their credit business, and advocated the strengthening of insider trading rules. It also recommended that information about all board memberships be published annually.

German universal banks justify their share ownership, share voting, and supervisory board roles as follows:

1. It permits orderly restructuring of enterprises and saves jobs. Firms that get into trouble are taken over by banks, restructured, and then resold to new shareholders.
2. It supports poorly capitalized mid-size companies (*Mittelstand*) directly though bank shareholdings and lending that would not otherwise be bankable.
3. It can efficiently prepare government-owned enterprises for privatization.
4. It provides an efficient vehicle for the sale of privately-held companies to the public, with shares taken over by the bank and subsequently sold in a public offering.

The first two of these points relate to the insider information issue as it bears on reducing asymmetry of information problems between banks and business (discussed earlier).

Universal Banking and Economic Restructuring

Economic restructuring in Germany has always heavily reflected bank-oriented corporate finance, with financial institutions having universal banking powers engaged in corporate lending as well as the aforementioned equity investments for their own and fiduciary accounts. This pattern has provided the universal banks with both nonpublic information and (indirectly and through their external board memberships) potential influence over management decisions involving corporate restructuring activities. Firms that do not meet bank performance expectations find themselves under pressure to restructure—activity that may be initiated, orchestrated, and implemented by the banks [Rybczynski 1989]. Indeed, the German universal banks have repeatedly been relied upon to carry out industrial restructurings in the absence of well-functioning capital markets in the past, following periods of war or economic collapse, and so are accustomed to this role [see Calomiris 1993].

This is clearly at variance with the experience in the United States and the United Kingdom, where banks have not had a comparable tradition in corporate finance, and where capital markets have played a constructive role in industrial development for well over a century. Corporate debt financing has relied much more heavily on the securities markets, with debt-holders exerting limited influence on managerial decisions, and public equity holders exposed to the agency costs associated with management pursuing interests other than those that would maximize the value of their shareholdings. At the same time, accounting and disclosure standards are such that the financial affairs of public companies are relatively transparent, while banks under the Glass-Steagall provisions in the United States and pre-Big Bang activity restrictions in the United Kingdom were limited in their ability to exert influence on management even remotely comparable to that of some of their German counterparts—notwithstanding their traditionally powerful exertion of control in the context of restructuring via loan workouts. Consequently, changes in corporate control have been exerted by the capital market, often through hostile takeovers by unaffiliated parties that lead (if successful) to changes in corporate ownership and control. Even if unsuccessful, existing management may engage in corporate restructuring activity similar to what an unaffiliated acquirer would do.

The merits and demerits of the two systems—Anglo-American and Germanic—have been widely debated. Bank-oriented systems are often said to be less crisis-prone, to favor long-term as opposed to short-term views in corporate decision making, and to provide superior continuous monitoring of corporate performance leading to preemptive structural adjustment. Market-oriented systems are often credited with greater efficiency, financial innovation and dynamism, superior resistance to inherent conflicts of interests among the various stakeholders involved, and (through better transparency) less susceptibility to major uncorrected industrial blunders.

In the 1990s, there is likely to be some degree of convergence between the two approaches. Financial liberalization and wider use of the securities markets by continental European corporations—including German companies—together with increasingly performance-oriented portfolio management on the part of mutual funds, insurance companies, and other institutional investors, is leading to a gradual shift away from bank finance, and the appearance of unwanted takeover attempts through acquisition of shareholdings by unaffiliated (often foreign) investors [Walter and Smith 1989]. At the same time, easing of bank activity limits in the United Kingdom and the United States is beginning to allow banks to play a larger role in industrial restructuring transactions and to exploit some of the information and relationship advantages they have as lenders [Walter 1993].

Universal Banking and German Unification

German reunification is not likely to alter the structure of the country's universal banking system. Figure 4–5 depicts the new banking system of East Germany as reconstituted from the preexisting system that was an integral part of the central planning apparatus. German financial institutions of all types struck deals with counterpart financial institutions in East Germany in specialized banking, universal banking, and insurance, most notably rapid penetration of the market by the three big universal banks and the Allianz insurance group. The Deutsche Bank venture with Deutsche Kreditbank took in 122 branches throughout East Germany along with 8,500 employees. Dresdner Bank relied on aggressive branching across East Germany and likewise established a joint venture with Deutsche Kreditbank, which added a further 72 branches. There is little doubt that the East German financial system is rapidly being absorbed into that of the Federal Republic. Other Eastern European countries, which

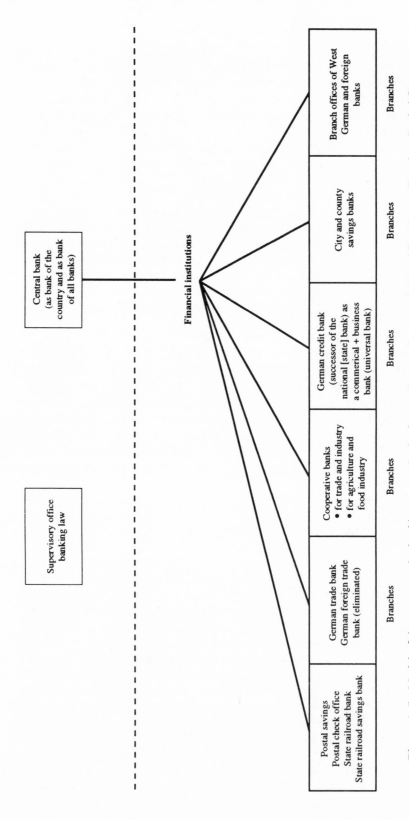

Figure 4–5 Model of the new, two-tier banking system in the former German Democratic Republic. (*Source:* Dresdner Bank AG)

will retain independent financial systems, also appear to look to the German universal banking approach as a model [Smith and Walter 1993].

Universal banking may thus provide significant competitive advantages in servicing, at acceptable risk levels, the burgeoning capital needs of Eastern Europe. If it is true that the Eastern European capital stock must be valued at or near zero at market prices—and given the skilled labor, locational, and resources endowments that may be necessary—the marginal product of investment in the region may prove to be extraordinarily high. The cross-border financial services involved are likely to be equity-related transactions (facilitating foreign direct investment flows, including foreign participation in privatizations), project financing, and corporate bank lending—in many cases backed by Western governments or agencies. Eventually the emergence of debt and equity markets in Eastern Europe will permit the development of securities services as well.

In the case of the former German Democratic Republic, such flows effectively become interregional within a unified Germany, involving only credit risk and obviating currency, transfer, and sovereign risk. Retail financial services and deposit-taking activities, as well as securities services, will be undertaken on the ground by German and foreign-based players on the same basis as in the Federal Republic, and the unified financial system will probably be a clone of the latter—with preexisting West German banks dominating. They know the territory, the language, the institutions, and the West German investors. Furthermore, the German universal banking "style" is well suited to the probable structure of financing needs. Foreign-based firms will compete as they do in the Federal Republic, and will have competitive advantages largely associated with contacts to non-German investors in the East. For example, a non-German bank may help finance a French food products company establishing distribution channels, or an American or Japanese investment bank may help find a Western buyer for a privatized enterprise.

In the case of the remainder of Eastern Europe, all of the aforementioned risks are present. Cross-border bank lending is therefore likely to involve credit enhancements from Western governments or international agencies, or other financial structures mitigating such risks, especially with the threat of "another Latin America" prominent in the minds of bank shareholders and regulators. Nevertheless, once the legal and economic infrastructures are in place (particularly in the Czech and Slovac Republics, Hungary, and Poland), it is likely that foreign direct investment will follow. This will provide opportunities to foreign banks and securities firms similar to those in East Germany, most of which will be well suited to the capabilities of German and other European universal banks.

Besides financing needs, opportunities should involve M&A services related to privatizations in a number of Eastern European countries. Again the German universals, as advisers and co-owners of German industrial enterprises, are expected to be among the most active in Eastern Europe.

In terms of taking positions in transactions that have only long-term potential, they are likely to be among the most successful in this respect.

Finanzplatz Deutschland

As the financial fulcrum of the new Europe, Germany's role as a financial center is clearly linked both to the strengths and the weaknesses of the universal banking system. Despite the preeminent position of the deutsche mark in Europe, the core strength of German industry, and the high savings rate, we have noted that Germany remains a significant importer of financial service innovations from abroad. The fact, as noted, that the German authorities have historically restricted the use of commercial paper and prevented development of an active domestic money market. Debt and equity securities denominated in deutsche marks are traded heavily in London, where derivatives markets developed early and transactions costs have been comparatively low. The German share of cross-border lending at 4% of the world total is smaller than that of France and about one-third that of Japan. German stock market capitalization amounts to only 5% of the global total. Modernizations already undertaken include the introduction of a computerized futures and options exchange, an auction process for government debt issues, and the abolition of the securities transfer tax [see Levich and Walter 1988], but the full development of a creative, diverse financial market has traditionally run counter to the interests of the dominant German universal banks. Further liberalizations—as well as measures to establish the country's first regulatory body for the securities industry and its first insider dealing law were announced by the Ministry of Finance in 1992. Other initiatives in late 1992 involved creating a single stock market holding company (*Deutsche Börse*) and further development of electronic stock trading via *Ibis* for 30–50 of the most actively traded stocks and bonds, alongside floor-based trading for less actively traded shares. These issues are discussed further in the context of EC financial integration later in this chapter, as are the implications of the German form of universal banking for U.S. regulatory reform.

Switzerland

Swiss banking has traditionally been oligopolistic in nature, international in scope, and universal in character. While banking historically existed in a carefully controlled competitive environment, the Swiss banking industry has gone through a rapid evolution in an effort to maintain its place in world financial markets.

According to one description of the Swiss financial system, Swiss banks ". . . offer a broad, strongly structured range of services and facilities. Legislation in Switzerland, unlike that in other countries, has never attempted to implement strict specialization or to order the banks to abandon the idea of a full-range service product. The banks have been largely free in the past to decide which banking services they wish to offer to the public, and continue to enjoy this freedom to this day. This offers considerable leeway for the evolution of the industry. . . . [It] makes it possible to satisfy a wide range of banking needs and at the same time enables these institutions to spread the risk and even out earnings from the various kinds of activity" [Wyler, 1986]. In addition to on-balance sheet business, Swiss banks manage some $4 trillion of domestic and $2 trillion of offshore assets for clients.

Categories of Banks

There are more than 600 Swiss banks in existence, which are divided into eight main categories (see Table 4–4). The five largest banks account for half of all banking assets.

Big Banks

The big Swiss financial institutions—four large, universal banks—dominate the Swiss banking system. The proportion of total banking assets accounted for by the big banks has increased steadily from about 25% in 1945 to almost 50% in 1990. The three largest, Union Bank of Switzerland, Zurich (with assets of SFr 186 billion in 1990); Swiss Bank Corporation, Basel (SFr 166 billion); and Crédit Suisse, Zurich (SFr 125 billion), all rank within the top 100 banks in the world in terms of assets and within the top 25 in terms of shareholder equity. The fourth and fifth largest banks, Swiss Volksbank and Bank Leu, have been acquired by

Table 4–4 Assets of Swiss Banks at Year-end 1990
by Type of Bank (S Fr Millions)

	Assets	% of Assets	No. of Companies
Big banks	523,526	48.4	4
Cantonal banks	213,879	19.8	29
Regional and savings banks	93,595	8.7	204
Mutual credit associations	34,042	3.1	2
Other banks	167,737	15.5	218
Finance companies	24,809	2.3	130
Branches of foreign banks	18,479	1.7	16
Private banks	5,581	0.5	22
Total	1,081,648	100.00	625

Source: Banque Nationale Suisse, *Annual Report, 1990.*

Crédit Suisse in 1993 and 1990, respectively. The big three dwarf all other banks in the economy.

The activities of the big banks encompass commercial banking, trade finance, and the money, note, bond, foreign exchange, precious metals, and stock markets of Switzerland. They also compete with other categories of Swiss banks by engaging in mortgage lending, consumer finance, leasing, and factoring. The big banks are active in foreign and Eurocredit and capital markets, including derivatives.

Cantonal Banks

The 29 cantonal banks (1 for each Swiss canton except Bern, Geneva, and Vaud, each of which has 2) in general are cantonal government-owned or government-guaranteed corporations dating from the last half of the nineteenth century. They are constituted under cantonal law. Dividends from operations accrue to the cantons. Although they pursue a number of regional economic and social goals, the cantonal banks are managed as commercial concerns. The advantages gained from their government guarantee, however, are generally more than offset by restrictions, especially on foreign transactions (which in aggregate accounted for about 5% of assets and 2.5% of liabilities in 1989).

The cantonal banks vary widely in size and scope with the largest, Zürcher Kantonalbank, having assets of about SFr 40 billion (making it the fourth largest bank in the country) and competing in many areas of commercial and investment banking directly with the big banks, while the smaller cantonal banks remain strictly regional in character. Since 1907, the Union of Swiss Cantonal Banks has been the coordinating, lobbying, and public relations instrument of the cantonal banks.

Regional and Savings Banks

The 204 regional and savings banks in Switzerland are domestically oriented and small in scale. Although not legally restricted from becoming universal institutions, a bank in this category often remains specialized as a savings, land, or mortgage bank. Founded in 1971, the Union of Swiss Regional Banks is a forum in which regional banks discuss and coordinate their activities.

Mutual Credit Associations

Two rather different financial organizations—the Schweizer Verband der Raiffeisenkassen (with assets of about SFR 30 billion and 1,228 affiliated mutual banks, the sixth largest bank in Switzerland) and the Fédération Vaudoise de Crédit Mutuel (with assets of more than SFr 180 million and 13 affiliated mutual banks)—comprise this category of banks. They are strictly regional and extend preferential credit to members who are jointly liable for the obligations of the association.

Other Banks

The 218 "other banks" in Switzerland (as of end-1990) are subdivided into two main classes: those owned by Swiss nationals and 124 institutions which, while constituted as Swiss banks, are owned by non-Swiss. The first category is further subdivided into (1) commercial banks, which are miniuniversals whose major activity is domestic secured lending but which also perform domestic and foreign investment management; (2) investment banks, which are active primarily in foreign-client portfolio management; (3) consumer credit banks, whose foreign activities are negligible; and (4) banks that cannot be classified elsewhere. Control of one of the large banks in the first category, Banca della Svizzera Italiana (BSI) was acquired by Swiss Bank Corporation in 1990.

Finance Companies

Finance companies are composed of 4 retail institutions and 126 wholesale finance companies. Because they solicit deposits, the retail finance companies are considered to be banks. The vast majority of the finance companies are Swiss subsidiaries of non-Swiss firms—mainly banks—with the two largest being Renault Finance SA (with 1989 assets of SFr 7.3 billion) and Sumitomo International Finance SA (SFr 1.1 billion).

Swiss Branches and Affiliates of Foreign Banks

As of 1991, 16 foreign banks had branches in Switzerland, comprising 1.7% of Swiss banking assets. Virtually all large international banks have a presence in Switzerland, either through branches, finance companies, or foreign-owned Swiss banks.

Private Banks

The oldest and perhaps most reputed sector of Swiss banking comprises the 22 unlimited liability private banks, which focus on a global client base of wealthy individuals and families. Swiss private banks have traditionally provided a full range of financial services to their clients, emphasizing discretion and the preservation of capital over performance. Several, notably Lombard Odier Cie. and Pictet & Cie., have pushed into institutional funds management with some success. Their importance in terms of assets is not great, however: The private banks' collective balance sheets account for one-half of 1% of total Swiss banking assets, while their fiduciary accounts account for a respectable share of total fiduciary business in Switzerland.

The International Character of Swiss Banking

The internationalism and global prominence of Swiss banking is particularly striking in view of the country's size. While the Swiss franc is the payments mechanism and accounting measure of a relatively small economy—1991 gross national product (GNP) of $228.7 billion versus $1,714.6 billion for Germany and $1,018.5 billion for the United Kingdom—it has for at least a century been a preferred, long-term, safe haven for wealth. Moreover, Swiss armed neutrality and Swiss bankers' reputation for competence, honesty, and confidentiality have combined to make Swiss institutions preferable in the view of many clients to other nations' banks. The confidentiality characteristic has undergone some degree of change in recent years, however [Walter 1990].

In general, Swiss authorities have worked to bolster the country's international role as a financial center, especially since the financial sector accounts for about 5% of total employment. However, in order to prevent loss of control of the money supply, the Swiss National Bank has (1) limited the development of the domestic money market; (2) prevented the opening-up of a Euro-Swiss franc market; and (3) used the foreign exchange swap market as one of its main tools in monetary policy.

Swiss Financial Markets

The money market in Switzerland is largely composed of interbank borrowing and lending, trade bills, acceptances, and government short-term paper. Banks have not used negotiable certificates of deposit in order to raise funds due to the traditional high liquidity of Switzerland and the country's position as a net capital exporter. A commercial paper market has not developed for four main reasons: (1) The Swiss corporate sector is relatively small; (2) a stamp tax has made secondary market transactions in domestic securities less attractive than the easily accessible Euro and foreign markets; (3) Swiss corporations have tended to be very liquid themselves and have met short-term capital needs from low-cost bank loans; and (4) as noted, the Swiss National Bank has discouraged financial markets in short-maturity securities for fear that international participation in such markets would swamp its ability to control the money supply.

Banks maintain an on-tap market in medium-term notes (MTNs), whose maturities range from 3 to 8 years. The market provides about one-tenth of the funding needs of the banking system and provides an econ-omywide interest rate benchmark, used especially in the mortgage market. Increases in the interest rate on MTNs are subject to the approval of the Swiss National Bank. Cantonal governments are the main participants in the MTN market.

Switzerland's deficiencies at the short end of the securities markets are offset by its highly developed market for long-term bonds, an outgrowth of the country's historically stable currency. Prospective issues, both domestic and foreign bonds, must be approved by the Central Bank's Issues Committee, which has the task of assuring that no temporary oversupply of new issues gluts the market. Approved issuers are then scheduled for issuing. The Swiss foreign bond market is second only to the U.S. foreign bond market in size. Bonds are typically in bearer form and typically represent fixed rate, straight securities with maturities ranging from 5 to 10 years—although in recent years increasing numbers of issues have been convertibles or linked to equity options.

Underwriting Swiss franc bonds had traditionally been the profitable preserve of an underwriting syndicate dominated by the three big banks, but including as well the lead bank of the Association of Swiss Cantonal Banks and the Association of Geneva Private Banks and, later, certain foreign banks. The syndicate in effect constituted a cartel, with a "fidelity clause" preventing members from participating in syndicates organized by nonmembers and obliging them to invite all others into their own deals. During the first 8 months of 1990, the syndicate accounted for 77% of all Swiss franc bond issues. This syndicate has since been dissolved by action of the Swiss Supreme Court.

In contrast to its deep, and highly international, long-term debt markets, Swiss equity markets are restricted, fragmented, and domestic. Local companies typically limit the ownership of their shares by non-Swiss or separate their equity tranches into Swiss and international shares, with the latter having subordinate rights as bearer versus registered shares. There have traditionally been six stock exchanges in the country, formed under cantonal law and without a central regulatory body (except the joint dominating influence of the big banks) overseeing their activities. In February 1990, the report of an independent commission set up by the federal Finance Ministry recommended the creation of a single nationwide electronic stock exchange—similar to the Swiss Options & Financial Futures Exchange (SOFFEX), a joint venture between the big banks established in May 1988—under a single federal supervisory body. Since then, the stock exchanges of Bern, Lausanne, and St. Gallen have been closed, with Basel, Geneva, and Zurich eventually due for electronic hookup.

Regulatory Environment

All credit institutions doing business in Switzerland are subject to the Federal Banking Act, authorized and supervised by the Federal Banking Commission, whose members in turn are elected (but not instructed) by the Federal Council. The Swiss National Bank has no supervisory powers, but does set reporting requirements. Bank managers and employees are personally liable under Swiss law for violation of fiduciary responsibility and dereliction of duty as defined under the Federal Banking Act. The cantons regulate the stock exchanges, with authorization and supervision carried out by self-regulatory bodies—although all of the significant players are universal banks and therefore also subject to the Federal Banking

Act. Capital ratios are defined and set at conservative levels that more than comply with the BIS standards, making Swiss universal banks among the most heavily capitalized in the world. Liquidity ratios are similarly set at conservative levels.

Bank supervision is thus shared between the Swiss National Bank (SNB) and the Federal Banking Commission (FBC). The SNB's concerns are primarily of a monetary policy nature. The FBC is empowered to grant licenses to, supervise the activities of, and enforce its decisions with respect to all banks and investment trusts.

The FBC grants licenses subject to satisfaction of capital adequacy requirements (SFr 2 million), articles of association, detailed internal controls and viable business plan, "fit and proper" criteria based on integrity and Swiss nationality of ownership and/or Swiss management. The latter restriction does not seem to have significantly reduced foreign bank entry.

The law (and implementing ordinance) specifies detailed capital adequacy and liquidity provisions and reporting requirements to both the SNB and the FBC, both of which may request additional information. Funding exposure to individual customers in excess of given proportions of capital must be specifically approved by board resolutions. FBC loan loss reserves of one-fifth of capital or one-twentieth of assets must be maintained, in addition to the total surplus of share issues (after costs) and one-tenth of distributed profits after other provisions. Foreign currency positions are monitored but not restricted. The SNB provides collateralized lending to banks with liquidity problems. In addition, banks have the legal right to petition the federal government for relief in the event of any inability to meet their obligations.

There are no legal restrictions on the scope of Swiss banks' activities from the side of the regulators, only that ". . . the scope of a bank's business and of its activities must be defined in detail and must correspond to its financial resources and its administrative organization" [Swiss Bankers Association 1990]. Limits on activities and geographic scope are specified by the banks themselves in their articles of association, which must be submitted to the FBC prior to granting a license. Although the federal government has the power to prevent mergers if they are considered to have potentially adverse economic or social effects, the FBC has no specific authority to concern itself with such mergers.

Swiss banks are not limited in their equity holdings in nonfinancial firms. However, there is a capital requirement of 40% on all nonconsolidated participations and 100% on all consolidated participations. Unlike the German case, Swiss banks do not have a tradition of using equity ownership for purposes of corporate control.

Any bank must notify the SNB before it participates in an international syndication or primary securities issue, or in foreign investments with a maturity of more than 1 year; the SNB maintains the right to prevent such participations.

Switzerland has no formal deposit insurance system, although the

Swiss bankruptcy law extends legal protection to individual savings accounts up to SFr 10,000, which are accorded first priority in claims over bank assets. In addition, there is a "gentlemen's agreement" signed under the auspices of the Swiss Bankers Association and encompassing most of the banks, which guarantees savings and salary accounts up to SFr 30,000 per client. These accounts make up about 15% of bank liabilities and capital (10% for the big banks). There are no insurance premiums, and total payouts during the 1980s amounted to only SFr 120,000 [Swiss Bankers Association 1990]. Most cantonal banks are guaranteed by their respective cantons. The failure in 1991 of a small, regional bank in Thun shook confidence in the Swiss system of depositor protection.

Swiss banking law holds bankers to a high standard of conduct by imposing criminal liability for violations of legal statutes. The best-known clause, Article 47.1, enshrines discretion in banking. Others, relating to defamation of banks, misrepresentation regarding banking, and negligence in the preparation and submission of reports, written in a similar spirit, attest to the special place banks occupy in the Swiss economy.

Insurance

Swiss banks may engage in insurance activities, but only though separately capitalized subsidiaries: The Private Insurance Act does not permit them to engage directly in insurance. Most major Swiss banks have preferred so far not to compete with the large insurance companies such as Zurich, Swiss Re, Swiss Life, and Winterthur even in mass products such as life insurance. In part this may be a manifestation of a gentlemen's agreement to stay out of each others' businesses, as long existed in Germany, which will ultimately break down. Crédit Suisse, for example, has begun vigorous life insurance operations, while Swiss Bank Corporation has created a strategic alliance with an insurance company—paralleling the Deutsche Bank-Dresdner Bank approaches to *Allfinanz* in Germany. In the past, Swiss bankers have tended to see the combination of banking and insurance as a zero-sum game. That is, if a bank is to be highly competitive in the insurance business as against the major established players, it is likely to have to cross-subsidize that business from its banking and securities operations. Swiss banks traditionally viewed the existing insurance industry in Switzerland as being highly competitive, and Swiss universals largely stayed out of the life underwriting business despite the absence of regulatory barriers. This has now changed and the separation of banking and life insurance in Switzerland seem to be subject to the same integrative moves as in Germany.

Politics and Banking

In contrast to the United States, Japan, and Germany, the debate on the social value of bank universality—whether banks can be engaged in both commerce and banking without adverse social consequences—is not an issue in Switzerland. With the exception of Crédit Suisse Holding's interests in several nonfinancial enterprises, no German-style industrial–financial alliances are in evidence in Switzerland—notwithstanding the big banks' board of directors, which invariably include prominent industrialists. The Swiss view has been that "bankers should be bankers and industrialists should be industrialists." And since banking interests are generally perceived to be coincident with the national interest, the power of the big banks and their role in the industrial structure is not widely questioned; however, there are pressures for change in the direction of greater competition and greater disclosure.

In 1986, the Swiss Cartel Commission acquired enhanced powers to enforce its decisions. International deregulation and the 1992 EC initiatives led many Swiss to conclude that competition-restricting practices applied by the big banks and the government were simultaneously weakening Swiss markets and were unfairly advantageous to the big banks. In early 1989, the Cartel Commission recommended that banks annul 18 cartel-like agreements—a recommendation implemented by the Swiss Ministry of Economic Affairs. As already noted, those agreements included the Swiss franc foreign bond underwriting syndicate (incorporating the "fidelity" clause to prevent banks from underwriting outside it), dividend, interest and documentary credit fee collusion, fixed brokerage commissions, custody and foreign exchange fees, and agreements on advertising. The Swiss Bankers' Association agreed to implement ten of the recommendations—forcing pricing and costs to be brought into line—but resisted the more substantive recommendations to annul the syndicate for Swiss franc-denominated foreign bonds and fixed brokerage, documentary credit, and custody fees. Moreover, the Association of Swiss Exchanges simultaneously introduced a new fixed commission structure, in defiance of the Cartel Commission's recommendation. But the banks' resistance to increased competition appeared to be a rearguard action. With the cartel system in retreat, the strongest argument was not against the reforms, but against promulgating those reforms with such haste as to destabilize or weaken markets and institutions in the absence of tax and other reforms affecting banks.

However, on 31 December 1990 the issuing syndicate, which had dominated the Swiss bond market for 40 years, was dissolved under the ultimately successful influence of the Swiss Cartel Commission as a further step in liberalizing the market. Despite this action, the three big banks indicated that they would continue collective underwriting and cooperation on an ad hoc basis.

These pressures on Swiss banks have been compounded by a series of bank-related scandals that tarnished the reputation of Swiss banking with revelations of money laundering and insider trading cases facilitated by banking secrecy. In response, legislation was introduced that would make a bankers' complicity and negligence in money laundering a criminal offense. The Swiss Banking Commission also bowed to criticism of bank accounting practices (particularly consolidation and the treatment of hidden reserves), which allowed considerable discretion to bank managements in the reporting of income. And legislation to increase the competitiveness of Swiss secondary markets by repealing the stamp duty was repeatedly put forward, notwithstanding the opposition of the Swiss Social Democratic Party.

An active debate in Switzerland thus continues as to whether these) deregulation moves would proceed far enough to maintain Switzerland's unique competitive position in world finance. Given the strong traditions of government guidance of finance through the big banks, conflicting social goals, and the rise of foreign competition, the likely outcome continues to be actively debated.

United Kingdom

Three characteristics of U.K. banking stand out. The first is that the industry is made up of roughly equal foreign and domestic sectors. As the traditionally undisputed center of international banking and the capital of the Euromarkets, the United Kingdom has long kept its doors open to the world's banks, yet its domestic markets remain largely a domestic preserve. The second is that the United Kingdom has historically, but not legally, separated the activities of its banking industry into commercial banking (dominated by the four large clearing banks) and investment banking, the preserve of a dozen or so merchant banks in the City of London. The third is that self-regulation and moral suasion of the authorities have historically predominated over explicit laws and regulations of government agencies.

Classifications of Banks

In the United Kingdom, the more than 600 deposit-taking institutions can be separated into five categories: clearing banks, merchant banks, other British banks, foreign banks, and other deposit-taking institutions. Table 4–5 shows the relative importance of these sectors under Bank of England authority (i.e., including foreign-currency deposits but excluding other deposit taking institutions). The numbers and the categories, however, are somewhat deceptive, as we will discuss later.

Clearing Banks

The clearing banks (sometimes called "high street" or "retail" banks) are those institutions with extensive branch networks in the United Kingdom or those participating directly in the U.K. clearing system. The category is dominated by the four big clearers, Barclays Bank (assets of £ 135 billion end 1990), National Westminster Bank (£ 110 billion), Midland

Table 4–5   Assets of U.K. Authorized Depository Institutions

	No. of Banks (1991)	September 1991		December 1979	
		£ Million	%	£ Million	%
Clearing banks	21	443,932	34.32	62,198	23.57
Merchant banks	33	56,983	4.40	10,251	3.89
Other british banks	142	56,035	4.33	39,025	14.79
British banks subtotal	196	556,950	43.05	111,474	42.25
American banks	39	128,335	9.92	59,228	22.45
Japanese banks	32	233,572	18.06	29,165	11.05
Other overseas banks	273	374,829	28.97	63,977	24.25
Foreign banks subtotal	344	736,736	56.95	152,370	57.75
Total banks	540	1,293,686	100.00	263,844	100.00

Source: Bank of England. *Quarterly Reports.*

Bank (£ 62 billion), and Lloyds Bank (£ 55 billion), which together account for about 80% of the total assets of the clearing banks. At the end of 1990, all of the four big clearers internationally ranked in the top 50 worldwide in terms of assets and in the top 20 in terms of shareholder equity.

The category "clearing banks" excludes Citibank as a foreign bank—notwithstanding its extensive U.K. branching and its role as a de facto clearing bank. However, if one considers only the assets of the clearers compared with the assets of all U.K. banks, the clearers appear to be less dominant than they really are.

The four big clearers are essentially universal banks. In addition to taking deposits, offering checking accounts, performing clearing functions, and lending to businesses, the clearing banks are active in consumer finance, mortgage lending, credit card networks, documentary credits, international lending, fiduciary services, and investment management. They pursue investment banking activities mainly through wholly owned subsidiaries. Various clearers have moved into life insurance, travel services, real estate, and trust management.

Merchant Banks

The 33 U.K. accepting houses or merchant banks (actually only 17 in number if one omits multiple corporate identities of single businesses) were historically merchants engaged in international trade. Their names were sufficiently well recognized in the financial community for them to be able not only to sell (as discounted short-term securities) their own trade bills in the market but, for a fee, to "accept" (by signing) and sell bills of lesser-known merchants as well.

As commercial banks displaced much of this trade financing role over the years, the merchant bankers used their expertise in placing securities to expand into what Americans call investment banking and what the British now call merchant banking—that is, investment management, underwriting and trading of securities, M&A services, bullion, financial advisory work, personal banking, and lending to clients (usually in connection with specific corporate finance, syndication, or project financing transactions). Acceptance business is at present a very minor part of their operations.

Other British Banks

The 142 "other banks" in the United Kingdom comprise a diverse group. Some provide services indistinguishable from those of merchant banks (as is the case of Barclays de Zoete Wedd Ltd.). Others are finance houses providing consumer finance, hire-purchase, leasing, and personal lending. Of these, the 48 largest finance houses (many of which are subsidiaries of British clearing banks or foreign banks) are grouped together into the Finance Houses Association (FHA), accounting for 85% of the finance house business. As of December 1989, total FHA credit outstanding stood at £ 38 billion.

Foreign Banks

Due to the presence of Euromarket banks in London, the banking assets of foreign banks in the United Kingdom slightly exceed those of domestic banks. All of the major banks in the world are represented in London, and the foreign banks employ 72,000 people (1989). In terms of the U.K. domestic market, however, the level of penetration is much lower. The focus of this massive foreign presence has thus been largely international, although some foreign banks have made commercial banking inroads in the United Kingdom, and Citibank competes directly with the clearing banks with its consumer banking activities. With the British financial deregulation of Big Bang in 1986, moreover, a number of foreign banks have begun competing in British capital markets as well, albeit not always with success.

Other Deposit-taking Institutions

The most important nonbank deposit takers (whose deposits are not reported in the Bank of England figures) are the *building societies*. These are generally mutual organizations designed to mobilize savings for members' home mortgages. The building societies are estimated to account for just over half of the new mortgages in the United Kingdom. They come under the purview not of the Bank of England, but of the Building Societies

Commission. Financial deregulation, however, has allowed them to expand their activities into check clearing, personal loans, and credit cards, and to finance their activities on wholesale money and capital markets.

The Department for National Savings, with deposits gathered through some 22,000 post offices throughout the country, operates the Post Office Savings Bank (formerly called the National Girobank). This institution invests its regular savings and investment deposits of about £ 8 billion in government securities.

The Markets

Banks are active in the U.K.'s varied and deep money markets, where short-term instruments such as eligible commercial bills, treasury securities (gilts), bank bills and, since 1986, sterling commercial paper are traded. The traditional vehicle for U.K. monetary policy has been the market in eligible bills that are acceptable for rediscount at the Bank of England. The eight discount houses, which are committed to making a market in bills, deal with banks on one side and the Bank of England on the other. Discount houses function more as administrative arms of the Bank of England than as independent commercial businesses, which, under law, they are. U.K. banks offer medium-term (1–5 year maturity) certificates of deposit (CDs), which are traded in active secondary markets.

The long end of the U.K.'s debt markets is dominated by gilts and Eurobonds—international bearer bonds that are typically listed on the London or Luxembourg stock exchanges. The domestic U.K. bond market effectively has been rendered redundant by the less-regulated Eurobond market. On the equities side, the International Stock Exchange (ISE) in London makes markets in U.K. and foreign stocks. Foreign investment in U.K. stocks is largely unrestricted, and the United Kingdom has the only active market for corporate control in Europe.

The U.K. capital markets experienced unprecedented deregulation through Big Bang in October 1986 (under discussion since 1983), which opened the previously sheltered domestic investment banking to free competition. Big Bang focused on four regulatory reforms: (1) The ISE did away with fixed commissions on purchases and sales of securities; (2) The ISE ended the division between brokers and jobbers, whereby jobbers made markets in stocks and brokers completed orders for their customers through the jobbers; (3) The U.K. government changed the market in gilts from a monopoly of one broker and two jobbers to a U.S.-type primary dealer system with authorized dealers; and (4) The U.K. government allowed foreign financial firms to acquire 100% stakes in British securities houses. At the same time, the ISE implemented an automated quotation system. The immediate benefits of Big Bang included lowering fees and commissions for investors and enhancing the reputation of London as a financial center, although the subsequent fallout has included severely reduced profitability for firms competing in the market. Interestingly, many banks including universals (e.g., United Bank of Switzerland) and non-universals (e.g., Citicorp) have fared very badly in the intense competitive environment immediately after Big Bang.

Regulatory Environment

British regulation of financial institutions has been among the world's most well structured and carefully thought through, in a serious and relatively unpoliticized effort to balance safety and soundness with static and dynamic efficiency as a matter of the national interest. In the process, the United Kingdom has created an environment that is both highly competitive internationally (with significant employment, export, and growth benefits to the real economy) and one that has been free from the kinds of massive institutional failures and burdens on the general public that have characterized the U.S. financial system—with the notable exception (and special case) of Bank of Credit and Commerce International (BCCI).

Perhaps the U.K. regulatory-design process can be considered "technical and professional," whereas the U.S. process is dominated by self-interest on the part of individual institutions and groups of institutions, converted to political action or paralysis through the lobbying process. Nonetheless, there have been criticisms that the U.K. system has introduced a measure of overregulation that will have to be reexamined especially in the context of the evolving European single financial market.

The British approach is based on protecting individual investors and depositors, together with avoiding systemic risk, by assuring: (1) the "fitness and properness" of owners and managers of financial institutions; (2) the adequacy of capital appropriate to the nature of the financial activities undertaken; (3) the adequacy of continuing control systems; and (4) high standards of conduct of business, normally supported by insurance or other forms of contingent compensation arrangements. Once these standards are met, a financial institution is afforded maximum latitude to compete according to the dictates of the market and its own resources.

Founded in 1694 but not nationalized until 1946, the Bank of England acts as the central bank of the United Kingdom by controlling the money supply, serving as lender of last resort, and supervising the financial sector. Any institution—except building societies, the Postal Savings Bank, local government authorities, and insurance companies—wishing to market financial services to the general public must be authorized by the Bank of England. As of 1987, U.K. law recognized only one category of "authorized institution" for deposit taking. Of the authorized institutions, only those with capital and reserves over £ 5 million can use the word *bank* in their names.

No explicit restrictions apply to the scope of activities that banks may undertake. However, the Bank of England can require a bank to reduce its stake in another company if it deems the ownership to be a threat to the bank's stability. The Bank of England also expects to be consulted prior to a bank's acquisition of any significant share (over 15%) in another bank. Management must meet continuing stringent, but not always transparent, fit and proper criteria.

Banks submit periodic audited reports to the Bank of England and must submit to its rulings (e.g., with respect to third world debt provisions against credit losses). Although the Bank of England has no say in the appointment or removal of auditors, it must be informed when a bank changes auditors, presumably since such a move could indicate that the bank is experiencing difficulties or attempting to cover up dubious activities.

In general, the Bank of England has not set ratios for liquidity, solvency, or various types of exposures. Risk-based capital adequacy provisions, however, were adopted for the first time in 1988 according to the BIS' recommendations adopted by most of the developed countries at that time. The Bank of England and the U.S. Federal Reserve were the prime movers behind the BIS initiative. Moreover, exposures in excess of 10% of an institution's capital base must be reported to the Bank of England after the fact, and proposed exposures in excess of 25% must be reported in advance.

In a codification of the principle of self-regulation, the Financial Services Act of 1986 legislated that a series of self-regulatory organizations (SROs) be created in investment banking and placed under control of the Securities and Investments Board (SIB)—although SROs have come under severe criticism for an allegedly poor record of detecting fraud early and protecting individual investors.

Commercial banks and other financial services companies that conduct fiduciary business for customers and also run their own investment funds are subject to *polarization*; that is, they must demonstrate that their own products are indeed the best available if they purport to give independent advice and simultaneously sell proprietary products. Commercial banks in general have chosen to sell only in-house products.

A mandatory government deposit protection system under the Bank of England is in force, which covers 75% of the first £ 20,000 of a customer's deposits. It is funded by a levy on eligible institutions' deposit bases. A similar but separate scheme covering 90% of deposits is in force for building societies.

Insurance

British banks may engage in the insurance business through separately capitalized subsidiaries. The British life insurance industry is highly fragmented and relatively lightly regulated (especially with respect to capitalization) with several hundred firms from all kinds of strategic groups competing for business. A number of large players and syndications through Lloyds and other exchanges dominate commercial insurance. The Prudential, Norwich Union, Standard Life, Royal Insurance, Legal & General, Commercial Union, Sun Alliance & London, Guardian Royal

Exchange, and Eagle Star are among the major players on the life and nonlife sides of the business.

All of the British clearing banks and many other financial institutions, especially building societies, have established life insurance operations, Barclays Bank and Lloyds Bank both have captive life insurance subsidiaries while National Westminster Bank distributes insurance underwritten by others—all marketed through their banking offices as well as leads provided to salesmen through banking relationships. Lloyds Bank also holds a majority stake in Abbey Life, whose products are sold through brokers and an independent sales force. Besides the building societies, the Trustee Savings Bank is another institution that has established its own life insurance subsidiary.

As in the German case, there seems to be a strong view that life insurance underwriting is the activity most complementary to retail banking, and that nonlife retail products requiring more substantial servicing might come later. As far as is known, no clearing bank or building society has moved into the commercial risk insurance business.

Politics and Banking

In the United Kingdom, a consistent political theme has played since the early 1980s—denationalization, deregulation, and the rule of markets. With the Euromarkets in London providing a benchmark for financial deregulation, Big Bang brought international standards to domestic capital markets. Privatization of formerly state-owned corporations provided additional marketable equity transactions to the expanding financial sector, which, thanks largely to the prevailing bull market of the time, were highly profitable. Privatization of state-owned corporations included floating—along with such industrial concerns as British Petroleum, British Telecom, British Airways, and British Gas—Trustee Savings Bank, formerly a quasi-public sector savings institution. The Postal Savings Bank was also scheduled to be privatized.

The changes in the United Kingdom's financial structure carried out during the 1980s have given the British clearing banks the potential to evolve into true universal banks. No significant political lobby against such an evolution has emerged, although the Monopolies and Mergers Commission has reserved the right to review any merger likely to result in a restraint of trade. In addition, the Bank of England had a policy of preventing large clearing banks from falling into the hands of non-U.K. nationals—a stand that was significantly modified with the acquisition of Midland Bank by the Hongkong and Shanghai Banking Corporation in 1992—defeating a competing bid by Lloyds Bank.

Universal Banking and European Financial Integration

On 13 June 1988 the Council of Ministers of the EC authorized full capital-movement liberalization (including those regulations affecting short-term funds flows) by the end of July 1990—with an extended adjustment period to the end of 1992 granted to Greece, Ireland, Portugal, and Spain—although there are provisions for reimposition temporary restrictions on short-term capital movements under a "safeguard" clause in case these seriously disturb a member country's exchange rate or monetary policies.

The Second Banking Directive, intended to provide a consistent and level playing field for credit institutions within the EC, was proposed by the Commission in early 1988 and acted upon by the council in late 1989, and took effect at the beginning of 1993 [EC Commission 1988]. A parallel draft directive covering the securities industry—the Investment Services Directive (ISD)—was initially agreed in November 1992, and a Capital Adequacy Directive (CAD) covering both banks and securities firms and designed to create a level playing field for securities activities was still being circulated in late 1992. Rules governing the creation and EC-wide distribution of mutual funds (Undertakings for the Collective Investment of Transferable Securities, or UCITS) were adopted in 1989 as well [Dermine 1993]. By early 1993 the broad outlines of the EC financial markets for the remainder of the century had largely been set in place, although not yet fully operational.

Liberalization of intra-EC banking activities can be traced to the 1977 First Banking Directive, which allowed banks based anywhere in the EC to establish branches or subsidiaries in any other member country (freedom of establishment) on the condition that banking regulations in the host country were fully observed. It also required member states to establish a licensing system for credit institutions, including minimum "fit and proper" criteria for authorization to do business.

The Second Banking Directive was based on three concepts: (1) the "single passport," which allows credit institutions deemed "fit and proper" by the regulatory authorities in any EC country to open branches and provide banking services in all others; (2) agreed activity rules, which allow all EC credit institutions the right to provide a broad range of financial services, including deposit taking, wholesale and retail lending, leasing, stock and bond dealing, fee-based advisory services, portfolio management, custody, and transactions services; and (3) harmonization of capital requirements and supervisory standards. In line with the broader dictates of the Basel Concordat of 1986, prudential control over all banks authorized to do business in the EC is exercised by *home* countries, including subsidiaries (which come under a separate 1983 EC directive on consolidated supervision). The EC banking rules are thus broadly based on the German universal banking model, but are flexible enough to accommodate a wide range of institutional forms elected by individual firms according to the dictates of market competition. This is complemented by the Own Funds Directive and the Solvency Ratio Directive, which set forth minimum prudential standards.

Modeled on Britain's 1986 Financial Services Act and originally scheduled to go into effect in January 1993 [see Walter and Smith 1989] but now slated for 1996, the draft Investment Services Directive governs the activities of nonbank securities firms (in the British, Japanese, and U.S. traditions) and likewise involves a single passport. Again, home-country agencies (public authorities or professional associations appointed by public authorities) will retain the power of licensing, supervising, and regulating investment firms. Institutions duly registered and supervised by EC home countries will essentially be free to establish a commercial presence and to supply securities services in any member country without separate authorization. Investment firms holding membership in stock exchanges in their home countries are free to apply for full trading privileges on all EC stock, options, and futures exchanges. Membership access also applies to banks and requires a physical presence in the local market except in exchanges which do not have floor trading.

The draft ISD defines a broad range of investment activities: brokerage, dealing as principal, market making, underwriting, arranging financings, portfolio management, investment advisory, and custody services covering transferable securities, money market instruments, financial futures, and options as well as exchange rate and interest rate instruments (but not including transactions in commodities). It also provides unrestricted access to all major stock, bond, futures, and options exchanges throughout the EC. Close collaboration is envisaged between the EC Commission, the authorities responsible for securities markets and institutions, and banking and insurance authorities.

The draft ISD is complemented by a Draft Capital Adequacy Directive, which specifies the initial capital requirements for securities activities. It is applicable to both banks and nonbank securities firms, and it specifies the treatment of position risk involving exposure to adverse market movements, exchange rate movements, counterparty and settlement exposures, and "other risks" such as extended lack of firm profitability. The draft CAD defines "capital" as equity plus subordinated debt equal to 250% of equity, although the Germans argued that all capital should consist of equity to keep out unsound players. However, the draft contains some flexibility to account for the degree of liquidity of a securities firm's assets. Initial capital levels are set at ECU 500,000 for full securities firms, ECU 100,000 for firms that act only as brokers and portfolio managers, and ECU 50,000 for firms not authorized to hold customers money or securities. Pure investment advisers are exempt from the regulations altogether.

A problem with respect to the CAD has been whether the securities activities of universal banks ought to be treated separately or on a consolidated basis within the bank. Nonbank securities firms argued that bank capital adequacy standards were inappropriate and excessive, reducing their efficiency and competitiveness with non-EC players and leading to a solution that breaks out securities activities of universal banks for capital adequacy purposes. Under the CAD, banks would have a choice of either

(1) applying the book value risk-based capital ratio to both securities and banking business or (2) applying a market valuation to the securities business and the 8% risk-based ratio to the banking business. Under the second option, a universal bank's securities book would thus be broken out for regulatory purposes and capitalized according to the securities rules rather than the banking rules. It would not require, however, that banks place their securities activities in separately capitalized subsidiaries. Such a requirement would have moved still further in the direction of regulation by function and provided some degree of insulation for the banking parent. The compromise nevertheless represented, for the Germans, a significant break in the universal banking tradition. Indeed, this issue pitted the Germans against the British, given their historically different regulatory systems. This issue was of great concern since implementation of the EC regulatory structure for banking in the absence of a comparable structure for securities and capital adequacy could cause serious competitive distortions.

Liberalization of the rules governing the EC insurance industry lags well behind that applied to the banking sector, in part because much of the industry—notably life insurance—remains heavily localized and fragmented, both in terms of insurance underwriting and distribution. Consumer protection and fiduciary regulation play a critical part in setting the terms of competition in the EC countries and in some, notably Germany, have been used to fight a rearguard action against increased competition from foreign insurers.

Commercial risks—property and casualty insurance—are covered by a directive that came into force at the end of June 1990. Such insurance is typically placed in the wholesale markets and syndicated through reinsurance. The industry has traditionally been heavily international. Under this directive, commercial risk insurers licensed by the appropriate regulators in a EC member country may do business anywhere in the EC on a par with local firms. A nonlife directive for the retail sector was agreed in June 1992, to take effect in July 1994.

One difficulty with the life insurance sector is that life policies can be sold either through independent brokers, commission agents of the insurance carriers, or possibly other financial services firms commissioned by the insurance carrier, such as banks and building societies. Several EC draft insurance directives contained, *inter alia*, an "own initiative provision" that would permit the sale by brokers of foreign insurance policies to clients who specifically ask for them, and a "single passport" similar to those in the banking and securities sectors that would permit life insurance companies licensed in one member country to establish distribution channels for its policies in all others. Home-country licensing and host-country control of the conduct of business is exceedingly controversial in life insurance. Perhaps more than in other financial services sectors, consumer protection rules will have to be subject to significant harmonization before liberal EC market access is assured. In Germany, for example, life policies are rigorously standardized, and any new features are subject to painstaking examination by regulators and competitors before they can be marketed. Nevertheless, a life insurance directive was agreed in November 1992, to take effect in July 1994.

The EC Directive governing the operation and sale of mutual funds—UCITS—came into force on 1 October 1989, after 15 years of negotiation. It specifies general rules for the kinds of investments that are appropriate for mutual funds and how they should be sold. The regulatory requirements for fund management and certification are left to the home country of the firm, while specific rules for adequacy of disclosure and selling practices are left to the respective host countries.

Consequently, funds that are duly established and monitored in any EC member country, such as Luxembourg, and that are in compliance with UCITS can be sold without restriction to investors in local markets EC-wide. They can be promoted and advertised through local selling networks and direct mail, as long as selling requirements applicable in each country are met. Permissible investment vehicles include high-performance "synthetic" funds, based on futures and options, not previously permitted in some financial centers such as London. Under UCITS, 90% of fund assets must be invested in publicly traded companies, no more than 5% of the outstanding stock of any company may be owned by a fund, and only limited amounts may be borrowed by investment funds. Real estate funds, commodity funds, and money market funds are excluded from UCITS treatment.

As a consequence of these four building blocks of the EC financial services initiatives, the community by the mid-1990s should have a financial market that is not only unified, but also one that is governed by one of the most liberal and carefully thought-out regulatory regimes in the world.

True financial market integration involves freedom for savers to place their funds, for borrowers to finance themselves, and for banks and other financial firms to pursue profit opportunities anywhere within the EC, all within a reasonably consistent and coherent regulatory framework. This issue has been formally taken up relatively late in the evolution of the EC. It has, however, developed a powerful momentum, driven by political and economic events that began to come at a rapid pace during the 1980s and that promise to continue and perhaps strengthen further in the 1990s. The European financial services industry is thus caught in a dual revolution—geographic and sectorial restructuring, both of which are occurring simultaneously. According to Robin Leigh-Pemberton, former governor of the Bank of England, "The scale of the changes will be so great that in an American context it would almost be as if nationwide interstate banking and the repeal of the Glass-Steagall Act were to be effected at the same time" [Leigh-Pemberton 1989, p. 6].

In the process, the EC will become among the most competitive of the world's financial markets, with large numbers of indigenous and foreign-based players clustered in distinct strategic groups. Universal banks ranging across the spectrum from the German to the British model will play a major role in this structure, but—if Germany's own banking history is any guide—they will not monopolize it as an institutional form. Local and regional banks that can reach viable scale, maintain low costs, and tailor their services to local demand patterns will be able to survive; some of these grouped into cooperatives or strategic alliances may even stretch across borders, as will specialized banks focusing on niches such as mortgage credit. Full-service investment and merchant banks, as well as financial boutiques, are also likely to prosper, especially in various aspects of corporate finance and fast-moving capital market segments, where they may have an advantage against their more bureaucratic and slow-moving universal rivals. Insurance companies will take on a broad range of financial services, such as mutual funds and pensions, even as banks have penetrated retail insurance services. Different types of financial services companies such as Allied Dunbar of the United Kingdom and Compagnie Bancaire of France will offer unusual combinations of financial services based on customer market segments or particular approaches to financial services marketing.

Vigorous competition will dominate the financial services industry of Europe—competition among financial institutions, among EC financial centers, and with financial centers outside the Community. Japanese and American institutions will play significant, (but different) roles in the evolving structure. The EC will provide a new arena in which successful U.S. financial firms can test their mettle against the best of the competition. There is thus a good chance that the EC banking and financial markets in the 1990s will become among the most efficient and innovative in the world, possibly surpassing those of the United States in some respects. European financial market integration stands to play a role in the 1990s that is comparable to the creation of regional free trade some 30 years earlier. Besides creating internal static and dynamic benefits for the EC regional economy, European financial market integration will do much to enhance the standing of the EC in global finance and create a viable staging area for financing the economic restructuring of Eastern Europe. At the same time, the absence of geographic and activity limits in the EC will also make it one of the safest financial systems in the world, in contrast to the United States, where geographic limits have had a demonstrably adverse bearing on failure rates of financial institutions and where activity limits can likewise be argued to have had the same effect. Indeed, according to a position paper by Leigh-Pemberton [1990, p. 12], ". . . by reducing or removing certain distortions in the market, by encouraging some rationalization and concentration of investment, and by promoting efficiency, increased competition in the EC should help strengthen the capacity of EC financial institutions to compete in global markets with non-EC firms (particularly the large U.S. and Japanese groups)."

Some Further Controversies

The controversial issues surrounding universal banking in Europe, as elsewhere, broadly reflect the internal German debates discussed earlier. Issues include the following points, some of which are addressed in later chapters.

Concentration of economic power: Universal banks, by holding large blocks of stock in industrial companies, may be able to influence the structure of the national economy in ways that run counter to the national interest. Counterarguments generally refer to the vigor and sophistication of current antitrust enforcement, the absence of such concentrations in Swiss universal banking, and arguably anticompetitive Japanese *keiretsu* linkups even under prohibition of universal banking in that country.

Concentration of political power: The argument is that universal banks, through dominance of client relationships and degree of economic control, have the ability to suborn the political process and ram through political action that shifts the balance of risks and returns in their favor. This may include favorable tax legislation, access to government guarantees, etc. Counterarguments focus on the fact that special-interest pressures from other types of financial institutions (e.g., U.S. S&Ls) are no less capable of co-opting the political process and that the root of any problem thus may lie in the political process itself.

Conflicts of interest: The probability of conflicts of interest that arise from serving various clients increases with the breadth of activities of a financial services firm. Examples include conflicts between the fiduciary responsibilities of a bank and its role as investment banker; conflicts between its interest in completing a hostile M&A transaction where the target company is a client; and conflicts that result in stuffing and churning portfolios are only a few of a range of issues extensively explored in the literature [Gnehm and Thalmann 1990]. Economists generally rely on adverse reputation effects and on legal sanctions to check the incentives to exploit such conflicts.

Risk-taking: Universal banks may use their powers to undertake securities and insurance activities in order to enhance their risk-taking (and thus risk exposure). Counterarguments focus on the benefits derived from greater diversification and the observation that bank lending itself is often a more risky activity than securities and/or insurance underwriting.

Access to the safety net: Large universal banks will not be permitted to fail due to the social costs of such failure ("too big to fail"), and they therefore have an artificial advantage in competing with institutions that have no such access. Even in cases of failure of separately incorporated affiliates, it may be necessary to bring the safety net into play, leading to unfair advantages in funding costs. If the market perceives this to be the case, the safety net effectively stretches under such affiliates as well. Counterarguments focus on the view that a broader range of activities increases the stability of the financial institution and therefore decreases the likelihood that the safety net will come into play.

Supervision and regulation: Complex and heterogeneous financial institution are more difficult to regulate than those that are more narrowly defined. Counterarguments relate to the need to regulate by function in any case.

Local Monopolies: In efforts to compete, financial services firms view size as a weapon (see Chapter 2), leading to erosion of competition in regional or national markets, such as the Netherlands where the four-bank concentration exceeds 90% following the mergers of ABN-AMRO and NMB-Postbank–Algemene Nederlanden (ING Bank). Counterarguments focus on the pro-competitive impact of actual and potential rivals from other EC countries under a single-market regime.

Conclusion

This chapter has reviewed the universal banking structures of three countries: Germany, Switzerland, and the United Kingdom. Each is unique— Germany's emphasis on industrial holdings and corporate control, Switzerland's focus on fiduciary business and banks' long abstinence from insurance, and the U.K. bank's avoidance of industrial control and functional separation of merchant banking activities. All have in common, however, the broad-gauge ability of banks to choose the organizational form activity set that best suits them from a market perspective. This same freedom to choose is in the process of being implemented at the EC level as well. As we shall reemphasize in the final chapter of this study, absent a significant, coherent and long overdue reordering of the U.S. financial regulatory system, the EC initiatives could lead to a serious erosion in the competitive position of American financial institutions and markets.

5

The Risk of Nonbank Activities

The decade of the 1980s was a traumatic time for U.S. banks. Major federal legislative initiatives, such as the Depository Institutions Deregulation and Monetary Control Act (DIDMCA, 1980) and the Garn-St.Germain Act (1982), eroded bank-thrift barriers to competition while statewide initiatives, such as regional banking pacts, significantly reduced the importance of barriers to interstate banking that include the McFadden Act.

At the same time, competition for banking-type products intensified outside the domestic banking sector in at least three areas.

1. Competition from money market mutual funds (on the liability side) and commercial paper (on the asset side) challenged the profitability of banks' core business activities, that is, deposits and loans.
2. The growth of nonbank banks (at least until the Competitive Equality in Banking Act of 1987) posed a further threat to the value of banks' retail banking franchises.
3. The growing entry of foreign banks into the United States captured significant markets with, for example, foreign banks at the end of 1990 holding more than 21% of total U.S. bank assets in California alone.

As noted in Chapter 2, at the end of 1991 no U.S. bank made the top 10 list of banks worldwide (measured by asset size) as global competition in financial services intensified. The largest U.S. bank (Citibank) ranked 25th at year-end 1991. Among the top 50 by this measure, 20 were Japanese, 8 were German, 6 were French, and 2 were American.

Despite erosion of U.S. banks' global charter values, the United States still retained, largely intact, its historic restrictions on banks' entry into many potentially profitable nonbank areas of activity in both the financial and real sectors of the economy. Thus, U.S. banks continue to be prohibited from underwriting both life insurance and property and casualty insurance, and have very limited ability to act as insurance brokers, while their corporate securities underwriting activities continue to be limited by the Glass-Steagall Act of 1933. Where nonbanking activities have been allowed, many are required to be "closely related to banking" and invariably undertaken in separately capitalized subsidiaries of the holding company under a restrictive set of *firewalls*—thereby limiting the potential economies of scope available from engaging in the sale and distribution of multiple financial service products.[1]

Background

Historically, regulators have justified the bank holding company structure and the philosophy of separating bank affiliates within the corporate structure on the grounds of safety and soundness [see Saunders 1988 for an extensive discussion of this issue]. Basically, it is argued that by requiring nonbank activities to take place in separately capitalized subsidiaries of the holding company, any risk-increasing effects of these activities can be insulated from the bank and will not impose additional claims on the federal safety net—deposit insurance, the discount window, and payment system guarantees. As will be discussed in Chapter 7, however, such insulation via regulatory imposed firewalls can never be perfect.[2] Moreover, separation and firewalls may impose their own costs, such as reducing potential economies of scope, as well as limiting the ability of U.S. banks to compete with other U.S. financial firms and large foreign universal bank competitors. And it is by no means certain that expanding the permitted range of banks' financial services activities increases the risk of the banking organization as a whole even if certain nonbank activities are risky when viewed in isolation: If returns from nonbank activities are imperfectly correlated with banking activities, overall risk of the firm can actually decrease as long as certain conditions hold with respect to the scale of the nonbank activity undertaken and its total risk level relative to banking.

The objective of this and the next two chapters is to evaluate the case for universal banking as the appropriate organizational form for U.S.

---

[1]Broadly defined, firewalls are regulatory or legally imposed limitations on relationships between insured depositories and their affiliates.

[2]For example, it is impossible to control for informational contagion effects among subsidiaries and affiliates of a holding company [see Benston 1989; Eisenbeis 1988; Flannery 1986; and Saunders 1988].

banking, focusing largely on the safety and soundness (risk) issues surrounding a radical reform of the system. In so doing, it is hoped to move the debate away from piecemeal ad hoc tinkerings with the existing one-bank holding company structure, and towards considering the implications of adopting more universal configurations for financial service firms similar to those found in Germany, Switzerland, Britain, and the EC in general, as discussed in Chapter 4.

Universal banking in its fullest or purest form would allow a banking corporation to engage "in house" in any activity associated with banking, insurance, and securities. That is, these activities would be undertaken in departments of the organization rather than in separate subsidiaries.

Recall from Figure 4–1 the two variants of universal banking that result from actual practice. In Germany, while bank and securities activities are usually undertaken in departments of the universal bank *itself*, insurance activities must be undertaken in a bank subsidiary. In the United Kingdom, on the other hand, securities activities and insurance activities both are usually undertaken in separate subsidiaries of the bank.

Apparently, in the view of U.S. bank regulators, the capital of the banking organization and the federal safety net would be more seriously exposed to losses on securities and insurance activities under either of these forms of universal banking than under traditional one-bank holding company structure, where a bank and its securities (or insurance) affiliate are organized as separate subsidiaries of a parent holding company. As a result, any in-depth consideration of the case for (or against) universal banking must evaluate the potential riskiness of the organization form—both its insolvency risk and other risks such as conflicts of interest—as well as implication (if any) for the federal safety net.[3]

While 1992 was an exceedingly good year for U.S. banks, partly due to the very low level of interest rates (and relatively wide interest margins) it is arguable that this might have been a special case that bucks the secular trend. Specifically, evidence on the declining value of U.S. bank charters over the decade of the 1980s can be found by analyzing both accounting and stock market data. With respect to accounting data, *Forbes* [1990] has

---

[3]In this book, we do not consider in depth the benefits and risks to the United States from the equity control aspect of universal banking. Indeed, one of the facets of universal banking that has gained attention is that by taking long-term equity positions in firms either directly or indirectly via customer proxies, universal banks can better monitor and discipline managers and thereby achieve better industrial performance [see Cable 1985; Steinherr and Huveneers 1989; and Cable and Dirrheimer 1983 for evidence in the context of German universal banking]. See the discussion of this issue in Chapter 4. It is assumed here that the United States will continue to seek a separation from banking and commerce and that nonbank equity positions of financial universal banks will arise out of trading, investment trustee, underwriting, and agency considerations, rather than from nonbank managerial control considerations. Of course, if such a separation is relaxed, this may provide additional potential benefits from universal banking [see Saunders 1990 for a full discussion of the issues relating to the separation of banking from commerce in the United States and Berlin, John, and Saunders [1992] for a theoretical modelling of the advantages of banks holding equity stakes in firms].

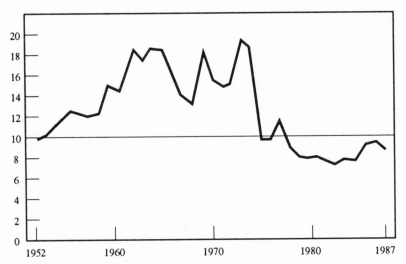

Figure 5–1 Ratio of market value of equity to book value of equity, 1952–87.
The twenty-five largest bank holding companies. (*Source:* Boyd and Rolnick
1988)

shown that for the years 1980–89, the U.S. Generally Accepted Accounting Practice (GAAP) average return on equity was lower for multinational
(i.e., money center) banks (at 10.4%) than for any of the three insurance
sectors (an average return of 14.4%), or large thrift institutions (15.2%),
brokerage and commodities firms (13.4%), and lease and finance companies (15.9%). Regional banks (14.5%) outperformed brokerage and commodity firms, life and health insurance firms, in addition to money center
banks.

An alternative way to view the secularly declining value of bank charters is to plot over time the ratio of the market value of bank equity to the
book value of bank equity. A high value for this ratio indicates high
profitability for the industry.[4] As can be seen from Figure 5–1, for the
period 1952 to mid-1970s for the 25 largest banks the market-to-book
ratio exceeded 1. However, since 1975 (until at least 1987), the market-to-
book ratio has been less than 1. Indeed, Salomon Brothers analysts have
reported that as of the third quarter 1990, the market-to-book ratio for
their 11 money center bank composite stood at .666, while their 24
regional bank composite stood at .788.[5] See Table 2–10 for market-to-
book ratios for the top 50 U.S. and foreign banks in 1991.

Figures for 1990 from the FDIC also confirm a downward profitability trend for all FDIC-insured banks in the 1980s with the exception
of 1988, a year of exceptionally high bank profitability (see Table 5–1). In
addition, the FDIC data reveal a second trend in the 1980s, namely,

---

[4]That is, current assets of the industry are valued more than its book values.

[5]See Salomon Brothers, *Commercial Bank Stock Research*, 15 October 1990. These ratios
were, however, significantly above 1 in 1992.

Table 5-1 Selected Indicators, Federal Deposit Insurance Corporation (FDIC)-Insured Commercial Banks

	1991[a]	1990[a]	1990	1989	1988	1987	1986
Return on assets	0.60%	0.61%	0.49%	0.49%	0.82%	0.12%	0.63%
Return on equity	8.92	9.59	7.63	7.78	13.30	2.00	9.94
Equity capital to assets	6.71	6.45	6.46	6.21	6.28	6.04	6.20
Noncurrent loans and leases plus other real estate owned to assets	3.07	2.63	2.90	2.26	2.14	2.46	1.94
Net charge-offs to loans	1.51	1.35	1.41	1.16	1.00	0.92	0.98
Asset growth rate	1.48	5.06	2.73	5.37	4.36	2.01	7.71
Net operating income growth	−13.33	12.95	3.72	−35.84	1,905.16	−91.04	−20.65
Percentage of unprofitable banks	11.25	11.46	13.35	12.50	14.65	17.66	19.79
No. of institutions	12,072	12,409	12,340	12,707	13,139	13,696	14,200
No. of problem banks	1,005	1,006	1,012	1,092	1,394	1,559	1,457
No. of failed/assisted banks	82	134	159	206	221	201	144

[a]Through September 30; ratios annualized where appropriate. Asset growth rates are for 12 months ending September 30.
Data: Federal Deposit Insurance Corporation, 1992.

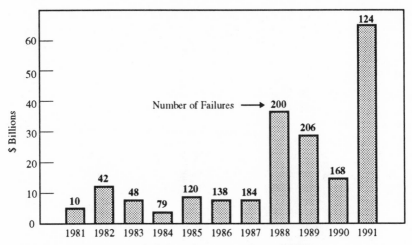

Figure 5-2 America's bank failures by assets. (*Data:* FDIC)

increased bank risk. Specifically, in the period 1975–79, an average of 10.4 banks per year failed; between 1981 and 1991 banks failed at an average annual rate of 120 (see Figure 5–2) with 124 failures in 1991 alone. Other indicators also show an increase in bank risk exposure. In 1989, for example, the number of banks on the FDIC's problem list was 1,092 (compared to 800 in 1984), net charge-offs on loans were 1.16% in 1989 versus 0.75% in 1984, and nonperforming assets to totals assets were 2.26% in 1989 versus 1.60% in 1984.

At least some of the increase in bank failures and problem banks may be attributable to bankers undertaking more risky *banking* activities per se, in attempts to maintain profitability and to exploit the risk-taking incentives inherent in a mispriced FDIC safety net. However, one might reasonably question whether the same number of failed and problem banks would have occurred if: (1) banks had been allowed to diversify into *non*bank activities—such as certain insurance lines (e.g., personal automobile insurance or whole life insurance) and securities activities—as might have been their reaction to increased competition in a universal banking environment; and (2) They had been able to diversify on a national basis in lending, that is, if they had not been restricted by the McFadden Act and other interstate banking restrictions.[6]

The expansion of banking organizations into insurance and securities activities raises a number of controversial issues regarding the associated risks and their effects on the overall safety and soundness of the banking

---

[6]Again, more universal banking systems, such as those found in Germany and the United Kingdom, historically have had no restrictions on the ability of banks to branch nationwide. The absence of this restriction is exhibited, in general, by a smaller number of banks in such systems. Further, as Benston [1989] notes, a very large proportion of U.S. bank failures are unit banks, that is, those who choose not to, or, in many cases, could not, branch.

system. In this chapter, we examine the inherent riskiness of life insurance, casualty and property insurance (brokerage and underwriting), and securities activities (brokerage and underwriting). Since considerable analysis of the risks inherent in securities activities has already been made [see Walter, ed., 1985; Benston 1989; and Saunders 1988], more attention will be placed here on the insurance sector. We concentrate on the fundamental types of insolvency risk facing a financial institution that engages in these activities. This will allow a fuller understanding of the risk exposure of banking organizations entering such activities and of the value-added or skills they can bring to these markets as risk managers.

We first examine life insurance, concentrating on the ability of universal banks to manage risks associated with the business of life insurance. We next conduct a similar analysis for property–casualty insurance, and for securities activities. Finally, we analyze issues relating to conflicts of interest and insolvency risk.

Banks and Life Insurance

Life insurance contracts allow people to protect themselves and their beneficiaries against losses in income, either through premature (untimely) death or retirement. Their essential feature is that, by pooling risks, the insurance mechanism allows income-related risks to be transferred from an individual to a group. While life insurance may be its core activity, the modern life insurance company usually also engages in (1) the sale of annuity contracts, (2) the management of pension plans, and (3) the provision of accident and health insurance.

Current Regulation

Historically, banks in the United States have been granted very limited permission to *sell* life insurance and virtually no permission to *underwrite* life insurance. However, more recently the courts, state, and national bank regulators have widened these powers somewhat. Nevertheless, the scope of permitted activities remains narrow, and is dependent on the type of bank charter and on whether insurance activities are conducted by the bank or its parent holding company.

For nationally chartered banks, the National Bank Act allows the sale of (1) all types of insurance in towns of less than 5,000 residents; (2) insurance activity lines related to banking—such as credit insurance, title insurance, and certain annuities; and (3) customer lists to outside insurers. States have taken varying restrictive actions regarding the insurance activities of state-chartered banks. Since 1987, however, there has been a clear trend towards a broadening of banks' insurance selling powers. The General Accounting Office (GAO) [*Banks Selling Insurance*, 1990] reported that 22 states in 1989 introduced bills expanding insurance sales by state-chartered banks. Indeed, Delaware in 1990 passed legislation allowing state-chartered bank affiliates to sell and underwrite insurance nationwide. This would have allowed a number of large banking organizations with operations in that state, such as Citicorp and Chase Manhattan, to engage in insurance underwriting and selling through direct subsidiaries of the Delaware-chartered bank, for example, Family Guardian Life Insurance Company of New York as a subsidiary of Citibank, Delaware. However, both the Federal Reserve and the FDIC have vigorously sought to prevent banks from exploiting the Delaware law.

In general, the 1956 Bank Holding Company Act and its 1970 amendments restrict bank holding companies from engaging in insurance activities through affiliates. The major life insurance exceptions are that: (1) a bank holding company may sell credit insurance, (2) a bank holding company may sell all types of insurance in towns of less than 5,000 residents, and (3) a bank holding company selling insurance on 1 May 1982 may continue those activities—this is a grandfather clause under the Garn-St. Germain Act of 1982.

Banks and Life Insurance Risk

The limited nature of banks' permitted life insurance activities reflect concerns among regulators that any expansion in insurance activities will result in new and more managerially complex risks that could ultimately harm the bank itself, causing it to fail and imposing increased potential claims on the deposit insurance fund and the safety net in general.

There are three organizational ways in which banks could engage in insurance activities: (1) in house, via a department of the bank, (2) via a separately capitalized subsidiary of the bank, or (3) via a separately capitalized affiliate of the bank holding company. Clearly, the risks to the bank will depend on the degree of integration and the organizational structure chosen in which to engage in insurance activities. As noted in Chapter 4, even in Germany—the most universal of banking systems—insurance activities are conducted either through subsidiaries of the parent bank or through cross-selling joint ventures with insurance companies.

Here, we shall assume that underwriting is conducted via a direct subsidiary of the bank, so that a bank has a direct capital stake in the insurance subsidiary. We then ask whether there is anything exceptional, in terms of risk, when the underwriter and seller of life insurance is operated as a bank subsidiary rather than as an independent life insurer. Three central issues that arise in this case concern:

1. The potential for conflicts of interest arising, for example, from banks tying loan customers to their subsidiaries life insurance products.

2. The potential for deposit insurance and other safety net guarantees either explicitly or implicitly being extended to the bank's insurance affiliate, so that it gains a competitive advantage.

3. The degree of earnings diversification between bank product lines and insurance product lines.

These three risk-related issues will be addressed later in this book. Here we focus on direct life insurance risk management issues. What new types of risk do life insurance activities create that are relatively unfamiliar to bankers? What types of risk, on the other hand, are quite familiar to banks and bankers? What skills, expertise, resources, and experience can banks bring to the management of life insurance activities? What risk management gaps remain to be filled?

The first, and perhaps most important, distinction in evaluating the insolvency risk of life insurance activities is between the *agency* function of selling and marketing insurance policies and the *principal* function of underwriting different types of life insurance policies.

Agency Risk

Insurance products can be marketed or sold through three delivery systems: (1) independent agents, (2) exclusive agents, or (3) direct writers. An independent agent represents, and seeks to sell, the products of a number of different insurers and earns fees and commissions from the insurance companies whose policies are sold. An exclusive agent (or captive agent) represents the products of one insurer and earns commissions and other income from that insurer. Direct writers have employees who generally use direct mail and telephone solicitation, as well as mass-media advertising, to solicit sales of policies for a single insurer.

As long as the *agent* selling insurance is separate from the principal underwriting the insurance, the *direct* risks of agency activities are likely to be small—regardless of delivery system used—since policy losses are the financial responsibility of the underwriter. A GAO study [1990] concluded that the direct risks of the agency function (including banks selling insurance products underwritten by unaffiliated firms) is minimal. However, the GAO also suggested that some *indirect* risks may indeed arise. There may be economic losses if agency business is unprofitable, as well as potential for conflicts of interest and a diversion of scarce managerial skills into new activities. And an insurance agency may be liable to policyholders for errors in marketing the insurance, although this is usually hedged by agents purchasing "errors and omissions insurance" [GAO 1990].

Principal Risk

Although a detailed discussion of the nature of the underwriting function and the role played by actuaries in determining premiums is well beyond the scope of this chapter, we shall endeavor to describe here the essential sources of risk in life insurance underwriting and to explain how banks could manage such risks if they were permitted to engage in life insurance activities.

The primary function of an actuary, within a coverage group and contractual type, is to determine a net premium that is sufficient to cover the risk of loss (claims cost). At the heart of this calculation are assumptions about the mortality probabilities of the group being insured and the interest (yield) on investments made between the time premiums are paid in and the time benefits are paid out. The gross premium—which is the actual premium the consumer pays—adds a loading factor to the net premium. This factor can include an element to cover operational and distribution costs, a profit element (determined by competitive conditions for the contract), and a "safety margin" element (in the case of so-called participating policies).

It is clear that losses on the underwriting function can result from any or all of the following three factors: (1) unexpected increases in mortality probabilities, (2) unexpected declines in investment yield/returns, or (3) unexpected increases in insurers operating costs and other expense factors relative to the loading factor. Life insurance underwriting thus has three essential risk sources: mortality risk, investment risk, and loading or expense risk [see *inter alia* Black, 1987; Mehr and Gustavson, 1987; and Vaughan, 1989]. In addition, life insurers face the risk of adverse selection, reinsurance risk, liquidity risk, and the risk to the guarantee fund. We can take a closer look at the implications of these risks for insurance subsidiaries of banks.

Specific Risks and Banks' Ability to Manage Them

Mortality Risk

At the core of evaluating mortality risk are mortality tables that express the probabilities of individuals living or dying at any given age. Using such tables, which reflect past experience based on the law of large numbers, the actuary seeks to predict future death (loss) rates at given ages for the insured. These tables may either be firm-based (i.e., based on the experience of the individual insurer) or national-based, such as the mortality tables produced by the Society of Actuaries, that reflect the experience of a large group of insurers over a number of years. Based on these tables, the National Association of Insurance Commissioners often determines "safety margins" that overstate the actual death rate experience. Given the experiential and "law of large numbers" base for mortality tables, the risk in setting future premiums is that the mortality rates are shifting, and will shift significantly, over the coverage period by a rate that exceeds any built-in safety margin in the premiums. For example, fixed premiums that were set on a 10-year term life policy at the beginning of the period, based on mortality experience as of that time, may be rendered insufficient by large upward shifts in mortality probabilities.

Recent research has highlighted the potentially high-risk consequences of acquired immunodeficiency syndrome (AIDS) and human immunodeficiency virus (HIV) infection on life insurers. For example, Cowell and Hoskings [1987] estimate that of the 1 million to 1.5 million Americans infected with AIDS/HIV, the majority would die over the next 10 years. They also estimate that AIDS-related claims would amount to some $50 billion just from customers already covered. Given incomplete medical screening, long and variable latency periods, and uncertainty over the rate of diffusion of the disease, the risk of misestimating mortality probabilities has in all likelihood increased for most life insurers.

Mortality risk is the feature of life insurance contracts that is probably the least familiar to bankers, other than those directly concerned with the credit life insurance product traditionally offered by banks. It suggests that the actuarial basis of risk and premium setting would require additional (external) expertise in this area. Since there is no reason to believe that the market for actuarial talent is uncompetitive, banks willing to pay market salaries should have equal access to actuarial skills. As a result, the uniqueness of mortality risk should be viewed as neither a barrier to entry nor to appropriate risk management by banks.

Investment Risk

Since life insurers normally receive premiums before benefits are paid, and since the insurer generates interest (returns) on premium flows, premiums are set to reflect expected investment returns. As in the case of mortality tables, the insurer often has considerable freedom in selecting the expected interest rate assumption underlying investment earnings, with many insurers assuming rates in the 4.5–5.5% range. These conservative assumptions mean that only if interest rates drop below this low level—for example, in periods of very low inflation—will the "compounding" assumptions on premiums paid be insufficient to meet the expectations of the company.

This emphasis on yield and the low-yield assumption for premium setting, however, may create incentives for insurers to shift into higher-yield investments, since interest earnings that exceed assumed yields potentially add to an insurers profits and increase the firm's surplus and reserves. This incentive is enhanced by regulators' use of Statutory Accounting Principles (SAP), under which most bonds are carried at amortized (historical) cost rather than at market value. As a result, capital gains and losses are not fully reflected on the insurer's balance sheet.

While state insurance regulators seek to put limits on the asset mixes that can be chosen to back most types of life insurance policies—the major exception being separate-account types of policies, such as variable life—insurers still have a considerable degree of investment discretion.

Moreover, the growth of asset-return-sensitive policies, such as universal life and variable life, as well as interest rate or yield guarantees provided to private pension plan through Guaranteed Investment Contracts (GICs), have accelerated and augmented those incentives in the 1980s. These were heavily promoted by life insurance companies, and sold to pension funds and other long-term investors. In its most simple form, the GIC guarantees the holder a fixed interest rate on invested funds over a number of years. Because of intense competition, insurers often had to invest GIC-committed funds in long-term and more risky assets such as low-grade corporate bonds, so as to try to make the target return. As a result, they subjected themselves to significant interest rate and default risk. In addition, they often made forward commitments by agreeing to GICs at some fixed rate over some fixed time period. If market rates then dropped during the commitment period, "off balance sheet" exposure was added to basic risk exposures associated with these instruments, sometimes leading to a negative spread—with GIC rates exceeding market rates and creating corresponding losses for insurers.

The pursuit of high *ex ante* yield has caused a number of problems for life insurers which have had to face the realization that high *ex ante* yield is not the same as high *ex post* return on investments. For example, the problems that Executive Life, First Capital, and Mutual Benefit Life had in the early 1990s stemmed, at least in part, from risky investment policies in which junk bonds were relied on to enhance yields.

Specifically, life insurance companies face two additional sources of investment risk, over and above the risk that investment yields will fall below those assumed in premium calculations:

1. *Duration-mismatch or gap risk* arises whenever the insurer mismatches the respective durations of its portfolio of assets and liabilities. Since duration is a direct measure of the sensitivity of the market value of assets and liabilities to interest rate shocks, a balance sheet mismatch will result in market value gains or losses on assets and liabilities that directly affect the economic value of net worth, or true solvency position, of the insurer. Whereas SAP-based net worth calculations will, in general, fail to reflect such shocks, they nevertheless affect the true solvency position of the insurer—since economic net worth is the difference between the market values of the insurer's assets and its liabilities. For example, to the extent that pursuit of high yields drives insurers to invest at the very long end of the bond yield curve—when the yield curve assumes its normal upward-sloping shape—it is likely that the duration of assets will be greater than the duration of liabilities. In this case, the economic net worth (solvency) will be adversely affected by any unexpected increase in yields.

2. *Asset-quality or default risk* arises from investments in risky assets. While state regulators have often imposed stringent limits on life insurers' investments in common and preferred stocks—so that at the end of 1990 they accounted for a mere 4.2% of assets—considerably more discretion has been allowed for real estate and

bond investments. Indeed, excessive investments in commercial real estate and junk bonds have been viewed as central to a number of large life-insurer insolvencies and problems. Moreover, Value Line and Investors Diversified Services Corp. (IDS), among others, have issued investor warnings regarding the junk bond and commercial mortgages portfolios of life insurers. Concerns about such investments have prompted states such as New York to restrict investments in junk bonds to 20% of life insurers' portfolios. They have also prompted National Association of Insurance Commissioners (NAIC) to propose a model law restricting junk bond investments. A number of insurers divested large proportions of their junk bond holdings in the early 1990s.

While life insurance companies do own approximately 30% of the junk bonds outstanding, these holdings have been quite heavily concentrated among a few insurers. Further, the default risk performance and relative return performance of junk bonds versus investment grade bonds is the subject of considerable dispute [Altman 1989]. It is the area of real estate and mortgage loans, that may pose greater longer-term asset quality problems to life insurers.

The types of interest-rate and credit-related investment return-risk trade-offs faced by life insurers should be fully familiar to bankers. Indeed, like life insurance companies, banks hold few (if any) equity investments in their portfolios and concentrate on fixed income securities such as bonds and loans. While regulators have limited bank holdings of junk bonds, banks' participation in the Highly Leveraged Transactions (HLT) loan market has involved credit risk assessments of a similar nature to the valuation of assets underlying junk bond issues. Indeed, the credit risk assessment tools for corporate bonds and commercial loans are generally very similar, involving subjective and objective evaluations of the assets and cash flows of the issuing (borrowing) firms. In a related fashion, the tools and methods of duration gap management were largely innovated by banks. Thus, the growth of banks' off-balance sheet positions in interest-rate futures, options, swaps, and caps can be explained, in part, by concerns relating to the hedging of their interest risk exposures. Nevertheless, gap management in life insurance may be complicated by the multiple option features inherent in newer types of life insurance contracts.

Loading or Expense Risk

The third component of risk in setting premiums relates to the cost elements in setting the loading factor—or the difference between the *gross* premium and the *net* premium. For example, rapid increases in inflation may cause underlying assumptions incorporated in existing premiums to be unrealistic about the costs of insurance distribution and administration. Since premiums on most traditional policies cannot be altered once they are put into effect, this risk can only be hedged by incorporating a sufficient margin or premium in the loading factor to account for expected inflation and cost-pressure risk.

To this end, insurers often market so-called *participating policies* that have a bigger "cost" safety margin than nonparticipating policies. Participating policies return dividends to policyholders when the safety margin is not needed (as in low inflation periods), often after adding a part of the unused margin to reserves while using the extra premium margin to meet rising costs in more inflationary periods.

The exposure of banks to risks associated with operating costs will most likely depend on the chosen method of life insurance distribution. If they choose to distribute their insurance products through either independent or exclusive agents, they may have a more difficult time in monitoring and controlling costs and commissions than if they were to use salaried employees to sell insurance directly via their branches. Although direct selling may involve training costs for staff to familiarize them with insurance products and their risk characteristics, direct selling may offer the best opportunity for a banking organization as a whole to generate cost-economies of scope—for example, through a shared customer information base and input resources—as well as economies of scope in revenues through joint marketing of products. Of course, failure to achieve sufficient sales may rapidly escalate operational costs and cast doubt upon the adequacy of premiums, especially given the old adage that insurance is "sold" rather than "bought."

Adverse Selection Risk

While insurers consider mortality, investment return, and loading when calculating premiums, an important component of underwriting risk is the question of whom to accept or deny coverage. To the extent that the idiosyncratic characteristics of each individual covered (age, health, job, education, etc.) could be exactly identified, precise pricing of insurance contracts should be straightforward. However, given the costs of information collection, premiums are often predicated on a narrow set of observed characteristics such as age and sex. Despite the use of such selection screens, individuals often have private information regarding their own longevity and health prospects. The weaker the prescreening, the more apparently equivalent any group becomes, and the greater the problem of *adverse selection*.

For example, with premiums set according to the average age and sex characteristics of the group, those individuals who are more risky than average—that is, who privately expect to live shorter lives—will be more likely to buy insurance than those individuals who have private beliefs/information of longer than average life expectancy. Such a problem can result in adverse selection in that the good risks do not join the insured pool while the bad risks do join. If premiums are based on some average population life expectancy, the insurance rate may be set too low given the impaired quality of the actual pool being insured. As a result, the potential for adverse selection is often considered to be greater in group life insurance than in ordinary life insurance—since many screening devices such as medical examinations are often forgone in group life coverage.

One technique that insurers use to avoid adverse selection in such cases is to require a large percentage (e.g., 75%) of employees to join a group plan before it begins operation. In this way, both "above average" and "below average" risks are more likely to be covered and the adverse selection problem is reduced as compared to group coverage where membership is voluntary. Where the employee does not personally pay for the coverage, in the case of noncontributing group plans, it is also common practice for the insurer to require a 100% coverage of all employees.

As in the case of insurers, adverse selection risk is a common problem faced by bankers seeking to make loans to an observationally equivalent pool of potential borrowers. In particular, raising loan rates often results in "good" borrowers dropping out of the potential pool of borrowers, leaving behind a poorer quality pool of actual borrowers. Like life insurers, bankers expend substantial resources seeking to distinguish among borrowers according to characteristics such as age, sex, occupation, and salary so as to minimize adverse selection problems. Such credit-screening mechanisms are of course costly. Interestingly, many of the characteristics or attributes used in prescreening individual life insurance applicants to avoid adverse selection also go into credit-scoring models used by banks to sort among individual prospective borrowers in credit card and mortgage loan applicants. While there is unlikely to be a one-to-one mapping between an individual life insurance screening mechanism and a credit screening mechanism in banks, they are sufficiently similar to suggest important potential economies of scope in risk management.

Reinsurance Risk

Insurers generally set retention limits on the amount of risk exposure they are willing to face on any given individual or group life policy. To facilitate their ability to write large contracts while limiting their risk exposure, primary insurers can cede some of the risk and premium income to one or more reinsurers. In the United States, an estimated 4% of gross life insurance premiums are ceded to reinsurers [Witt and Aird 1990; Swiss Re, *Sigma*, May 1990] which is far less than the percentage of property–casualty premiums ceded in this manner (as discussed later).

By its very nature, reinsurance has a number of potentially risk-reducing benefits for a primary insurer; however, it also has some inherent risk-increasing features [Witt and Aird 1990]. The principal benefits are that it allows the insurer the ability to increase capacity by taking on large exposures (contracts) while retaining only a portion of the risk. It also allows an insurer to spread or diversify its portfolio of risks better, and therefore to reduce overall underwriting exposure. It provides protection against extreme risks or catastrophic losses, and allows the primary insurer to generate fee income or commissions that can potentially add to its surplus by creating and then ceding business. Finally, it allows an insurer the ability to exit a given line or area of activity more easily than if there were no reinsurers. For example, an insurer may wish to cede all ordinary life policies written in a given state should it wish to withdraw from that market.

Nevertheless, reinsurance itself has some risk-increasing attributes as well:

1. Reinsurance contracts may encourage an insurer to pursue an excessive growth policy in terms of premiums written. In so doing, it may become less careful about underwriting standards—especially if it has entered into a treaty reinsurance contract, where it knows that it can automatically place risks in a certain contract-class with the reinsurer before the contract is written.

2. The wider the discretion the primary insurer has in writing contracts and ceding them to reinsurers, the greater are its incentives to place "bad risks" with reinsurers and retain the "good risks"—the moral hazard problem.

3. Related to moral hazard, the reinsurer can dispute a claim, especially where it asserts fraudulent behavior on the part of the primary insurer. This creates a problem because the claim of insurance beneficiaries is legally against the primary underwriter, even when part of the coverage is ceded to reinsurers. The policyholder cannot sue the reinsurer for failure to meet its share of a claim.

4. Reinsurers themselves have retention limits and often seek reinsurance with so called retrocessionaries. This leads to a complex web of claims that is extremely sensitive to solvency problems among reinsurers or retrocessionaries.

5. There is also the relatively unregulated nature of the reinsurance market. One reason for lack of regulation is the difficulty in accurately assessing the precise nature of the liabilities and risks faced by reinsurers. Another is the fact that a significant portion of reinsurance capacity is located offshore (e.g., Munich Re, Swiss Re) and is not subject to state examination or enforcement, which itself is viewed as comparatively weak [see GAO 1989].

Reinsurance can thus have both risk-reducing and risk-increasing effects. The fact that life insurance risks are generally more predictable and less catastrophic than property–casualty risks has meant that the demand for life-related reinsurance has been low as a percent of gross premiums. So any net risk exposure emanating from reinsurance activities is probably very low.

With respect to banks' ability to deal with this issue, Witt and Aird

[1990] note that reinsurance, under which a life insurer cedes part of a policy to another insurer, is quite similar to loan selling or securitization in which a bank originates, packages, and sells all or part (strips) of its mortgage and commercial loans. The similarity is stronger if loan sales are made with recourse, under which the banker retains a contingent long-term liability should the credit risk of the loan change.

As noted earlier, insurance policies ceded in part to reinsurers remain a liability of the insurer from the perspective of the policyholder. Moreover, reinsurance (like loan sales) allows a financial institution to expand capacity, achieve greater diversification, and generate fee income. Furthermore, contractual incentive issues, such as the moral hazard incentive to sell bad loans, arise in a similar fashion to the moral hazard incentive to cede questionable insurance policies.

This similarity probably should not be taken too far, however, since the contingent liability risk of reinsurance for a primary insurer may be much greater on average than for a bank engaging in loan sales. For example, for regulatory reasons most bank loan sales are made without recourse for the buyer of the loan. This would be similar to the reinsurer having a binding obligation to pay the policy claims on any and every policy ceded to him.

Liquidity Risk

Like any financial institution (such as banks), life insurers are potentially exposed to liquidity risk. In the case of insurance, liquidity risk emanates from a sudden demand for cash by policyholders when the balance sheet assets of the insurer are relatively illiquid. In many cases, cash demands can be met by selling off assets such as Treasury securities, representing approximately 8% of life insurers' assets in 1989 (according to *Best's*). But such actions may involve capital losses on securities, since cash demands tend to increase in high-interest environments. In extreme cases, when large numbers of policyholders demand cash simultaneously, a liquidity crisis can develop and result in eventual insolvency as the insurer seeks to sell off less liquid assets such as commercial real estate or corporate bonds at "fire sale" prices. That is, cash demands of policyholders have in recent years resulted in "run"-type situations and rendered insurers insolvent, as in the case of a state bailout of Mutual Benefit Life in New Jersey during 1990.

A number of different types of liquidity risk can be identified:

1. Requests by individual policyholders to borrow against their policies. Most individual life insurance contracts allow such borrowings or "policy loans" to be made. This risk is greatest when the costs of policyholder loans lie below market interest rates and offer arbitrage opportunities. To limit this subsidy and its profit-eroding effects, insurers have attempted to lift the rates charged for such loans. Many states have placed an upper cap, or limit, of 8% on

policy loan rates. Again, this type of cash withdrawal risk is clearly greatest in high interest rate environments.

2. Liquidity risk can emanate from partial withdrawals of funds under universal life contracts. Such contracts enable individuals to withdraw funds without terminating policies. This risk is greatest when market yields exceed the yields on the investment element of the universal policy.

3. Policyholders may become unsure of the ability of the insurer to meet promised future benefits and claims. This is the most serious type of liquidity risk—and the one that can develop into a "run" and subsequent insolvency. In such a situation, "place in line" can matter in that the first policyholders seeking to cash in their policies are most likely to receive payment in full. Those last in line may be left holding claims against an insolvent insurer. As a result, there is an incentive to "run" on the insurer and to be the first to withdraw whenever there is doubt about the ability of the insurer to meet policy commitments. This may be due, for example, to large investments in poor quality assets which come to the attention of policyholders. Moreover, runs might develop not only among smaller "less informed" policyholders, but also among sophisticated ones such as group pension plan sponsors, who may doubt the ability of an insurer to meet promised funding commitments (especially returns on guaranteed investment contracts) and therefore seek to switch their pension plan business to other financial institutions.

4. While the risk of runs is potentially smaller for life insurers than for depository institutions—because of the less liquid and, *ex ante*, longer-term nature of life-insurance policyholder contracts as compared with deposit contracts, and the fact that termination of the contract usually involves a penalty—it is a risk that has raised considerable concern among industry analysts and regulators.

Like life insurers, banks are exposed to cash withdrawal demands as part of the contractual rights of their main liability holders, depositors. Like policyholders of life insurance, bank depositors may engage in run-like behavior and push the institution into insolvency. But liquidity risk pressures are, on average, always likely to be more ominous for banks because of the short-term nature of their contractual liabilities. That is, demand deposit accounts give the contract holder an instantaneous putable claim on the bank, with virtually zero transaction cost. So bankers have traditionally been very conscious of liquidity risk problems and the need to retain sufficient liquid assets, such as cash reserves and government bonds to meet customer demands for cash withdrawals. Consequently, bankers are likely to be highly conscious of the potential liquidity risk problems faced by an affiliated insurer.

Guarantee Fund Risk

In the event of life insolvencies, insurance regulators have organized guarantee funds to meet residual claims by small policyholders. With the exception of New York State, which has a permanent fund, most states have organized contingent funds which can impose *ex post* levies on surviving insurers to meet the claims of the failing company's policyholders. In general, *ex post* levies on surviving insurers are charged on a pro rata basis, according to the share of premiums written by each surviving insurer in the state.

As in the case of deposit insurance, guarantee funds have both potential risk-reducing and risk-increasing facets. The presence of such funds may reduce the incentives of small policyholders to engage in run-type behavior. At the same time, the credibility of guarantees provided by such funds appears to be less than for deposit insurance (even among small policyholders) because: (1) the guarantee fund may not be considered permanent, and (2) the explicit and implicit backing of these funds in the U.S. is by the state rather than by the federal government.

The risk-increasing incentives arise from the *ex post* premium structure of insurance guarantee funds and from surviving firms picking up the tab for failed firms. That is, risky insurance firms face no explicit price discipline—such as an *ex ante* guarantee fund risk-related premium schedule—to punish egregious risk-taking behavior. To the extent that discipline is in fact imposed on them, it has to come from state regulators placing restrictions and surveillance on insurers' activities and from competitive pressures imposed by sound and solvent insurers which attracts business away from low-quality players. However, it should be noted that the GAO [1987; *Insurance Regulation*, 1990] has been extremely critical of the ability of state insurance examiners to detect solvency risk problems at a sufficiently early stage. There consequently appears to be a direct subsidy or wealth-transfer effect from relatively safe insurers to relatively risky insurers under current state guarantee fund structures in the United States.

As with deposit insurance for banks, the existence of state guarantee funds can potentially deter runs and extreme cases of liquidity risk. However, the state-backed and nonpermanent nature of these funds is probably a weaker deterrent to a run than federally organized deposit insurance schemes for banks, even though it is more costly for insurance policyholders to engage in a run than it is for bank depositors, in terms of transaction and liquidation costs. Apart from run deterrence, state guarantee funds and their contractual features contain risk-increasing incentive effects such as size-related "premiums," rather than risk-related premiums. These risk-taking incentives were removed (in part) by the adoption of a risk-related deposit insurance pricing scheme by bank regulators in 1993 (as an outcome of the 1991 FDIC Improvement Act). However, "too big to fail" implicit guarantees, which some claim exist under bank deposit insurance for the largest banks, appear to be absent (or at least weaker) in the case of life insurance, where this doctrine has yet to be fully tested by a really major firm failure such as one of the top 10 national life insurers.[7]

In summary, perhaps with the exceptions of mortality risk and expense risk (for nondirect selling), many of the core risks central to selling and underwriting life insurance—interest rate, credit, adverse selection, and liquidity risks—are quite familiar to bankers. So are the available methods for managing such risks. Moreover, risk issues relating to the costs and benefits of reinsurance and state guarantee funds are quite similar to those raised by loan sales/securitization and deposit insurance. This suggests that the types of risk and the level of risk exposure among banking and life insurance activities may be less different than those claimed by opponents of bank entry into life insurance.

Banks and Property and Casualty Insurance

Property insurance involves coverage related to losses of real and personal property while *casualty*—or perhaps more accurately *liability*—insurance concerns protection against legal liability exposures. Indeed, distinctions between the two broad areas of property and liability insurance have become increasingly hazy due to the tendency of property–casualty (P/C) insurers to offer multiple activity lines and combining various features of property and liability insurance into single policy packages such as Home Owners Multiple Peril.

In a manner parallel to the life insurance section of this chapter, we shall look at the current regulation of banks seeking to enter P/C insurance lines of business and then go on to evaluate the ability of banking organizations to manage P/C risks. We seek to identify, in particular, whether bankers would face new or exceptional types of risk in the P/C insurance underwriting business.

Current Regulation

The regulations covering the ability of national banks, state banks and bank holding companies to engage in P/C insurance activities are quite similar to those relating to life insurance. In general, the scope of such activities is highly restricted. National banks in towns with populations not exceeding 5,000 are free to sell all types of insurance. In addition they can sell title insurance incidental to their primary business. They also have powers to lease space to an insurance agency, and to advertise for and sell customer lists to insurance agencies. Over half of all states allow state-chartered banks to sell some form of insurance.

Under Title VI of the 1982 Garn-St Germain Act, bank holding companies or their subsidiaries may engage in certain P/C activities. They may: (1) Act as brokers or agents for credit-related property insurance in

[7]The 1991 FDIC Improvement Act also circumscribed large banks' access to "too big to fail" bailouts.

connection with small loans; (2) act as insurance agents in towns with a population not exceeding 5,000; (3) continue any insurance activities engaged in by the holding company and its subsidiaries on or before 1 May 1982; (4) act on behalf of insurance underwriters as a supervisor of retail insurance agents who sell fidelity insurance and casualty insurance on bank holding company assets; (5) continue any insurance agency activity performed prior to 1 January 1971, pursuant to approval of the Federal Reserve Board; and (6) bank holding companies, or their subsidiaries, with assets of $50 million or less may engage in any insurance agency activity.

Banks and P/C Insurance Risks

What types of risk are likely to be familiar to bankers, and what types are likely to be relatively new or exceptional, should banking organizations be given wide powers to underwrite and sell P/C lines through separately capitalized subsidiaries? As in the case of life insurance, an important distinction has to be made between the risks of selling P/C insurance (agency function) and the risks of underwriting P/C insurance (principal function).

Agency Risk

Perhaps the major distinction between selling life and P/C insurance is the stronger tendency in the case of P/C insurance to use the direct writing and exclusive agent distribution channels as the least costly methods. The GAO [*Insurance Regulation,* 1990] reported that 64% of personal auto insurance and 52% of homeowners insurance was sold through these channels. This suggests that an insurer marketing P/C lines through independent agents and brokers may be at an increasing cost disadvantage. The potential risks to the safety and soundness (or solvency risk) of an affiliate marketing P/C insurance would generally relate to: (1) losses from its inability to sell enough policies, that is, to earn sufficient commissions to cover fixed and variable costs of operations; (2) the potential opportunity cost of diverting scarce management resources toward an unprofitable area of business; (3) the possibility that P/C products may substitute for products already sold by the agent, for example, bank products in the case of commercial banking; and (4) potential legal liability for errors and omissions made in marketing such policies.

This suggests that any associated risks would most likely arise when insufficient business volume is generated, as is the case for most agent/broker type operations where the volume potential facing a new entrant depends on the competitive structure of the line of business that it enters. The ability of a new player to survive may well depend on its ability to generate economies of scope and scale, on both the cost and revenue sides, between the insurance products it seeks to sell and any existing (noninsurance) products it is marketing or originating.

Principal Risk

The major risks of underwriting any given P/C line as in the case of life insurance, can be conceptually divided into three components. The premiums generated on a given P/C line should be sufficient to cover:

1. The expected claims losses incurred in insuring the peril, and
2. The expected expenses related to the provision of that insurance (legal expenses, commissions, taxes, etc.), *subject to*:
3. The expected investment income generated between the time at which premiums are received and the time when claims are paid.

Consequently, insolvency risk may be the result of: (1) unexpected increases in loss rates, (2) unexpected increases in expenses, and/or (3) unexpected declines in investment yields/returns. We can look more carefully at each of these three areas of risk and at the effect on banks should they in engage in insurance underwriting.

Loss Risk

The key feature of claims loss exposure in underwriting P/C lines is the actuarial predictability of losses relative to premiums earned. This predictability will depend on a number of characteristics or features of the perils insured.

Property versus Liability. The maximum level of losses that can be incurred is generally more predictable for property lines than for liability lines. For example, the monetary value of the loss or damage to an auto is relatively easy to calculate, while the upper limit to the losses an insurer might be exposed to in a product liability line—such as asbestos under general (other) liability insurance—might be difficult if not impossible to estimate.

Severity versus Frequency. In general, loss rates are more predictable on low-severity but high-frequency lines than on high-severity but low-frequency lines. For example, losses in fire, auto, and homeowners peril lines tend to be events that might be expected to be independently distributed across any pool of insured. The dollar loss of each event, in terms of the insured pool, will tend to be relatively small. Applying the law of large numbers, the expected loss potential of such lines—the likelihood that a loss will occur (frequency) times the extent of the damage (severity)—may be estimated within quite small bounds (variance). Other lines, such as earthquake and financial guarantee insurance, tend to insure very low probability events, where the probabilities are not stationary, the individual risks in the insured pool are not independent, and where the severity of the loss could be potentially enormous.

Long-Tail versus Short-Tail. Some liability lines suffer from a long-tail risk exposure phenomenon that makes estimation of expected losses difficult. This long-tail risk arises in policies where an event (peril) occurs during a coverage period although a claim is not made or not reported until many years in the future. Losses that have been incurred but not reported have caused insurers significant problems in lines such as medical malpractice and general (other) liability insurance where product damage suits (e.g., the Dalkon shield IUD and asbestos pollution cases) have emerged many years after the event occurred and the coverage period expired.[7]

Babbel and Staking [1989] argue that Schedules O and P of insurers' annual financial statements provide a direct measure of the long-tail (Schedule P)–short-tail (Schedule O) activity mix of existing insurers. In particular, long-tail Schedule P items account for approximately 65% of all premiums and cover activities such as auto liability, medical malpractice, workers compensation, ocean marine, aircraft, boiler and machinery, and homeowners and commercial multiple peril. Writers of policies in these areas have traditionally sought to limit the nature of their exposures either by: (1) issuing so-called *claims form* policies, where the policy in existence at the time of the claim is reported (rather than when the event occurred) applies to loss coverage, or (2) by withdrawing completely from writing insurance in those lines with high long-tail risk—which has been especially true in the product liability area.

Product Inflation versus Social Inflation. Unexpected increases in inflation—as were triggered, for example, by the oil shocks of 1973 and 1978—can result in adverse affect loss rates on all P/C property policies. However, in addition to a systematic unexpected inflation risk in each line, there may be line-specific risks as well. While the inflation risk of *property* lines will likely reflect (approximately) the underlying inflation risk of the economy, *liability* lines may be subject to what is often called *social infla-tion*. This is reflected in a willingness of juries to award punitive and other liability damages at rates far above the underlying rate of inflation. Such social inflation has been particularly prevalent in commercial liability and medical malpractice insurance, and has been directly attributed by some analysts to faults in the U.S. civil litigation system.

Actual Loss Ratios. The above features are reflected in the left half of Table 5–2, which shows the mean and variability (coefficient of variation) of loss ratios on 21 different P/C lines, as reported in Best's *Aggregates and Averages: Property-Casualty* [1989] for the period 1979–88. The loss ratio measures the ratio of losses incurred to premiums earned. A loss ratio that is less than 100 means that premiums earned were sufficient to cover losses incurred on that line. The data in the table can be viewed as measures of the loss exposure the average industry underwriter faced in writing busi-ness in each line.

During this period, the mean loss ratio for all lines was 69.35, with the highest loss ratio (92.41) in the case of medical malpractice. However,

---

[8]In some product liability cases, such as asbestos, the nature of the risk being covered was not fully understood at the time many policies were written.

Table 5-2 Different Insurance Lines (Summary Statistics: 1979–88)

Line	Loss Incurred				Combined Ratio			
	Mean	Sigma	COV	Rank	Mean	Sigma	COV	Rank
Fire	54.91	5.617	.102	7	97.44	6.577	.068	7
Allied lines	55.33	8.964	.162	15	95.75	10.394	.109	13
Farmowners	69.12	7.857	.114	8	108.76	8.706	.080	9
Homeowners	63.21	3.961	.063	2	103.38	3.984	.039	2
Commercial	59.15	11.674	.197	17	107.74	14.480	.134	18
Ocean marine	70.79	6.512	.092	5	108.52	5.108	.047	3
Inland marine	55.73	8.483	.152	13	95.64	8.931	.093	11
Workers' comp	75.20	7.689	.102	6	112.14	8.019	.072	8
Other liab'ty	69.18	12.101	.175	16	122.40	16.982	.139	20
Med Malprac	92.41	14.504	.157	14	139.36	17.259	.124	17
Aircraft	69.21	5.728	.083	4	101.11	6.776	.067	6
PVT auto liab'ty	75.65	5.732	.076	3	112.31	5.847	.052	4
Comm auto liab'ty	77.51	9.488	.122	10	119.04	12.125	.102	12
PVT auto dam	65.08	3.103	.048	1	97.61	3.680	.038	1
Comm auto dam	58.69	8.563	.146	12	95.55	10.699	.112	15
Fidelity	51.71	12.500	.242	19	94.95	17.760	.187	21
Surety	42.63	13.825	.324	21	100.68	11.584	.115	16
Burgl & theft	31.29	7.654	.245	20	79.60	10.771	.135	19
Boiler & mach	38.13	8.654	.227	18	95.79	10.701	.112	14
Reinsurance	80.48	9.628	.120	9	114.46	10.583	.092	10
Other lines	79.48	10.533	.133	11	118.75	6.747	.057	5
Total all lines	69.35	4.350	.063	xx	108.36	5.360	.049	xx

Note: Investment Income (1979–88): Mean 8.92; Sigma 1.183; COV 0.133. COV = analysis of coefficient of variation of rates of return.

in terms of *predictability*, the variability of the loss ratios are of interest as well. Table 5–2 ranks the coefficients of variation of loss ratios (the standard deviation of the loss ratio divided by its mean) from lowest (rank 1) to highest (rank 21). As the foregoing discussion suggests, prominent among the highest variability ranking lines are medical malpractice, other general liability, and commercial multiperil, that is, lines with a higher degree of social inflation, long-tail and/or high-severity low-frequency exposures.

Finally, it should be noted that few P/C insurers today are monoline carriers, specializing in only one (or a few) lines. Most large P/C insurers diversify across many lines. In so doing, they can avoid the unsystematic or idiosyncratic component of the loss ratio in any given line. In a fully and *optimally* diversified P/C line portfolio, the insurer could diversify away all line-specific idiosyncratic risks, leaving only its exposure to the systematic risk of the line—those risks related to overall macroeconomic/market movements such as general inflation risk. The gains from product-line portfolio diversification increase as the correlations among these loss ratios decrease. The range of the correlation coefficient is from plus unity to negative unity. As is evident in Table 5–3, which shows the correlations among loss ratios for the 1979–88 period, the high number of low positive and negative correlations among loss ratios is consistent with the view that there is a large potential for risk diversification from writing multiple P/C lines.

Certain features of the claims loss–risk distribution functions of P/C lines will be relatively new to bankers, especially in P/C lines that are more concerned with insurance per se rather than certification of default-type risks, as in surety, fidelity, and financial guarantee insurance. It may be argued that loan losses have a maximum upper bound (loss of loan principal and interest) whereas losses on some low-frequency high-severity lines such as earthquake insurance have an extremely high and uncertain upper bound.

Furthermore, losses related to default risk for the banker normally occur within the loan contract period, so that long-tail type losses—claims on bank resources beyond the normal contract or loan coverage period—are unusual. Such exceptional losses might occur only if a loan gets into trouble and the courts view the bank as taking an equity-type interest in the firm, as in some loan workout situations, for example. Under these circumstances, a bank may face a future liability for actions taken by the borrowing firm during the loan workout period, that is, during the period over which the bank was assumed to have an "ownership" stake in the firm. Overall, it might be expected that specialized actuarial expertise will be needed by bank affiliates for premium setting in most, if not all, P/C lines they plan to offer.

Expense Risk

There are two major sources of expense to P/C insurers: (1) loss adjustment expenses (LAE) and (2) commission expenses. Loss adjustment expenses relate to the costs surrounding the loss settlement process. Many P/C insurers employ adjusters who determine the liability of the insurer and the size of the adjustment (settlement) to be made. These adjusters may be salaried employees of the company. Alternatively, they may be contracted from a bureau, engaged as independent adjusters, or represent public adjusters working for a fee.

Adjusters have two basic options when confronted by a claim. They can either settle the claim or contest it. In the case of contested claims—for example, because of disputes over coverage or possible fraud—additional costs may be incurred in arbitration or court settlement of disputes, especially lawyers' fees.

The second major area of expense occurs in the commission costs paid to brokers and agents, and other expenses related to underwriting.

The two sources of expense noted earlier can account for quite significant portions of premiums. For example, in 1990 the ratio of loss adjustment expense to premiums (earned) was 12.9% and the ratio of commis-

Table 5–3 Correlation Matrix—Loss Ratio, 1979–88

	1	2	3	4	5	6	7	8	9	10	11	12	13	14	15	16	17	18	19	20	21
1 Fire	1.00	.75	.69	.70	.87	.65	.80	-.17	.52	.62	.51	-.22	.77	.68	.88	.77	-.16	.30	.61	.66	-.58
2 Allied lines	.75	1.00	.57	.75	.70	.82	.89	-.55	.27	.45	.76	-.54	.49	.77	.87	.73	-.21	.61	.05	.21	-.65
3 Farmowners	.69	.57	1.00	.79	.78	.60	.76	-.38	.51	.80	.06	-.09	.70	.61	.80	.78	-.13	.57	.35	.39	-.79
4 Homeowners	.70	.75	.79	1.00	.77	.52	.71	-.20	.61	.77	.39	-.04	.64	.66	.71	.59	.20	.40	.23	.35	-.60
5 Commercial	.87	.70	.78	.77	1.00	.46	.71	-.12	.79	.89	.28	.08	.96	.64	.86	.90	-.04	.25	.60	.72	-.58
6 Ocean marine	.65	.82	.60	.52	.46	1.00	.94	-.83	-.14	.17	.67	-.82	.21	.73	.83	.63	-.59	.87	-.06	-.07	-.78
7 Inland marine	.80	.89	.76	.71	.71	.94	1.00	-.70	.19	.48	.61	-.58	.50	.81	.95	.79	-.45	.80	.12	.18	-.85
8 Workers' comp	-.17	-.55	-.38	-.20	-.12	-.83	-.70	1.00	.42	.06	-.42	.81	.12	-.50	-.55	-.42	.72	-.96	.46	.47	.72
9 Other liab'ty	.52	.27	.51	.61	.79	-.14	.19	.42	1.00	.91	-.14	.64	.89	.22	.39	.54	.49	-.25	.62	.83	-.13
10 Med malprac	.62	.45	.80	.77	.89	.17	.48	.06	.91	1.00	-.06	.39	.91	.46	.63	.72	.27	.14	.48	.69	-.49
11 Aircraft	.51	.76	.06	.39	.28	.67	.61	-.42	-.14	-.06	1.00	-.69	.04	.72	.55	.26	-.28	.41	-.09	-.10	-.22
12 P A liab'ty	-.22	-.54	-.09	-.04	.08	-.82	-.58	.81	.64	.39	-.69	1.00	.33	-.46	-.42	-.18	.66	-.74	.40	.47	.43
13 C A liab'ty	.77	.49	.70	.64	.96	.21	.50	.12	.89	.91	.04	.33	1.00	.44	.70	.83	.09	.01	.73	.84	-.43
14 P A dam	.68	.77	.61	.66	.64	.73	.81	-.50	.22	.46	.72	-.46	.44	1.00	.84	.60	-.29	.62	.12	.13	-.53
15 C A dam	.88	.87	.80	.71	.86	.83	.95	-.55	.39	.63	.55	-.42	.70	.84	1.00	.91	-.39	.65	.32	.39	-.78
16 Fidelity	.77	.73	.78	.59	.90	.63	.79	-.42	.54	.72	.26	-.18	.83	.60	.91	1.00	-.35	.48	.45	.53	-.72
17 Surety	-.16	-.21	-.13	.20	-.04	-.59	-.45	.72	.49	.27	-.28	.66	.09	-.29	-.39	-.35	1.00	-.57	.02	.34	.49
18 Burglary & theft	.30	.61	.57	.40	.25	.87	.80	-.96	-.25	.14	.41	-.74	.01	.62	.65	.48	-.57	1.00	-.40	-.33	-.80
19 Boiler & mach	.61	.05	.35	.23	.60	-.06	.12	.46	.62	.48	-.09	.40	.73	.12	.32	.45	.02	-.40	1.00	.79	-.02
20 Reinsurance	.66	.21	.39	.35	.72	-.07	.18	.47	.83	.69	-.10	.47	.84	.13	.39	.53	.34	-.33	.79	1.00	-.05
21 Other lines	-.58	-.65	-.79	-.60	-.58	-.78	-.85	.72	-.13	-.49	-.22	.43	-.43	-.53	-.78	-.72	.49	-.80	-.02	-.05	1.00

Correlation Matrix—Combined Ratio, 1979–1988

	1	2	3	4	5	6	7	8	9	10	11	12	13	14	15	16	17	18	19	20	21
1 Fire	1.00	.76	.68	.48	.85	.76	.85	-.02	.67	.60	.47	-.24	.84	.66	.89	.88	-.58	.56	.78	.68	-.70
2 Allied lines	.76	1.00	.52	.57	.66	.81	.91	-.43	.45	.48	.71	-.53	.58	.78	.88	.84	-.57	.72	.29	.31	-.75
3 Farm-owners	.68	.52	1.00	.74	.79	.57	.69	-.02	.73	.83	-.03	.09	.78	.58	.75	.75	-.23	.63	.50	.49	-.64
4 Home-owners	.48	.57	.74	1.00	.70	.30	.50	.15	.72	.84	.13	.19	.62	.53	.55	.50	.09	.28	.07	.44	-.71
5 Commercial	.85	.66	.79	.70	1.00	.49	.72	.22	.95	.91	.18	.17	.99	.63	.86	.87	-.37	.43	.62	.81	-.75
6 Ocean marine	.76	.81	.57	.30	.49	1.00	.91	-.59	.21	.23	.67	-.66	.44	.67	.81	.77	-.75	.84	.51	.11	-.52
7 Inland marine	.85	.91	.69	.50	.72	.91	1.00	-.48	.48	.51	.63	-.51	.66	.82	.95	.90	-.71	.86	.46	.35	-.75
8 Workers' comp	-.02	-.43	-.02	.15	.22	-.59	-.48	1.00	.47	.33	-.56	.86	.29	-.43	-.29	-.22	.57	-.75	.23	.60	.06
9 Oth liab'ty	.67	.45	.73	.72	.95	.21	.48	.47	1.00	.96	-.09	.47	.95	.41	.65	.69	-.08	.17	.50	.87	-.67
10 Med malprac	.60	.48	.83	.84	.91	.23	.51	.33	.96	1.00	-.11	.41	.90	.50	.67	.69	-.04	.30	.36	.73	-.71
11 Aircraft	.47	.71	-.03	.13	.18	.67	.63	-.56	-.09	-.11	1.00	-.76	.07	.64	.50	.40	-.67	.44	.11	-.11	-.26
12 P A liab'ty	-.24	-.53	.09	.19	.17	-.66	-.51	.86	.47	.41	-.76	1.00	.24	-.46	-.33	-.25	.56	-.60	.01	.39	.06
13 C A liab'ty	.84	.58	.78	.62	.99	.44	.66	.29	.95	.90	.07	.24	1.00	.55	.82	.85	-.34	.39	.68	.86	-.70
14 P A dam	.66	.78	.58	.53	.63	.67	.82	-.43	.41	.50	.64	-.46	.55	1.00	.85	.75	-.63	.71	.27	.25	-.45
15 C A dam	.89	.88	.75	.55	.86	.81	.95	-.29	.65	.67	.50	-.33	.82	.85	1.00	.97	-.67	.79	.56	.53	-.72
16 Fidelity	.88	.84	.75	.50	.87	.77	.90	-.22	.69	.69	.40	-.25	.85	.75	.97	1.00	-.66	.76	.64	.56	-.71
17 Surety	-.58	-.57	-.23	.09	-.37	-.75	-.71	.57	-.08	-.04	-.67	.56	-.34	-.63	-.67	-.66	1.00	-.71	-.48	.00	.24
18 Burglary & theft	.56	.72	.63	.28	.43	.84	.86	-.75	.17	.30	.44	-.60	.39	.71	.79	.76	-.71	1.00	.27	-.03	-.52
19 Boiler & mach	.78	.29	.50	.07	.62	.51	.46	.23	.50	.36	.11	.01	.68	.27	.56	.64	-.48	.27	1.00	.62	-.23
20 Reinsurance	.68	.31	.49	.44	.81	.11	.35	.60	.87	.73	-.11	.39	.86	.25	.53	.56	.00	-.03	.62	1.00	-.53
21 Other lines	-.70	-.75	-.64	-.71	-.75	-.52	-.75	.06	-.67	-.71	-.26	.06	-.70	-.45	-.72	-.71	.24	-.52	-.23	-.53	1.00

sions and other underwriting expenses to premiums (earned) were 11.3% and 14.8%, respectively. These compare to a simple loss ratio on all lines of 69.4%.

In addition to these two major sources of expense, insurers need sufficient premium and other income to cover general operating expenses. Clearly, sharp rises in LAE, commissions, other underwriting expenses, and general operating costs can rapidly render an insurance line unprofitable. Consequently, a major risk for insurers is a sharp and unanticipated increase in price (cost) inflation. And the tendency for courts to make large punitive damage awards has led to an increased tendency for insurers to contest awards. This has resulted in an escalation of court and legal expenses that have only recently reached a plateau.

A widely followed measure of the overall underwriting profitability of a line, one that includes both expected loss and expense experience, is the *combined ratio*. Technically, the combined ratio is equal to the loss ratio plus the ratios of LAE (to premiums earned), commissions, other acquisition costs, and general expense costs to premiums written, adjusted for dividends paid to policyholders. If the combined ratio is less than 100, premiums alone are sufficient to cover both losses and expenses related to the line.

The right-hand side of Table 5–2 shows the combined ratios for 21 lines covered by *Best's* over the 1979–88 period. For 13 out of the 21 lines, the mean combined ratio *exceeded* 100 over this period with the highest combined ratio being the medical malpractice (a combined ratio of 139.36). This suggests that on a gross underwriting basis (considering underwriting losses and expenses alone and ignoring net investment income) a number of P/C lines were unprofitable. Indeed, the combined ratio for all lines averaged 108.36 over this period.

In terms of risk, the coefficients of variation for the line-specific combined ratios suggest that the least predictable were fidelity, other (general) liability, burglary and theft, commercial multiperil, and medical malpractice insurance. With the exception of burglary–theft, these lines are of the long-tail and/or high-severity low-frequency type. The correlation matrix for the 21 combined ratios over the 1979–88 period is shown in Table 5–3. As with the loss ratios, the large number of low positive and negative correlation coefficients are consistent with the notion that there is significant potential risk reduction associated with multiline diversification. That is, combined ratios appear to exhibit important line-specific or idiosyncratic risk elements.

Expense risk can arise from unexpected increases or cost overruns in P/C insurance provision. As discussed here, there are two major expense costs related to P/C lines: (1) commission costs and (2) loss adjustment expenses. Commission costs have been established to be higher for insurance sold through independent agents rather than direct writers. Indeed, there is a strong trend in the P/C insurance industry towards the use of direct writers [see GAO, *Insurance Regulation*, 1990]. If banks are allowed full P/C underwriting and selling powers, they would probably market many, if not most, lines on a direct writing basis by employees of the banking organization. This should keep costs in line with industry trends and, at the same time, increase the potential for revenue (cross-marketing) and cost synergies that underlie many of the arguments in favor of the expansion powers by banks.

The second major area is loss adjustment expenses. These costs have accelerated in line with what we have termed *social inflation*—the tendency of juries to make large damage awards and the increased incentives for insurers to challenge such awards. While legal defense costs are clearly part of LAE, a further important slice of such costs are expenses related to the claims adjustment process itself. On entry into P/C underwriting, a banking affiliate would need either to employ its own claims adjusters or to use external consultants or adjustment firms. Its choice will probably be mandated by the volume of business it underwrites in any given line, along with concerns about the quality of claims service it should provide. High volume business and pursuit of a high quality of service would probably require banks to establish their own claims adjustment divisions.

Investment Yield/Return Risk

Besides premiums, another integral component of the insurers' earnings is generated from the returns on its asset portfolio. Because there is an interval between the time the insurer receives premiums and when it pays claims, the insurer can expect to earn investment income that has a direct and positive effect on overall profits. For example, as Table 5–2 shows, while the average combined ratio for all P/C lines between 1979 and 1988 was 108.36 (%), the ratio of net investment income to premiums earned (the investment yield) averaged 8.92%. As a result, the overall operating ratio, which takes investment income into account, as well as underwriting losses and expenses, averaged 99.44%. This is consistent with overall (if modest) profitability of the P/C business over this period.

While high actual yields are clearly good for a P/C insurer, since such income can compensate for expected (and unexpected) losses and expenses from underwriting, the pursuit of high yields *ex ante* can represent risky behavior. That is, pursuit of high yield investments can result in: (1) an underwriting cycle risk, (2) increased default risk, and (3) increased gap-duration risk.

Underwriting Cycle Risk. One of the most common regularities in P/C insurance has been the cyclical behavior of the loss ratio and the combined ratio in the United States and in a number of other countries. This behavior has been called the *underwriting cycle*, with a duration (peak to peak) that varies between 6 and 10 years [see, for example, Cummins and Outreville 1986; and Harrington 1988].

Two major peaks for these ratios in the U.S. P/C underwriting cycle were the "crises" of 1974–75 and 1984–85. For example, over the 1978–

85 period, the combined ratios for most insurance lines rose, peaking in 1985, when the all-line combined ratio reached 116.3 and more risky (high coefficient of variation) lines such as other (general) liability and medical malpractice reached 145.8 and 166.9, respectively. After 1985, loss and combined ratios fell dramatically. By 1988, the all-line combined ratio had fallen to 105.4, other (general) liability had fallen to 109.9, and medical malpractice had dropped to 119.7.[9]

One possible explanation (certainly not the only one) for this type of cyclical behavior is that it reflects a reaction by insurance underwriters to changes in the level of yields/interest rates on investment assets. This so-called cash flow theory of underwriting [see Rappaport 1989; Vaughan 1989; and Clarke et al., 1988] views insurers and underwriters as following a systematic behavioral pattern in response to yield changes. It is argued that in a period like 1979–82, when the Federal Reserve tightened the money supply and interest rates rose on short-term instruments to levels up to 18%, underwriters cut normal underwriting standards in pursuit of premium income (cash flow), which they could invest in high-yielding assets. So high interest rates/yields made underwriters willing to accept more marginal underwriting business. New entrants accelerated this phenomenon.

However, in step with the decline in underwriting standards, the loss and combined ratios of insurance lines rose, putting an increasing squeeze on insurers' profits. This was reinforced as interest rates reached a peak and then started to fall. As a result, a crisis materialized and the insurance market changed from being "soft" to "hard," as insurers reacted to the profit squeeze in one or all of three ways: (1) raising premiums, (2) rationing availability, and (3) exiting some lines. As insurers responded in this way, loss and combined ratios started to fall and the insurance market moved into a more profitable phase of the cycle.

While there are other competing theories of the causes of underwriting cycles, such as collusive behavior among insurers [Angoff 1988] or constraints on surplus limiting premiums being written, a number of analysts give the cash flow theory credence—especially in explaining behavior surrounding the 1984–85 crisis [Rappaport 1989].

Nevertheless, the evidence supporting the cash flow theory of insurance cycles is far from concrete. For example, the correlation coefficient between the combined ratio and the contemporaneous average annual interest rate on 3-month Treasury bills was only .319 over the full 1972–88 period—although using a 1-year lagged Treasury bill rate brings this correlation up to .639. The cash flow theory also ignores the fact that modern insurers can hedge themselves against subsequent declines in interest rates by buying financial futures, interest rate floors, or other synthetic hedging instruments.

Default Risk. Pursuit of *ex ante* high-yielding investments can also result in high-risk, low-return investment outcomes. However, unlike life

---

[9]However, since 1988 the combined ratio has risen, reaching 116 at the end of 1992.

insurance companies, P/C insurers invest very small proportions of their assets in mortgages and other real estate assets (usually less than 2%) and they have not, in general, invested in junk bonds. They invest relatively more in bonds (59%) and common and preferred stocks (10.5%). As a result, their major asset exposures in terms of default risk arise in recessionary periods, when their investment-grade corporate bond and stock portfolios decline in value as corporate profits decline and the market reassesses the bankruptcy risk of firms in general.

Duration (Gap) Risk. Gap exposure occurs when the P/C insurer mismatches the durations of its assets and liabilities. An example of this is the pursuit of higher yields when the yield curve is upward-sloping. Such duration mismatches expose the insurer to shocks in interest rates that can adversely impact the firm's net worth and solvency. Papers by Babbel and Staking [1989] and Lamm-Tenant, Starks, and Stokes [1990] have attempted to assess the degree of interest rate risk exposure caused by balance sheet duration mismatches of P/C insurers. Their findings suggest that the durations of assets and liabilities of P/C firms are both relatively short term, and their duration gaps tend to be small. On average, the duration of liabilities exceed the duration of assets. The direction of this duration gap is the reverse of that normally found in banks [see, e.g., Flannery and James 1983] and suggests that positive (upward) interest rate shocks will not adversely impact P/C insurers' net worth.[10]

While the management of default risk and duration gap exposures are familiar problems to bankers, the techniques available to avoid exposures in periods of "hard" markets during insurance cycles may be less (but not totally) unfamiliar. At least one of the many theories of the underwriting cycle attributes its cause to the incentives facing P/C insurers to engage in cash flow underwriting—relaxing normal underwriting quality and loss standards to generate higher premium flows—in periods of high interest rates. Perhaps the closest parallel to banking might be the temptation to relax collateral standards in order to pursue greater loan volume in periods of high interest rates. Just as poorly collateralized (or uncollateralized) lending can result in lower (not higher) *ex post* returns to banks, cash flow underwriting can result in lower overall operating income for insurers. Moreover, just as prudent bankers can avoid the temptation to pursue greater uncollateralized lending in higher interest rate environments, so prudent insurers can avoid excessive cash flow underwriting and its hazards.

Other Direct P/C Risks

As in life insurance, adverse selection problems can reduce the returns and raise the risks faced by P/C insurers. In recent years, two major trends have increased the adverse selection exposure of P/C insurers.

The first has been the trend towards self-insurance by corporations [see Mayers and Smith 1990]. This has been done either through internal

---

[10]Mei and Saunders [1993] find similar results using an asset pricing model.

hedging/retention of all but catastrophic risks and/or establishing captive insurance organizations. Indeed, the Risk Retention Act Amendments of 1986 encourage self-insurance by corporations by simplifying the ability of businesses to act as a group in purchasing insurance or in establishing captive insurance companies. One estimate [Kuffel 1989] is that corporate insurance, through risk retention groups, took a one-third share of the commercial insurance market by the end of 1991. A move toward corporate self-insurance means that independent P/C insurers will increasingly be asked to provide coverage for extreme types of risk, rather than "normal" risk, and that the average quality of the corporate risk coverage pool is declining as "good firms" establish their own insurance captives and leave "bad firms" to seek coverage with independent insurers.

The second trend has involved states and politicians viewing the availability and provision of insurance at an "affordable price" as a social right. This is similar to the debate over banking services for the poor—the so-called "lifeline banking" debate. This pressure is particularly strong in rate-regulated personal lines such as automobile insurance, where special pools have been developed to insure high-risk applicants. Political pressure to make insurance available to everyone at low prices—even if under reasonable risk criteria certain individuals should be excluded or required to pay much higher premiums—lowers the average quality of the risk pool facing insurers and their expected returns, unless bad risks can be cross-subsidized by charging higher rates to good risks. However, attempting such cross-subsidization tends to drive good risks out of the insured pool, for example, into seeking self insurance where possible or legally allowed. That is, the more good risks are required to subsidize bad risks in a given insurance line, the greater the potential for adverse selection.

As discussed in the section on life insurance, the general nature of adverse selection and its effects on risk selection and pricing are well known to bankers. It was noted that the risk of P/C insurance may be particularly affected by the growth of corporate self-insurance and the increased trend by regulators toward making some regulated personal lines (especially automobile insurance) available to all parties at socially or politically acceptable prices rather than at market prices.

While not intending to push the comparison too far, the trend towards corporate self-insurance has been mirrored in banking markets by the trend towards disintermediation. This has resulted in better quality corporations raising funds directly in markets such as those for commercial paper, leaving more risky and/or smaller corporations (with no access to such markets) as the lending opportunity set available to banks.

It has thus been argued that the average quality of the pool of potential corporate borrowers facing banks has declined over the years. Similarly, it is arguable that political and regulatory pressure to increase the availability and to lower the cost of personal insurance mirrors the debate over lifeline banking services to the poor. As we have discussed, the resulting cross-subsidization involved in requiring good risk groups to subsidize bad risk groups can lower the overall quality of the portfolio of risks, as those in the good risk groups seek insurance services elsewhere, including self-insurance.

Reinsurance Risk

Reinsurance plays a more important role in P/C than in life insurance. Whereas approximately 4% of gross life premiums in the United States are reinsured, 9.9% of nonlife premiums are reinsured [Swiss Re, *SIGMA*, May 1989]. The P/C areas with the highest incidence of reinsurance are marine (14.8%), general (other) liability (13%), and fire (11.7%). As discussed in the section on life insurance, reinsurance allows the primary insurer to lay off (cede) a share of large risks, so as to improve its ability to diversify and to expand capacity. However, reinsurance has some explicit risks as well, especially in terms of exposure to overseas reinsurers, exposure to reinsurers that go bankrupt or fail to honor their contracts, and the incentives that reinsurance creates for pursuit of premium growth rather than quality of business.

In the late 1980s and early 1990s, the reinsurance market appears to have entered difficult market conditions, with rising loss and combined ratios. This has been due partly to increased competition, as U.S. reinsurers have begun to compete on a more aggressive basis with overseas ("alien") reinsurers such as Lloyds of London and Swiss Re. This has limited the rate at which reinsurance premiums have risen. It is also attributable in part to primary insurers increasingly laying off catastrophic risks with reinsurers and to an "unusual" number of catastrophes. For example, the period since July 1988 saw the Piper Alpha oil platform disaster (insured loss $1.5 billion), Exxon Valdez ($.8 billion), Hurricane Hugo ($4.2 billion), Hurricane Andrew ($10 billion) and four major European storms ($10 billion). These losses resulted in a number of companies withdrawing from the reinsurance market and underwriting syndicates (such as at Lloyds) to shrink.

Reinsurers in the United States have traditionally held lower premium-surplus (net worth) ratios than P/C insurers in general. The premium-surplus ratio in a given line of business is the key ratio monitored by state regulators in analyzing the ability of insurers to withstand unexpected losses. In most states, the maximum permitted premium-surplus ratio is 3 to 1. This basically means that, ignoring investment income, an unexpected rise of up to 33% in the loss rate on a given line of insurance can be met from the capital surplus/reserves of the insurer, and insolvency avoided. The Reinsurance Association of America conducted a survey of 57 U.S. reinsurers covering the period 1984–88, which reported annual average premium surplus ratios of between 1.1 and 1.6. A premium surplus ratio of 1.6 implies that an unexpected increase in losses of 62.5% can be met by the reinsurers capital reserves [see Reinsurance Association of America 1989]. It thus appears that U.S. reinsurers have historically held considerable capital surplus reserves, in recognition of its special type of risk exposure of the activity.

We have noted that the writing and ceding of insurance to reinsurers has some similarities to securitizing assets in banking—originating, packaging, and selling loans—in order to improve loan capacity and diversification, as well as to improve gap exposures and reduce regulatory costs. The analogy should not be taken too far, however. While most bank loans are sold without recourse, primary insurers retain their underlying exposure to the insured, even when part of the coverage is ceded to a reinsurer. Moreover, given the more extreme "outcome" risk of certain coverages under P/C insurance, there is a greater reliance on reinsurance for P/C lines than for life insurance lines. This underlying contingent risk-retention makes primary P/C insurers sensitive to failures of reinsurers. They thus may be exposed to a form of contagion failure risk unless they diversify across many independent reinsurers in order to limit their exposure to any individual firm or organization. Nevertheless, since many reinsurers cover similar catastrophes (storms, earthquakes, etc.), there is a stronger degree of systematic risk across reinsurers than across primary insurers [see Witt and Aird 1990].

Finally, bank-affiliated insurers may seek to provide reinsurance themselves as one line of business. For example, it is estimated that 40% of total P/C reinsurance premiums are written in departments of primary insurers [Swiss Re, *SIGMA*, May 1989]. As noted earlier, one way for existing reinsurers to deal with their exposure to catastrophic perils is to hold greater capital and surplus reserves, as a percent of premiums, than those held for coverage in other P/C lines. Just as in banking, where greater capital and loan loss reserves are often set aside against more risky assets—now formalized in the BIS risk-based capital standards—prudent P/C insurers set aside greater reserves and capital against more risky lines of business.[11]

It might also be noted that, as measured by the coefficient of variation of loss and combined ratios over the 1979–88 period, risk associated with reinsurance has not in fact been greater than lines such as fidelity and other (general) liability insurance. Indeed, while many states have required that the fidelity insurance line be "walled off" from other activity lines in a separate monoline insurance affiliate, this sort of separation has not been required for reinsurance. This suggests that, given appropriate capital and reserves, reinsurance might be offered by a bank's insurance affiliate as part of a multiline portfolio of P/C activities without significantly increasing its insolvency risk.

Liquidity Risk

P/C insurers tend to face different liquidity risk problems than do life insurers. On the one hand, the need to meet cash (liquidity) demands—due to policyholders' borrowings or surrender of policies for cash—is generally absent. On the other hand, the shorter-term nature of P/C policies relative to life policies leads to greater exposure to policy switching or nonrenewal risk. Similar to the case of time deposits in banking, there is a

---

[11]Such provisioning is likely to be required under the risk-based capital standard, to be introduced for P/C insurers in 1993.

risk that on maturity the insured will not renew a policy with the company, but rather switch premiums elsewhere. In making the decision to renew or not to renew, the insured will weigh the costs of switching such as premium costs, foregone bonuses/rebates (if any), and reputation costs against the perceived benefits. A significant benefit might be a higher probability that a new insurer will not fail during the coverage period.

While there has been an increased number of P/C insolvencies in recent years (e.g., 23 in 1989 compared to 12 in 1988 and 14 in 1987), the failures appear to have been due to a variety of reasons unrelated to liquidity risk. For example, the GAO [April 1989] listed the following reasons for failures of P/C companies in the late 1980s: (1) underpricing premiums, (2) underreserving for losses, (3) problems with risk-sharing arrangements, (4) fraud or incompetence, and (5) overexpansion.

Although the number of liquidations remains relatively low (under 1% of all companies per year), the number of companies designated for regulatory attention has been increasing rapidly. In 1988, for example, 21% of P/C insurers were designated for regulatory attention by the NAIC.

The major tool for such regulatory attention consists of financial statement examinations and application of the NAIC's Insurance Regulatory Information System [Harrington and Nelson 1986]. This seeks to identify insurers with financial ratios outside normal ranges. Ratios that have implications for the liquidity of P/C insurers include: (1) investments in real estate to capital and surplus, as well as (2) the ratio of investments in affiliates to capital and surplus. In the view of the NAIC, large investments in real estate and affiliated companies represent less liquid assets that can expose the insurer to "fire sale losses" should they have to be liquidated in the face of runoffs in premium income due to policyholder cancellations, nonrenewals, and/or abnormally high payouts on policies.

As in the P/C insurance industry, liquidity risk is a common management problem faced by banks with short-term deposit liabilities and relatively illiquid assets. For the insurers, the major liquidity or cash flow risk appears to be nonrenewal of contracts on maturity—a risk that has similarities to time deposit withdrawals on maturity. Since contract renewal takes place at periodic intervals (e.g., annually) the probability of nonrenewal is usually predictable. However, concerns about the solvency of a P/C insurer can lead to a surge (an unexpected "run") of nonrenewals and policy cancellations and a sharp drop in net premium inflows. The magnitude of such risk nevertheless appears to be less than in banking, where transaction accounts can be "put back" to the bank instantaneously (on demand), and in life insurance, where policies can be quickly surrendered for cash in times of crisis. That is, all else equal, P/C insurers do not appear to be particularly susceptible to run-type liquidity risk.

Guarantee Fund Risk

State-organized guarantee funds exist to offset the loss exposure of small policyholders should P/C companies fail. The organization and insurance/

guarantee structure of these funds is virtually identical to those for life insurance companies, discussed earlier. Until 1990–91, guarantee fund assessments on surviving P/C insurers significantly exceeded those on life insurers. For example, between 1985 and 1989, guarantee fund assessments on P/C insurers amounted to approximately $2.9 billion compared to $ .38 billion for life insurance [*New York Times*, 3 November 1990, 50]. Since guarantee fund assessments are not based on the *ex ante* risk of P/C insurers, but rather levied *ex post* on surviving firms, perverse risk-taking incentives are created and low-risk insurers in effect subsidize high-risk insurers. These risk-taking incentives appear to have been amplified by a lack of monitoring, surveillance, and enforcement on the part of the administrators of state guarantee funds, which are usually run by private insurers in conjunction with boards of directors chosen or approved by the respective state insurance commission [GAO, July 1987].

While the risk of policyholder runs on P/C insurers is lower than the risk of runs by depositors on banks, the protection of the insured by P/C guaranty funds is probably weaker than for depositors under FDIC deposit insurance (and thus the deterrence to engage in runs is weaker). This is because: (1) there are no permanent funds in place to guarantee policyholders (with the exception of New York State), and (2) the funds are organized at the state rather than federal level, and thus have no contingent federal backing such as borrowing lines from the U.S. Treasury. However, it is also arguable that the weaker nature of the guarantee funds backing insurance policyholders mitigates against insurers exhibiting similar types of risk-increasing moral hazard behavior attributed to the deposit insurance contract in banking.

Summary: Insurance

Overall, it seems fair to conclude that the risks and risk management problems of multiline P/C insurers are *more different* from banking than those between life insurance and banking. These differences can mostly be attributed to (1) the frequency-severity and long-tail nature of loss functions on a number of lines, (2) the high proportion of expenses (such as LAE) in claims settlement, and (3) the tendency of P/C markets to follow hard and soft market cycles every 6 to 10 years. It does not necessarily follow that it would be imprudent to allow banks to enter P/C insurance underwriting. It does, however, suggest that the cost of entry in terms of putting the appropriate risk management personnel and tools in place are likely to be significantly greater than for life insurance.

Securities and Investment Banking Activities

A modern full-service investment banking firm engages in a broad range of securities investing, trading, distribution, custodial, and underwriting activities. While many activities are often sold or marketed in packages, it is possible to identify five key activity areas [Schwartz 1991; Bloch 1990; and Smith and Walter 1989]:

Investing: This involves managing of pools of assets such as closed- and open-ended mutual funds, as well as the management of pension funds and trusts. These funds can be managed either as agents for other investors or as principals for the securities firm itself. The objective in funds management is to choose asset allocations to beat specified return-risk performance benchmarks.

Securities underwriting: This refers to activities related to the origination and distribution of new issues of both debt and equity. These can be primary new issues (so-called initial public offerings, or IPOs) or secondary new issues (new issues of seasoned firms whose debt or equity is already trading). Securities underwriting can be undertaken through either public or private offerings. In a private offering the investment banker acts as a "placement" agent for a fee. In a public offering the securities may be underwritten on a best efforts basis or a firm commitment basis. With best efforts underwriting the investment banker acts as agent on a fee basis related to his success in placing the issue. In firm commitment underwriting, the investment banker acts as a principal, purchasing the securities from the issuer at one price and seeking to place them with public investors at a slightly higher price. Finally, in addition to investment banking operations in the corporate securities markets, the investment banker may participate as an underwriter (primary dealer) in government, municipal, and mortgage-backed securities.

Market making: This involves creating or participating in the secondary market trading of securities. Thus, in addition to being primary dealers in government securities and underwriters of corporate bonds and equity, investment bankers make a secondary market in these instruments as well. Market making can involve either *agency transactions*—conducting a two-way transaction on behalf of customers and acting as a stockbroker for a fee or commission such as the bid-ask spread—or *principal transactions*, where the market maker seeks profits on the price movements of securities and takes either a long or short (inventory) position for his own account (or takes an inventory position to stabilize the market).[12]

---

[12]In general, full-service investment banks can become market makers on National Association of Securities Dealers Automated Quotations System (NASDAQ), but have been prevented until recently from acting as "specialists" on the New York Stock Exchange (NYSE).

Trading: Trading is closely related to the market-making activities
described above, where the trader takes an active net position
in an underlying instrument or asset. There are at least four
types of trading activities: (1) Position trading involves purchases of large blocks of securities to facilitate smooth functioning of the secondary market; (2) Pure arbitrage entails
buying an asset in one market at a low price and selling it
immediately in another market at a higher price; (3) Risk
arbitrage involves buying blocks of securities in anticipation
of some information release—such as a merger or takeover
announcement; and (4) Program trading is associated with
seeking a (risk) arbitrage between a cash market price (e.g.,
the Standard and Poor, S&P 500 Index) and the futures
price of that instrument. As with many activities of securities
firms, such trading activities can be conducted on behalf of a
customer (as an agent) or on behalf of the firm (as a principal).

Back-office and other service functions: These include custody and
escrow services, clearance and settlement services, and research and advisory services such as mergers, acquisitions and
other corporate transactions. In performing these functions,
the securities firm normally acts as an agent in return for a fee.

Banks and Securities Activities

We now look at current regulations concerning banks securities activities.
This is followed by an analysis of the risks relating to securities activities
and which risks, if any, are new and unfamiliar to bankers and would
require the acquisition of additional risk-management techniques or expertise.

Existing Regulation

At the heart of the regulations covering the issue of U.S. banks engaging
in securities activities are the Glass-Steagall provisions of the 1933
Securities Act. Enacted in the midst of the Depression, Glass-Steagall
sought to impose a rigid separation between commercial banking (taking
in deposits and making commercial loans) and investment banking (underwriting, issuing, and distributing stocks, bonds, and other securities).
Sections 16 and 21 of the act limited the ability of (national) banks and
securities firms to engage directly in each other's activities. Sections 20 and
32 limited the ability of banks and securities firms to engage indirectly in
such activities via separately established affiliates.

There were three major exemptions to the Glass-Steagall Act. Banks
were allowed to continue to underwrite new issues of government (Treasury) bills, notes, and bonds. Thus, the largest banks such as Citicorp and

Morgan Guaranty compete with Salomon Brothers and Goldman Sachs in government bond auctions. Banks were also allowed to continue underwriting municipal general obligation bonds, as well as to engage in private placements. In a private placement, a bank seeks to find a large buyer or investor in a new securities issue. As such, the bank acts as an agent for a fee. The act thus made a distinction between private placements of securities (allowed) and public placements (disallowed).[13] Corporate pension plans and private pension plans were added in 1955 and 1970, respectively, as legitimate securities activities of banks.

Beginning in about 1963, commercial banks such as the large money center banks sought to challenge "gray areas" of the Glass-Steagall Act. Between 1963 and 1987, they challenged perceived restrictions on municipal revenue bond underwriting, commercial paper underwriting, discount brokerage, managing and advising open and closed-end mutual funds, and underwriting mortgage-backed securities. In some cases, the courts upheld these activities (e.g., discount brokerage in 1984). In others, the activity was deemed to be contrary to Glass-Steagall (e.g., municipal revenue bond underwriting).

In the face of this onslaught and erosion by legal interpretation, the Federal Reserve Board allowed commercial bank holding companies such as Citicorp, JP Morgan, and Bankers Trust New York Corporation to establish separate affiliates in which to place all their "ineligible" securities activities, such as commercial paper underwriting, mortgage-backed securities underwriting, and municipal revenue bond underwriting. These so-called "Section 20" subsidiaries were viewed as not being in substantive violation of Section 20 of the Glass-Steagall Act—which restricts bank-securities firm affiliations—as long as the revenue generated from the securities activities of these subsidiaries amount to no more than 10% of the total revenues generated by the subsidiary.

Moreover, very stringent "firewalls" were placed between a bank holding company's banking affiliate and its Section 20 securities affiliate. These were both legal and economic in nature. In particular, the bank could neither make loans to, nor buy assets from, its Section 20 affiliate. In 1989 the Federal Reserve Board expanded the set of permitted activities of Section 20 affiliates to include corporate bond underwriting and in 1990 to include corporate equity underwriting for *qualified* banks that applied for permission. Table 5–4 shows the list of 29 Section 20 subsidiaries of bank holding companies as of May 1992, and the notes indicate the extent of "ineligible" securities activities in which each is permitted to engage. Most of the largest commercial banks are represented, with JP Morgan Securities being the largest.

---

[13]The importance of the private placement exemption has been significantly increased by the passage of the Security and Exchange Commission's (SEC) Rule 144A in 1989, which has effectively enhanced the liquidity of the private placement market by easing the restrictions on secondary market trading.

Table 5–4 Section 20 Subsidiaries (as of 31 May 1992)

Banking Organizaton	Initial Order (mo./yr.)
Money Center	
Bankers Trust New York Corp[a]	4/87
Chase Manhattan Corp.[b]	5/87
Chemical Banking Corp.	5/87
Citicorp[a]	4/87
First Chicago Corp.	8/88
JP Morgan & Co., Inc.[a]	4/87
Security Pacific Corp	5/87
Regional	
Banc One Corp.	7/90
Barnett Banks, Inc.	1/89
Dauphin Deposit Corp[a]	6/91
First Union Corp.	8/89
Fleet/Norstar Financial Corp.	10/88
Liberty National Bancorp.	4/90
Marine Midland Banks	7/87
NationsBank Corp.	5/89
(original permission to NCNB Corp.)	
Norwest Corp.	12/89
PNC Financial Corp.	7/87
SouthTrust Corp.	7/89
Synovus Financial Corp.	9/91
Foreign	
Amsterdam-Rotterdam Bank N.V.	6/90
Bank of Montreal[a]	5/88
Bank of Nova Scotia[a]	4/90
Barclays Bank PLC[b]	1/90
Canadian Imperial Bank of Commerce[a]	1/90
Dai Ichi Kangyo Bank Ltd.	1/91
Long-Term Credit Bank of Japan, Ltd.	5/90
Royal Bank of Canada[a]	1/90
Sanwa Bank, Ltd.	5/90
Toronto-Dominion Bank	5/90

Data: Federal Reserve Board.

Note: Section 20 subsidiaries: Authorized to underwrite and deal in certain municipal revenue bonds, mortgage related securities, commercial paper, and asset-backed securities.

[a]Also has corporate debt and equity securities powers.

[b]Also has corporate debt securities powers.

The erosion of line-of-business barriers between commercial and investment banking has also been fostered by the fact that some 23 states allow state-chartered banks to engage in securities activities beyond those permitted by the Glass-Steagall Act for national banks (see Table 5–5). Moreover, some 19 foreign banks can continue to engage in (but not expand) those securities activities they were legally engaged in prior to the passage of the International Banking Act (IBA) of 1978. The act restricted the securities activities of post-1978 foreign bank entrants to the same ones permitted to domestic banks, that is, they too were subject to all Glass-Steagall restrictions. The act's grandfathering of pre-1978 foreign banks securities activities has meant that these foreign banks are at a potential competitive advantage relative to domestic banks. The grandfathered affiliates of foreign banks are shown in Table 5–6. In practice, some grandfathered foreign banks have found it necessary to "expand" their IBA rights, and thus go through the same Section 20 applications to the Federal Reserve Board as domestic holding companies.

Risk of Securities Activities

As with both P/C and life insurance, the activities of securities firms can be divided into agency-type activities and principal-type activities.

Agency Risk

Many activities of securities firms are of the fee-based agency type, ranging from stock brokerage activities to corporate advisory services. This has made the profits of securities firms sensitive to market volume. For example, in analyzing the stock return performance of publicly traded securities firms, Officer and Boyes [1984] found that stock market trading volume was a significant factor in explaining securities firms' stock returns. In low-volume periods, securities firms are still likely to have fixed expenses, even if salaries and commissions—essentially labor costs—tend to vary directly with market volume. In low-volume trading periods as well, gross fees earned related to back-office services such as clearance and settlement, custody, as well as from M&A advisory services are also likely to fall. For example, Petre [1986] estimated that three leading investment banks, Goldman Sachs, First Boston, and Morgan Stanley earned $200 million in the boom year of 1985 from M&A advice alone. Further, low-volume markets tend to be "cold markets" for new issues [Ritter 1984]. Thus, fees related to new issue services will also tend to fall with market volume.[14]

With respect to securities-related agency risk, banks are permitted to undertake most of the fee-related agency-type activities of securities firms.

---

[14]Investment bankers also face legal risks in their agency functions. For example, disputes with clients regarding stockbroker orders and over the due diligence underlying advisory services are commonly settled in courts.

Table 5–5 State Authorization of Selected Expanded Activities for State-Chartered Banks, May 1990

Insurance Underwriting	Insurance Brokerage	Real Estate Equity Participation	Real Estate Development	Real Estate Brokerage	Securities Underwriting	Securities Brokerage/No Underwriting
Delaware	Alabama	Arizona	Arizona	Georgia	Arizona	Arizona
Idaho	California	Arkansas	Arkansas	Iowa	California[d]	Connecticut
North Carolina	Delaware	California	California	Maine[p]	Delaware	Delaware
South Carolina	Idaho	Colorado	Connecticut	Massachusetts	Florida	Florida
Utah[a]	Indiana[m]	Connecticut	Florida	New Jersey	Idaho	Georgia
	Iowa[n]	Florida	Georgia	North Carolina	Indiana[e]	Idaho
	Nebraska	Georgia	Kentucky	Oregon	Iowa	Indiana[q]
	New Jersey	Kentucky	Maine	Utah	Kansas[f]	Kansas
	North Carolina	Maine	Massachusetts	Wisconsin	Maine	Iowa
	Oregon	Massachusetts	Michigan		Massachusetts	Maine
	South Carolina	Missouri	Missouri		Michigan	Michigan
	South Dakota	Nevada	Nevada		Missouri[g]	Minnesota
	Utah	New Hampshire	New Hampshire		Montana[h]	Nebraska
	Washington[o]	New Jersey	New Jersey		Nebraska[i]	New Jersey
	Wisconsin	North Carolina	North Carolina		New Jersey	New York
	Wyoming	Ohio	Ohio		North Carolina[j]	North Carolina
		Pennsylvania	Oregon		Pennsylvania[k]	Ohio
		Rhode Island	Rhode Island		Puerto Rico[i]	Pennsylvania[p]
		South Dakota	South Dakota			Texas

Tennessee[b]	Utah	Tennessee	Tennessee
Utah	Virginia	Utah	Utah
Virginia	Washington	Washington	Vermont
Washington	West Virginia	West Virginia	West Virginia
West Virginia	Wisconsin[c]		
Wisconsin[c]			

Source: Conference of State Bank Supervisors.

Note: Expanded activities above those permitted national banks and bank holding companies under the bank holding company act. Extent of practice unknown.

[a]Grandfathered institutions.

[b]Banks not allowed to be active partners in real estate development.

[c]Wisconsin: Enacted expanded powers legislation 5/86. New legislation authorized the Commissioner of Banking to promulgate rules under which state banks may engage in activities that are authorized for other financial institutions doing business in the state.

[d]Underwrite mutual funds; law silent on other securities.

[e]Underwrite mutual revenue bonds and market mutual funds and mortgage backed securities.

[f]Underwrite municipal bonds.

[g]Underwrite mutual funds and may underwrite securities to extent of the state legal loan limit.

[h]Limited to bonds.

[i]Underwrite U.S. government securities.

[j]U.S. government, federal farm loan act bonds and general obligation bonds of state and political subdivisions.

[k]Underwrite municipal and mortgage related securities to extent permitted savings banks.

[l]May underwrite bonds of the U.S. and Puerto Rican governments, their political subdivisions and instrumentalities, and agencies.

[m]Cannot broker life insurance, all other types permitted.

[n]Property and casualty only.

[o]Banks located in small towns (5,000) may conduct insurance agency activities withoug geographic limitations.

[p]May own or operate brokerage firm established for the purpose of disposing of bank-owned property.

[q]May conduct discount brokerage.

Table 5–6   Grandfathered Securities Affiliates of Foreign Banks Under Section 8
of the International Banking Act of 1978

Bank	Securities Affiliate	%
Julius Baer	Julius Baer Securities	100
Campagnie Financière de Paribas	A.G. Becker/Warburg	100
Bayerische Hypothekenbank	ABD Securities	25
Berliner Handels und Frankfurter Bank	BHF Securities	100
Bayerische Vereinsbank	Associated European Capital Corp.	95.1
Cho Houng Bank	Korean Associated Securities	9.1
Commerzbank	Europartners Securities	40
Crédit Lyonnais	Europartners Securities	40
Crédit Suisse	Swiss American Corp.	100
	Swiss American Securities, Inc. (First Boston Corp.)	80
Deutsche Bank	Atlantic Capital Corp.	100
Dresdner Bank	ABD Securities	75
	German American Securities (inactive)	100
Long Term Credit Bank	Sanyo Securities (Tokyo)	5.44
Société Générale (France)	Hudson Securities	100
Swiss BanCorporation	Basle Securities Corp.	100
Union Bank of Switzerland	USB Securities, Inc.	100
Westdeutsche Landesbank	RWS Securities	100
Bank Hapoalim	Ampal (best efforts for parent)	100

Data: Federal Reserve Board.

They can act as M&A advisory agents, custodial and settlement agents, trust and portfolio fund management agents, and discount brokerage agents, among other activities.

As in the case of insurance brokerage/agency activities, the safety and soundness risks of these activities are relatively small. Apart from concerns about conflicts of interest arising from mixing banking services with advisory services (see later), the major concerns appear to be that such activities will be unprofitable and drain valuable labor and capital resources from the banking organization.[15]

As discussed earlier, the returns from agency activities—such as stock-brokerage—are highly dependent on market volume, and the success of banks in agency roles depends critically on their ability to generate sufficient market share and volume to justify the fixed costs of entry. This in part depends on the employees of a commercial bank's securities affiliate possessing similar, if not superior, levels of expertise to those of traditional securities firms' employees supplying the same set of agency activities.

[15]It might be noted that Bank of America has sold off its Schwab discount brokerage subsidiary.

Doubts have been expressed concerning the ability of commercial bankers to offer the same level of expertise as traditional investment bankers [see Bloch 1991; and Smith and Walter 1989 for a review of these issues]. The major issue appears to be related to the different "culture" of traditional investment bankers, compared to commercial bankers, and the different types of reward or compensation structures. In particular, it has been argued that the fixed-type salary structure common to commercial banking may not induce the same level of effort as that induced in traditional investment banking where compensation is heavily commission-based and therefore volume-based. This argument, of course, assumes that labor contracts are somehow set in stone (i.e., that securities affiliates of commercial banks would not offer similar incentive contracts to those found in investment banking), and that commercial banks are unable to compete in the labor market for investment bankers. The recent experience and growth of the Section 20 subsidiaries of bank holding companies suggests that this limitation may not in fact be debilitating for commercial banks wishing to compete in the securities business (see, e.g., Tables 2–15 and 2–16).

Principal Risk

The two major principal activities of full-service securities firm's are underwriting and trading. We can briefly look at the risk of each activity, as well as two other risks faced by securities firms, liquidity, and guarantee fund risk.

Underwriting Risk. Risk related to underwriting arises mainly in the case of firm-commitment underwriting of public issues—which is the major method of corporate debt and equities underwriting. In firm-commitment underwriting, the securities firm bears the risk that the offer price, at which it endeavors to resell an issue it has underwritten, is too high relative to the market's assessment of the intrinsic value of that issue. In such a case, the underwriter's expected spread or profit from underwriting may be eroded and in some cases can become negative.

A classic (but exceptional) case was the British Petroleum share offering in October 1987. The price at which the new shares were offered to the market was set at £3.30 and the price paid to the issuer was £3.265—implying a gross spread of £0.035 per share. This price was set on 15 October 1987 when the market for existing BP shares was at £3.48. On 20 October, the day after the stock market crash, the price of BP shares had fallen to £2.83 and by 26 October it reached £2.65. As a result, four U.S. investment banks, which had underwritten 505 million shares in total faced massive losses—that is, the difference between the market's valuation of the shares (£2.65) and the price guaranteed to the issuer by the underwriter (£3.265) times 505 million shares. This case highlights that a major risk of firm-commitment underwriting is a sudden drop in the stock market after the offer price (and gross spread) on an issue has been fixed. It also raises the question as to how frequently such overpricing occurs, and the problem of pricing issues under different underwriting systems such as the United States versus the United Kingdom.

The question of the pricing of new securities issues is probably one of the most well-researched topics in finance. The studies can be divided into those looking at the pricing of new issues of seasoned companies (secondary issues) and those looking at new issues of companies approaching the public markets for the first time (primary issue or IPOs). Overpricing or underpricing is usually calculated by comparing the public offering price with the price observed for the security during its first day or week of trading in the secondary market. If the offer price is greater than the price observed on the first days of trading, the issue is viewed as being overpriced and the investment banker is exposed to the risk of loss.

With respect to secondary (seasoned) issues, Smith [1986] reviewed the evidence for various types of securities, ranging from equities to convertibles. Whatever the instrument, under- rather than overpricing was the experience on average—although the degree of underpricing is small. For example, the average degree of underpricing on secondary issues of equities was approximately 3% [see also Asquith and Mullins 1983]. Moreover, in a more recent paper examining 1,600 seasoned equity offerings, Loderer, Sheehan, and Kadlec [1991] found no evidence of over- or underpricing for equity issues on the NYSE and the American Stock Exchange (AMEX), and only a small degree of underpricing (less than 3%) on NASDAQ. These results are not surprising, since the investment banker can use the prices of the firm's securities that are currently trading to calibrate the offer price of secondary issues.

In the case of IPOs, the underwriting risk is potentially greater since, by definition, there is no established value for the securities of the issuer in the secondary market—although the investment banker can use price information (value) of similar firms' securities against which to calibrate prices. Saunders [March–April 1990], reviewing the findings of 22 studies that examined the pricing of *new equity* issues, found that (like secondary issues) they are *on average* underpriced rather than overpriced. Moreover, the degree of average underpricing found was much larger than that of secondary issues, varying from 5.9% to 48.4%.

Studies of the underpricing or overpricing of new issues have usually concentrated on the average experience. Conceivably, one or a few overpriced issues of the BP type could render an underwriter insolvent. Thus, a question not only arises about the mean degree of underpricing but also about the *distribution* or range of underpricing. Only one study [Giddy 1985] has fully analyzed the distribution of over- and underpricing of new equity issues. Covering 2,540 new equity issues (of which 604 were IPOs) over the period from 1976 through the third quarter of 1983, the findings were that a strong positive skew in the frequency distribution exists towards net underpricing. Indeed, using market prices on the first day after the issue, it was estimated that investors made gains on 2,439 of the issues and the underwriter made losses on only 96 issues (breaking even on 5). Only 4 issues out of 2,540 indicated a 1-day loss exceeding $5 million for the underwriter.

Finally, studies on the underpricing of corporate bonds are rare. This is largely because the thinness of organized secondary bond markets, such as the NYSE, raise doubts about the quality of market prices in these securities. Most corporate bonds are traded over the counter. Giddy [1985] conducted a rare study that used *matrix* secondary market prices established by Merrill Lynch for corporate bonds, to analyze the pricing performance of new issues. First, the study found that the gross underwriting spreads on new issues of bonds were very small, in the region of 0.5–0.8% compared to 4–7% in the aforementioned equity sample. Second, it found that the average profit or loss of the underwriter was highly dependent on the assumed syndication-offering period. Looking at the 1-week results, bonds appear to have been *overpriced* on average—347 issues being overpriced, 246 underpriced, and 72 correctly priced. Taken at face value, these findings are consistent with the view that corporate bond underwriting is more risky than corporate equity underwriting.

How have recent market and regulatory developments increased or decreased the risk of securities underwriting? The first major risk-reducing development has been the expansion of liquid markets in options and futures. As a result, an underwriter can potentially hedge the risk of a decline in the stock market over the offering period by buying a put option on the S&P Index. This allows the market-related systematic (if not unsystematic) underwriting risk of the issue to be hedged. Further, the unsystematic risk of a stock underwriting can be partially hedged by buying puts on the stocks of firms that have similar financial characteristics to those of the firm being underwritten. Similarly, the risk of bond underwritings— such as the risk of an increase in interest rates over the public offering period—can be hedged in the Treasury bond option or Treasury bond futures markets.

The second major development has been the adoption of SEC's Rule 415 concerning shelf-offerings of large firms' debt and equity issues. Introduced in March 1982 and approved in November 1983, Rule 415 has changed the risk profile of new issue underwriting. It allows large well-established firms to register with the SEC, at one time, all the public debt (or equity) securities they expect to sell over the following 2 years. The risk-reducing attribute from the underwriters' perspective is that it allows a new issue to be brought to the market more quickly (and in a more timely fashion) than under traditional public offerings. This reduces the underwriters' market risk exposure.

Offsetting this risk-reducing attribute is the fact that it is more difficult to syndicate (co-share) underwriting risks because of the speed with which shelf-offerings have to be made. Optimal market timing may preclude the delay involved in forming a sizable syndicate. For example, the Securities Industry Association (SIA) [1989] has shown that the proportion of nonsyndicated U.S. debt underwritings increased from 36% in 1983 to 89% in 1989.[16] This potentially increases the risk exposure of the lead underwriter in each issue.

A number of researchers have argued that the risk faced by securities underwriters in fixed-commitment underwriting is qualitatively similar to the risk faced by commercial bankers in commercial lending [see Giddy 1985; and Bloch 1990, e.g.]. In *securities underwriting*, the investment banker has a high probability of earning the spread between the offer price to the market and the price guaranteed to the issuer. But in the case of overpricing, there is some (small) probability of making losses—the size of which can be extremely large—depending on the degree of overpricing. Thus, the payoff distribution for securities underwriting has a fixed upside return and a range of downside losses of differing (small) probabilities.

In *commercial banking*, the lender has a fixed upside potential return, the spread between the loan rate and the cost of funds, which he will earn with a high probability and a range of loss outcomes of small probability varying from a minor loss, such as a default on interest payments on loans, to a potentially large loss, such as a default on both the interest and principal on the loan.

This suggests that the quantitative differences between the two exposures depend on: (1) the length of the principal's exposure period in the two activities, and (2) the underlying volatility of asset "prices" in the two activities over the exposure period. While the underlying volatility of equity prices and corporate bond rates may arguably be greater than bank loan values over any given time period, this is offset by the fact that, on average, the holding period for loans exceeds the "offering" period for securities, usually a maximum of 10 business days. Although loan securitization and loan sales are reducing the quantitative nature of this difference, many commercial and industrial loans (especially small loans) are difficult to securitize.[17] Thus, it appears that commercial lending is often riskier than securities underwriting.

Finally, bankers can use futures and options to hedge the credit risk on a loan or portfolio of loans in a similar manner to which investment bankers use these instruments to hedge the underwriting risk of new issues [see, e.g., Babbel 1989].

Trading Risk

Three key "principal risk" trading areas are position trading, risk arbitrage, and program trading.

Position trading involves securities firms taking a block of bonds or

---

[16]Moreover, gross underwriting spreads have dropped by approximately 50% over the same period.

[17]It is arguable that one of the motivations for loan sales was its similarity to commercial paper underwriting when activities in the latter area were restricted for banks.

equities into their portfolios usually in order to facilitate a large customer trade. For example, if an institutional seller wishes to dispose of 200,000 shares but can find buyers for only 150,000, the securities firm may temporarily take 50,000 into its own portfolio in order to consummate the trade. Such "block trades" clearly expose the securities firm to price risk. That is, an adverse price movement reducing the market value of the securities purchased in the block trade and held in the securities firm's portfolio. For example, academic studies of block trades find average price reversals of 0.7% following such trades [see Holthausen, Leftwich, and Mayers 1985].

Risk arbitrage is most commonly associated with M&As transactions. Traders anticipating a merger may take a large position in the target firm's stock in anticipation of a price rise in the value of that stock on the day of the merger announcement. Travlos [1987], Asquith and Kim [1982], and others have documented very large 1-day gains to target-firm shareholders on the day of a takeover or merger announcement on the order of 11% or more. The risk is that the predicted merger does not materialize and capital losses accrue as the securities firm and other risk arbitrageurs off-load the target firms stock and/or face the long-term costs of carrying the stock in their portfolios. Interestingly, Dodd [1980] examined 80 canceled mergers and tender offers and found that stakeholders in prospective targets still made cumulative gross abnormal returns of +3.68%, on average, over a period running from 10 days before the merger proposal to 10 days after its cancellation.

Program trading, as noted earlier, is a specialized form of arbitrage whereby a securities firm seeks to lock in the spread between the cash market index (such as the S&P 500 Index) and the traded futures on that index. This involves going long (or short) in a large basket of shares in the cash market and taking an offsetting short (long) position in index futures. The arbitrage produces profits as long as the spread between the futures and cash price on the "index" portfolio exceeds the cost of carry (the applicable short-term interest rate), net of any dividends earned on the cash portfolio plus transaction costs.

Program trading can involve a number of sources of risk [see Schwartz 1991; and Merrick 1987] including: (1) misestimation of cash dividends on the cash portfolio; (2) basis risk between the actual cash portfolio and the cash index portfolio it is meant to mimic; (3) misestimation of the scale of transaction costs involved in putting on a program trade; and (4) adverse market movements in the cash market when the program is unwound on the day the futures contract matures. Unwinding a cash position involves the sale of stocks that can put downward pressure on share values, and can increase the underlying volatility of the cash market. Similarly upward price pressure may be evident in the cash market when the program trade is instituted.

Although there have been recent institutional changes—such as basing futures settlements at the opening of the market rather than its close on futures expiration days and so-called circuit breakers defining the market conditions under which program trades cannot be instituted—concerns remain about the risks of program trading. This in spite of the fact that there is no convincing evidence that program trading significantly increases price volatility. For example, Stoll and Whaley [1986] concluded that the additional price fall of stocks involved in unwinding program trades amounted to only .05–.25% of the transactions value of the stock. This study also found that such price effects were less than those commonly experienced for block trades and that such price falls could be viewed as an "acceptable" price for the increased market liquidity engendered by program trades.

With respect to trading risk, banks are widely engaged in securities and asset trading. For example, the major money center banks are among the primary dealers in the government bond market and are major participants in the secondary market trading of government securities. They are also actively engaged in underwriting and trading in municipal securities within the relevant departments of the bank. Commercial banks, are moreover, dominant traders in foreign exchange markets, which have similar types of risk (when positions are taken) as those that occur in position trading and (pure) arbitrage type activities in securities markets. Indeed, in recent years, large commercial banks such as Citibank, Bankers Trust Company, and Morgan Guaranty Trust Company have made important contributions to their profits by taking active trading positions in the foreign exchange markets.

However, as a result of restrictions on banks' holding of equities, other than through their trust departments or in other agency type functions, banks may be less familiar with the risks of position trades as principals in equity instruments. We have noted that major losses can be incurred in risk arbitrage transactions when an expected event (e.g., a takeover or merger) does not materialize. While such adverse event risk can conceivably be hedged by buying put options on the underlying stock, the cost of hedging on a sufficient scale may be excessive. As a result, large-scale risk arbitrage positions will always carry some solvency risk for an investment bank or a securities affiliate of commercial bank. This suggests that in the short term, trading position limits might be imposed by regulators along the lines of the loan diversification requirements currently used in banking. This would prevent excessively risky and speculative positions being built up in any one "takeover" stock without unduly restricting banks' activities in this area.

Liquidity Risk

Like banks and insurance companies, securities firms are potentially exposed to liquidity risk. In the case of securities firms, the major source of liquidity risk emanates from the structure of their liabilities. Two principal sources of funds are overnight and short-term repurchase agreements

(RPs) and commercial paper. As long as RPs are fully collateralized, the collateral is appropriately transferred, and the ownership of the collateral in the event of bankruptcy is fully understood, then there is little incentive for an RP counterparty (undertaking a reverse RP) to terminate abruptly any long-term relationship with a borrowing securities firm—other than the fear of any (small) indirect transaction-unwinding costs relating to the potential bankruptcy or insolvency of the borrowing firm. By contrast, commercial paper holders are more likely to react in a fashion similar to large bank time depositors by withdrawing their funds (or not rolling over their commercial paper (CP) holdings) at maturity should there be concerns about the quality of a securities firm's assets and net worth. Thus, widespread concerns about the solvency of a securities firm can lead to a run-type situation in which the firm faces a cash flow crisis due to its inability to renew its short-term debt obligations. Haraf [1991] has noted that liquidity problems resulting from a run-type situation among CP holders (and RP holders as well) was an important factor underlying the demise of the Drexel Burnham Lambert group in 1990.

The types of potential liquidity risk that securities firms face—in particular, nonrenewal of funds provided by commercial paper investors—are likely to be very familiar to bank-affiliated securities firms. Bank holding companies themselves issue significant amounts of commercial paper, while large denomination, short-term maturity bank CDs have virtually the same maturity and payoff characteristics as commercial paper. And banks are also major participants in the RP market, which is the other major source of funds for securities firms.

Guarantee Fund Risk

Small-liability claimholders have been protected against broker-dealer insolvency risk by the Securities Investor Protection Corporation (SIPC) since 1970. In the event of the liquidation of a failed securities firm's brokerage activities, customers receive pro rata shares of the liquidated firms assets, with SIPC satisfying remaining claims up to a maximum of $500,000 per customer. Like the FDIC deposit insurance fund (and unlike the insurance industry guarantee funds), SIPC is a permanent fund. Each year, securities firms pay either a flat premium as a percent of their gross securities revenues or, more recently, a fixed dollar fee regardless of size. The maximum size of the fund has been approximately $400 million.

While SIPC has characteristics similar to deposit insurance, its actual operation has not been subject to the type of "too big to fail" or moral hazard criticisms of deposit insurance associated with FDIC and the Federal Savings and Loan Insurance Corporation (FSLIC). For example, as the commercial paper and other large liability holders of Drexel Burnham rightly believed in early 1990, they were not covered by implicit guarantees associated with SIPC, and in fact imposed market discipline on Drexel by withdrawing when their claims matured. Thus, while SIPC may deter small claimholder runs, it does not appear to deter large claimholder withdrawals, nor does it appear to expose the guarantee agency to moral hazard risk.

We have noted that the permanent nature of the SIPC fund is similar to deposit insurance. However, operationally it does not appear to have provided either explicit or implicit protection (guarantees) to large liability holders, or to the equity owners of securities firms—as shown in the Drexel Burnham failure. This contrasts with deposit insurance, where many (but not all) argue that large liability holders and equity holders are often protected by various implicit safety net guarantees that truncate exposure to insolvency risk—especially in large banking organizations. To the extent that so-called too big to fail guarantees exist in banking (notwithstanding the restrictions imposed under the FDICIA of 1991), they do not appear to exist for securities firms under the current guarantee fund structure. Indeed, some argue that the current regulatory approach to large securities firm insolvencies (as demonstrated in the Drexel case) offer important lessons to bank regulators [see Haraf 1991] on how to liquidate a large financial organization without imposing systemic risk on the financial system as a whole.

In summary, with possibly the important exception of position trading—especially risk arbitrage in individual stocks—the risk characteristics of the core agency and principal activities of securities firms appear to be largely familiar to commercial banks. Not only are the profit and loss characteristics and risks of underwriting qualitatively similar to the risks of commercial lending, but banks are already developing considerable expertise in underwriting through their role as primary dealers in government securities, through underwriting municipal bonds, and through dealing and underwriting in corporate securities through their Section 20 affiliates. Indeed, a study by Lockwood, Apilado, and Gallo [1991] found that there was a significantly positive announcement effect on large bank returns following the Federal Reserve Board's decision to allow banking organizations to establish Section 20 subsidiaries in April 1987, with no adverse effects on bank return variance (or risk).

Finally, it is unclear that underwriting of corporate securities is demonstrably more risky than commercial lending in general, given the greater holding period exposures of most loans compared to the relatively short offering periods for corporate securities underwritten.

Conflicts of Interest

Numerous potential conflicts of interest have been raised, both in the academic literature and by securities and insurance industry groups, in debates on the expansion of bank activity powers [see Tillman 1986; Saunders 1985; Kroszner and Rajan 1992]. Further, many of the issues raised, especially those involving tying of customers and information transfers, are raised whatever new (nonbank) powers are considered. We consider here only the potential conflicts of interest most commonly raised when the issue of banks securities underwriting powers are debated [see Saunders [1985] for a more detailed discussion].

Salesman's stake: It has been argued that when banks have the power to sell affiliates products, managers will no longer dispense "dispassionate" advice to their customers regarding which products to buy. Instead they will have a salesman's stake in pushing the affiliate's products, possibly to the disadvantage of the customer.

Stuffing fiduciary accounts: A bank affiliate that is acting as a securities underwriter and is unable to place the securities in a public offering—and is thereby exposed to a potential underwriting loss—may seek to limit this loss by "stuffing" unwanted securities in the accounts of trusts managed by its affiliated bank's trust department over which the bank has discretionary investment power.[18]

Bankruptcy-risk transfer: A bank with a loan outstanding to a firm whose credit or bankruptcy risk has increased, to the private knowledge of the banker, may have an incentive to induce the firm to issue bonds—underwritten by its affiliate—to an unsuspecting public. The proceeds of this bond issue could then be used to pay-down the bank loan. In this case, the bank has transferred debt-related risk from itself to outside investors, while the affiliate earns a fee or spread on the underwriting.[19]

Third-party loans: To ensure that an underwriting goes well, a bank may make cheap loans to third-party investors, on the condition that this finance is used to purchase securities underwritten by its affiliate.[20]

Tie-ins: A bank may use its lending powers to coerce or tie in a customer to the "securities products" sold by its affiliate. For example, it may threaten to credit-ration the customer unless it purchases certain investment banking services.

Information transfer: In acting as a lender a bank may become privy to certain material inside information about a customer or the customer's rivals that can be used in setting prices or helping in the distribution of securities offerings underwritten by its securities affiliate. This type of information flow could work in the other direction as well, that is, from the securities affiliate to the bank.

---

[18]This activity is illegal for any fiduciary.

[19]However, the bank might be exposed to future lawsuits by investors on the basis of lack of "due diligence."

[20]In this case, the banking organization is trading off underwriting profits against (opportunity) losses on the loan portfolio.

Conflict of Interest Control

Mechanisms to control conflict of interest risk, or more precisely, disincentives to exploit such conflicts, may be either market based, regulatory based, or some combination of the two. In most universal banking systems (e.g., Germany and Switzerland) the tendency has been to rely more on market disincentives, while in the United States the tendency has been to rely on regulations and in particular on *walls*.

Regulatory Approach to Conflict Control

The regulatory approach to conflict of interest control is perhaps best exemplified in the United States, which relies on a system of internal and external walls or controls to limit the ability of managers and stockholders to exploit potential conflicts. Thus, Chinese walls are normally established between the commercial bank, its trust department, and other securities activity areas internal to the bank.[21]

The role of such walls is to prevent the passage of material (inside) information among departments that might harm a customer's best interests. Various compliance rules and procedures are normally established and compliance personnel hired to monitor and manage conformance [see Herman 1980 for a full discussion of Chinese walls within U.S. banks]. External conflicts of interest—that is, those between the bank and its nonbank affiliates such as its Section 20 securities subsidiary—are also controlled by a set of walls, usually labeled firewalls.

While the primary objective of firewalls is to minimize the potential for safety and soundness problems for the bank resulting from its affiliation with a securities subsidiary of the holding company, the stringency of these firewalls have been so severe as to directly limit the scope for conflict exploitation. The firewalls between a bank and its Section 20 subsidiary prohibit lending and asset sale/purchase transactions, prohibit the sharing of personnel, as well as the sharing of information technology and transactions infrastructure such as computers. Given the stringency of these firewalls, it is perhaps not surprising that the GAO [*Bank Powers: Activities of Securities Subsidiaries* March 1990] found no evidence of conflicts of interest between Section 20 subsidiaries of bank holding companies and their affiliated banks.

Market Approach to Conflict Control

The U.S. approach to conflict control may be compared with the Swiss–German approach. In these countries, few internal Chinese walls exist

---

[21]It might be noted that Congress passed the Insider Trading and Securities Fraud Enforcement Act of 1988 requiring every registered broker-dealer to establish in writing and to maintain and enforce Chinese walls against misuse of inside information and required the SEC and other regulators to monitor with this act.

between bank and securities departments within the universal bank and, where relevant, few external firewalls exist between a universal bank and its nonbank subsidiaries such as insurance [see Gnehm and Thalmann 1989].

Instead, internally, there appears to be a primary reliance on the loyalty and ethics of bank employees, both with respect to the institution's long-term survival and the best interests of its customers. Externally, reliance appears to be placed on market reputation and competition as the disciplinary mechanisms. The concern of the bank for its reputational "franchise" and fear of competitors are viewed as enforcing a degree of control over the potential for conflict exploitation [see Gnehm and Thalmann 1989].

Regulatory Rules versus the Market Approach to Conflict Control

Each of these approaches has its strengths and weaknesses. The strength of the U.S. approach is that a clear set of rules and procedures are laid down for financial contracting between the bank, its affiliates, and its customers. The major disadvantage is that it imposes severe limits on the potential exploitation of synergies relating to economies of scope and scale, such as joint marketing and sharing of nonmaterial inside information. The strength of the market approach is that it allows banking organizations maximum flexibility to exploit economies of scale and scope. Its weakness lies in potential exposure to unethical behavior of managers and stockholders. While both a Monopolies Commission Report [1976] and the Gessler Commission Report [1979] found no evidence of conflict exploitation by universal banks in Germany, as discussed in Chapter 4, these findings have been treated with some skepticism [Steinherr and Huveneers 1989]. Further, Benston [1990], reviewing the historical record in the United States before 1933, could find few cases where conflicts of interest were actually exploited. Yet, it was the fear of these very conflicts that was a principle motivation for passage of the Glass-Steagall Act.

It is arguable that perhaps both systems have gone too far, either in the regulatory or market-mechanism directions. An appropriate disciplinary structure for U.S. universal banks that relies partly on a (weaker) set of internal Chinese walls and external firewalls—excluding those relating to resource transfers and marketing—and partly on market reputation, competition, and employee ethics may well capture the best features of both systems while allowing the banking firm to enjoy any available economies of scale and scope in providing a universal set of business activities.

Conclusion

This chapter has sought to identify and categorize, in a standardized way, the risks of life insurance, P/C insurance, and securities activities. A clear distinction was made between the risks relating to agency activities—

selling product lines for a fee or commission—and principal activities—incurring a direct risk of loss. In general, it was concluded that the risks of agency activities relating to life, P/C, and securities lines, were relatively low and implied a very limited degree of insolvency exposure to a bank engaging in such activities through a subsidiary or affiliate. The principal risk appears to be the potential for losses on an activity line when the volume of business is insufficient to cover the costs of operations.

The risks of principal activities—in particular underwriting risks—appear to be greater than agency risks since the provider of such services is more directly exposed to losses. However, the degree of risk related to life, P/C, and securities underwriting appears to differ, as do the types of risk faced, from those found in traditional banking activities such as commercial lending. In general, securities and life insurance underwriting are less risky activities than P/C underwriting (especially in long-tail liability lines). Moreover, the types of risk faced in underwriting securities and life insurance appear to be more similar to the risks faced in commercial bank lending than the risks involved in underwriting P/C lines.

While this conclusion should not be viewed as disqualifying a bank subsidiary from P/C underwriting, especially if it is undertaken on a well-diversified multiline basis, it does suggest that risk-based capital or "surplus" requirements should be established for the P/C underwriting subsidiary related to the different degrees of risk involved in writing premium business across individual property and liability lines, and that such activities should only be allowed for subsidiaries of well-capitalized banks (see Chapter 7). Interestingly, the NAIC has been working on a model "risk-based" capital requirement plan for P/C insurers similar in philosophy to that being phased-in for banks under the BIS Basle Agreement.

6

How Risky Would
Universal Banks Be?

In this chapter we review the potential return-risk advantages of a universal banking structure. On the one hand, universal banking can be potentially beneficial since it allows the commercial bank to diversify into other activity areas and thus reduces the risk of failure. On the other hand, some nonbank activities may be more risky than banking activities when viewed on a stand-alone basis. As a result, universal banking may increase the probability of bank failure.

Here we first consider the theoretical effects of universal banking on commercial banks risk and return. We then assess the empirical evidence on the potential gains from activity diversification and report some new results. By the very nature of its prominence and the importance of the ongoing debate on broadening commercial bank powers, most of the studies—as well as the new tests reported here—employ U.S. data. Because of the smaller number of banks and restrictions on information disclosure, little if any empirical research has been conducted into this issue for explicitly universal banking countries (such as Germany, Britain, and Switzerland, discussed in Chapter 4).

Expected Returns and Risks of a Universal Bank

From portfolio theory the (expected) mean returns $\overline{R}_u$ of a financial conglomerate or universal bank is a linear weighted sum of the returns from each activity it undertakes; that is,

$$\overline{R}_u = \Sigma_{i=1}^N \overline{R}_i X_i. \tag{1}$$

Here $\overline{R}_i$ = the mean return on activity i, (e.g., banking, insurance, securities activities), and X_i = the proportion of total activity measured by assets, allocated by the universal bank to activity i. The risk (variance of returns) of the universal bank is measured by σ_u^2:

$$\sigma_u^2 = \Sigma_{i=1}^N X_i^2 \sigma_i^2 + \Sigma_{i=1}^N \Sigma_{\substack{j=1 \\ j \neq i}}^N X_i X_j \rho_{ij} \sigma_i \sigma_j, \tag{2}$$

where σ_i^2 = the variance of returns from activity i, σ_{ij} = the covariance of returns between activities i and j, and ρ_{ij} = the correlation coefficient between the returns on activity i and activity j.

Thus, from equation (2), the risk[1] of a universal bank depends on the riskiness of each activity (σ_i^2) it engages in as well as on the proportion it invests in each activity (X_i), and the correlations (ρ_{ij}) among the returns from the different bank and nonbank activities (where $-1 \leq \rho_{ij} \leq 1$). As ρ_{ij} moves from $+1$ to -1 the risk benefits from diversification increase (for any given σ_i^2, X_i). Consequently, universal bank risk (σ_u^2) will be lower, other things remaining the same, the lower are bank–nonbank activity return correlations. That is, if commercial banking returns were independent or negatively correlated with the returns on securities activities, insurance activities, and the like, a strong case might be made for universal banking on the basis of its diversification benefits.

Previous Studies

A number of researchers have analyzed correlations among the returns on banking activities and the returns from nonbank activities using either accounting data or stock market return data. Accounting data have an advantage in that one can analyze the potential diversification benefits among a larger number of financial firms—even when the firms are not quoted on the stock market. There is a problem, however, in that accounting returns are not always comparable across firms and sectors, and can be "window-dressed" for regulatory and other purposes. Further, accounting information is issued at discrete intervals in time, with 3 months being the usual gap between observations. As a result the number of observations available for return-risk analysis is often severely limited.

Stock market return data, by comparison, have the advantage of reflecting market participants' views regarding a firm's current and expected future earnings. As such, they provide a standardized measure that allows a direct comparison of performance among firms and across industries. Moreover, stock return data are available on a daily basis, allowing far more observations to be generated—although this attribute was never exploited in previous studies. However, the stock-return approach is limited by the fact that one can only analyze firms in different sectors whose equities are

---

[1]The standard deviation of returns is simply the square root of the variance of returns. It is measured in the same units (e.g., percent) as mean returns.

widely traded on the stock market—typically the largest firms. Still, this should not be too much of a problem in universal bank simulations since, realistically, it is the larger financial services firms that will likely choose to become *full-service* universal banks if given the opportunity.

The COV Approach

Whether returns are estimated using accounting data or stock return data, a common approach used by academic researchers to measure "risk" has been to evaluate the potential coefficient of variation of returns (COV) when banks (or bank holding companies) are "synthetically" merged with nonbanking activities such as securities firms or insurance firms, where:

$$COV = \frac{\sigma_u}{\overline{R}_u}. \quad (3)$$

Inverting (3) produces, $\overline{R}_u / \sigma_u$ which can be interpreted as a firm's expected return (profitability) per unit of total risk.

The ROF Approach

A second commonly used approach to evaluating the risk exposure from nonbanking activities is to estimate the effect on a bank's risk of failure (ROF) from nonbank activities—controlling for the bank's capital position. Specifically a (universal) bank is insolvent when its capital (or equity)—denoted by E—is exceeded by the losses (or negative profits) from its activities.

As a result, the probability (Prob.) of insolvency can be written as:

$$\text{Prob. (Profits} < -E). \quad (4)$$

Dividing both terms by assets we have:

Prob. (Return on Assets $<$ – Capital/Assets ratio for the ith bank)

or

Prob. $(R_i < -E_i/A_i)$.

Standardizing this probability, under the assumption that the rate of return on assets is normally distributed, results in:

$$\text{Prob. } \frac{(R_i - \overline{R}_i)}{\sigma_i} < z, \quad (5)$$

where $\overline{R}_i$ = the mean (expected) return from the ith bank's set of activities, R_i = the ith banks actual return from those activities, σ_i = the standard deviation of return, and

$$z = \frac{-(E_i/A_i) - \overline{R}_i}{\sigma_i}. \quad (6)$$

The value of z is the number of standard deviations the actual return of the ith bank has to decline *below its expected return* before it becomes insolvent, that is, before its equity (E) is wiped out. As a result, high (negative values) of z indicates a bank with a low probability of insolvency. Thus z is the ROF measure used in many studies.

The Merger Simulation Approach

A third approach—one that has been used much less often—is to undertake an analysis of the return-risk characteristics that result from merger simulations among existing *individual* financial firms. That is, what would be the return-risk characteristics if Citicorp (a bank) merged with Salomon Bros., Inc. (an investment bank) and this combined organization then merged with Aetna Life & Casualty (an insurance company)? It is arguable that this type of simulated merger study (MS) gives greater insights into the potential risk effects of universal banking; that is, the likely return-risk trade-offs *before* any internal synergistic benefits or economies of scope are fully exploited. To some extent MS simulations can be viewed as providing a *lower bound* on the potential risk-reduction benefits or costs from universal banking.

Table 6–1 summarizes the findings of a number of previous studies regarding the risk of bank–nonbank activity combinations using COV, ROF, or MS studies as defined above. The periods covered, the level of data aggregation (firm versus industry) as well as the types of methodology, data (market returns or accounting returns) and sample period differ widely across studies. Nevertheless, they generally conclude that there are some, albeit sometimes limited, risk-reduction benefits from a traditional commercial bank's diversification into nonbank activities—with most finding that securities activities are relatively risky and should be confined to a small percentage of overall bank activities, often in the 5–10% range [see also Benston 1989].

Universal Bank Return-Risk Simulations Using U.S. Data

We now go on to provide some new insights into the potential risk-reduction benefits that would result from U.S. bank expansions into non-bank activities, especially securities brokerage/underwriting, life insurance, and P/C insurance. The data set we have used is based on daily stock returns for individual financial firms, thereby avoiding the overaggregation and limited time-series observation problem inherent in most of the previous studies. The period analyzed is 1984–88. This is important because this period *includes* (1) a major stock market crash (October 1987); (2) the change in emphasis of securities firms' activities towards greater risk taking (trading, junk bonds, etc.); and (3) an insurance underwriting cycle turning point, the P/C insurance crisis of 1984–85. This allows us to consider the potential for risk reduction, in a simulated universal bank, at a

Table 6-1 Review of Selected Studies of the Risk of Nonbank Activities

Study	Time Period	Methodology[a]	Do Nonbank Activities Reduce BHC Risk?[b]
Accounting			
Industry data			
Heggestad [1975]	1953–67	COV	Yes. Impermissible activities: insurance agents and brokers, and real estate agents, brokers, managers, holdings and investment companies, and lessors of R.R., oil, and mining properties. Banking is among the riskiest activities based on the coefficient variation in profits. (Studied activities of one-BHCs prior to 1970 BHC Act amendments.)
Johnson and Meinster [1974]	1954–69 (annual data)	COV and portfolio analysis	Yes. Impermissible activities: insurance agents and brokers, and real estate agents, brokers, and managers. Studies 13 activities. Portfolio analysis based on earnings and cash flow conclude there are diversification benefits into nonbank activities but that the benefits are sensitive to the percentage of assets in each activity.
Wall and Eisenbeis [1984]	1970–80	COV	Yes. Impermissible activities: S&Ls, security brokers and dealers, life insurance, general merchandise stores, lessor of R.R. property. Permissible activities: personal and business credit agency. Banking neither highest nor lowest risk based on coefficient of variation. Results are sensitive to time period.
Firm data			
Jessee and Seelig [1977]		COV	No. Risk reduction is not related to share of nonbank investment.
Meinster and Johnson [1979]	1973–77	ROF	Yes. BHCs effectively diversified but slightly increased probability of capital impairment with debt financing (Sample of only two BHCs in seven permissible activities of leasing, consumer finance, mortgage banking, bank management consulting, financial services, and foreign bank services.)
Litan [1985]	1978–83	COV	As likely to reduce volatility of BHC income as to increase it. (Sample of 31 large BHCs.)

continued

Table 6-1 (Continued)

Study	Time Period	Methodology[a]	Do Nonbank Activities Reduce BHC Risk?[b]
Wall [1986]	1976–84	ROF	Nonbank activity either decreases BHC risk slightly or has no impact. The positive relationship between nonbank risk and BHC risk, BHC leverage, and bank risk is consistent with the possibility that management preferences influence the riskiness of the BHC's subsidiaries and determine the use of leverage to influence overall risk.
Boyd and Graham [1986]	1971–83, (1971–77 and 1978–83)	ROF	Entire period: no significant relationship between nonbank activity and any risk or return measures. Less stringent policy period (1971–77): no, nonbank activity is positively related to risk. More stringent policy period (1978–83): weak negative relationship between nonbank activity and risk.
Boyd and Graham [1988]	1971–84 (annual data)	COV/ROF/MS	Study covers six impermissible activities. Yes for life insurance. The standard deviation and bankruptcy risk measures indicate risk is likely to increase for real estate development, securities firms, and property/casualty insurance activities, and increase slightly for other real estate and insurance agency and brokerage activities. BHC is lowest risk activity.
Brewer [1988]	1979–85	COV	Yes. One standard deviation increase in investment in nonbank subsidiaries leads to 6 basis point drop in BHC risk (approximately 7%).

Industry and firm data

Study	Time Period	Methodology[a]	Do Nonbank Activities Reduce BHC Risk?[b]
Stover [1982]	1959–68	Wealth maximization; debt capacity	Yes. Impermissible activities: S&Ls, investments banking, land development, fire and casualty insurance. Measures equity returns and diversification benefits of 14 permissible and impermissible activities in wealth maximization model.
Boyd, Hanweck and Pithyachari-yakul [1980]	1971–77	COV/ROF	Yes, but limited. Permissible activities: mortgage banking, factoring, consumer finance, credit card, loan servicing, investment advisors, leasing (except auto), community welfare, data processing, credit life, accident and health insurance agents and underwriters, and management consulting.

No (any investment increases probability of bankruptcy). Permissible activities: commercial and sales finance, industrial banks, trust services, auto leasing. (Study only covered permissible activities.) |

Market data			
Industry data			
Eisemann [1976]	1961–68 (monthly data)	Industry (portfolio) selection model (COV)	_Yes._ Banking is minimum risk activity. Lowest risk BHC includes permissible activity of sales finance and impermissible activities of insurance investment banking. Highest risk BHC includes permissible activity of data processing. Studies 20 activities.
Firm data			
Wall [1984]	Select dates	Bond returns	No significant effect.
Wall and Eisenbeis [1984]	Select dates (monthly data)	Bond returns	_No._ (Study only covered permissible activity of discount brokerage).
Boyd and Graham [1988]	1971–84 (annual data)	COV/ROF/MS	Studies six impermissible activities. Yes for life insurance, insurance agency and brokerage, and property/casualty insurance. Risk likely to increase for real estate development and securities firms, and increase slightly for other real estate. Based on standard deviation, bankruptcy and beta risk measures BHC is not lowest risk activity. Insurance agency and brokerage, and property/casualty insurance are lowest risk activities.
Brewer [1988]	1979–85 (daily data)	COV	_Yes._ One standard deviation increase in investment in nonbank subsidiaries leads to an 8–11% basis point drop in BHC risk. Resulta are sensitive to the time period studied.
Brewer, Fortier, and Pavel [1988]	1980, 1982 and 1986 and 1979–83	COV/MS	_Yes._ Impermissible activities of insurance agents and brokers, property and casualty and life insurance underwriting. Investment of 5% or less for any of the tested activities would not increase the variance of the BHC significantly, but investment of 25% or more for all but the above listed activities would increase the riskiness of the BHC significantly. Examination of the impact of total investment in nonbank activities regardless of the specific activities finds increases in nonbank activity tends to lower BHC risk significantly.

Source: Brewer, Frontier, and Pavel [1988].

Note: Permissible activities refer to those nonbank activities currently permissible (May 1988), whether or not they were permissible at the time of the study. Impermissible activities also include activities not yet ruled upon by the Board at the time of the study.

[a]COV = analysis of coefficient of variation of rates of return of banking and nonbanking activities; ROF = risk of failure (bankruptcy) analysis; MS = simulated merger analysis.

[b]BHC = bank holding company.

189

time when major changes in the returns and risks of nonbanking activities are indeed taking place.

The financial firms analyzed are listed in Appendix 6–1. The sample includes all national commercial banks, state commercial banks, life insurance companies, fire, marine, and casualty insurance companies, and security brokers and dealers (plus Salomon Bros. Inc.) listed on Compustat whose stocks were continuously traded on either AMEX or NYSE and were thus listed on the Center for Research into Securities Prices (CRSP) tapes over the 1984–88 period.

The bank group was also subdivided into 9 money center banks (as defined by Salomon Bros. Stock Research) and 24 other banks labeled regional banks.[2] Those banks that were merged[3] during the period were dropped from the sample, as was one regional bank due to missing returns on the CRSP tape.

In the initial tests, three large troubled Texas banks (MCorp, Bank Texas Group, and Texas American BankShares) were included in the regional bank sample. However, since their inclusion tended both to lower significantly the average return and increase the average risk of the regional bank group—thereby biasing the results *in favor of* finding potential diversification benefits from expanding into nonbank activities—these banks were dropped from the sample.

The life insurance group consisted of 13 companies; the fire, marine, and casualty group consisted of 8 companies; and the security brokers and dealers consisted of 11 companies.[4]

The sample as a whole therefore encompasses the largest financial service firms in the United States over the period of analysis.

Table 6–2 reports the compound daily returns (C), the mean daily returns (M), the mean standard deviation (S) of daily returns, and the return per unit of risk ratio (R) for these three financial groups.[5] Note that these figures reflect *average* returns for the firms in each industry group. For example, the *mean* money center return is the (unweighted) mean of the average returns of the nine money center banks comprising that group. The table reports C, M, S, and R for: (1) the entire sample period 1984–88,

---

[2]Dividing banks into money center and regional banks allows us to investigate both the product and geographic diversification benefits that are potentially available from full interstate (regional) universal banking.

[3]These mergers were First Wyoming Bancorp (acquired by Keycorp), Horizon Bancorp (acquired by Chemical Banking Corp.), and Irving Bancorp (acquired by Bank of New York).

[4]It is arguable that the securities firms in this group are rather heterogeneous, including both large full-service investment banks (such as Merrill Lynch) and financial service firms such as American Express that owned Shearson-Lehman-Hutton as well as retail brokers. Also, large private firms such as Goldman Sachs cannot, by definition, be included [see Benston 1989 for a similar point]. Of the "big securities firms," our group thus excludes Morgan Stanley (which went public during the 1984–88 period), Goldman Sachs (private), and Drexel-Burnham not listed on Compustat.

[5]The return per unit of risk ratio is the inverse of the coefficient of variation (COV = standard deviation of return/mean return).

Table 6-2 Compound Returns, Mean Daily Returns, Mean Daily Standard Deviations, and Return/Standard Deviation Ratios

		Value-weighted Returns	Money Center Banks	Regional Banks	Life Insurance	Fire & Casualty Insurance	Security Brokers & Dealers
1984-88	C	.93923	.71732	.96846	.54206	1.03702	−.00394
	M	.00058	.00061	.00065	.00047	.00062	.00027
	S	.01072	.02024	.01877	.01851	.01738	.02541
	R	.05410	.03014	.03263	.02539	.03567	.01063
1984-88 (excluding 1987)	C	—	—	—	—	—	—
	M	.00066	.00107	.00090	.00074	.00078	.00066
	S	.00781	.01727	.01688	.01658	.01563	.02347
	R	.08451	.06196	.05332	.04463	.04990	.02812
1984	C	.04916	.12126	.10555	.26912	.10656	−.15210
	M	.00022	.00058	.00049	.00091	.00047	−.00038
	S	.00734	.01729	.01772	.01648	.01749	.02770
	R	.02997	.03355	.02765	.05522	.02687	—
1985	C	.30882	.41921	.49315	.33425	.63482	.66358
	M	.00109	.00145	.00170	.00121	.00202	.00218
	S	.00581	.01475	.01518	.01570	.01451	.02148
	R	.18761	.09831	.11199	.07707	.13921	.10149
1986	C	.17011	.09731	.13328	.04817	.00480	.01014
	M	.00066	.00052	.00056	.00033	.00013	.00027
	S	.00834	.01864	.01741	.01749	.01618	.02262
	R	.07914	.02790	.03217	.01887	.00803	.01194
1987	C	.02634	−.33694	−.14322	−.19201	−.03216	−.36418
	M	.00028	−.00124	−.00037	−.00062	−.00002	−.00131
	S	.01821	.02900	.02461	.02453	.02290	.03177
	R	.01538	—	—	—	—	—
1988	C	.17595	.54056	.21976	.10812	.11252	.10414
	M	.00068	.00174	.00086	.00049	.00050	.00059
	S	.00932	.01766	.01589	.01589	.01389	.02121
	R	.07296	.09853	.05412	.03084	.03600	.02782

Note: Daily returns were compounded using the CRSP COMPND procedure. The mean daily returns and mean daily standard deviations are arithmetic means of the average daily returns and average standard deviations of the individual banks and companies.
C = compound annual and 5-year returns; M = mean daily returns; S = mean daily standard deviations; and R = M/S.

(2) the entire sample period excluding 1987 (the crash year), as well as for (3) each individual year. Looking at R, or return per unit of risk, the *higher* this ratio—or alternatively the lower is its inverse, the coefficient of variation—the *less* risky is the industry.

For the period as a whole, the highest R industries ranked in order were: (1) fire and casualty insurance, (2) regional banks, (3) money center

Table 6-3 Average Correlation Coefficients for Financial Firms

	Money Center Banks	Regional Banks	Life Insurance	Fire & Casualty Insurance	Security Brokers & Dealers
Money Center Banks	.51722	.30275	.31142	.31326	.32276
Regional Banks		.24840	.24953	.25316	.25417
Life Insurance			.27078	.28391	.27525
Fire & Casualty Insurance				.28537	.28923
Security Brokers & Dealers					.36537

Note: The average correlation coefficients are arithmetic means of all cross-correlation coefficients; for example, money center banks and regional banks have $9 \times 24 = 216$ cross-correlation coefficients and money center banks alone have $9 \times 9 \times 9 = 72$ cross-correlation coefficients.

banks, (4) life insurance, and (5) security brokers and dealers. Measured simply by standard deviation of returns alone (S), it is clear that both life and casualty insurance were less risky than banking over the 1984–88 period.

Recall that, in considering the gains from universal banking, it is not just the absolute levels of risk (S) or return per unit of risk (R) of different financial group activities that should be considered, but also the *covariance* or *correlation* coefficients (ρ_{ij}) among firms in each financial activity group and among firms in different groups. As discussed earlier, as ρ falls from $+1$ to -1, the potential gains from a bank diversifying into nonbank activities will increase.

Table 6–3 shows the average correlation coefficients for financial firms, both *within* each sector and *across* sectors. Note that the average correlation coefficient for returns among money center banks for 1984–88 was around .52, whereas the average correlations among money center banking firms and firms in *other* sectors (regional banks, life insurance, fire and casualty insurance, and security brokers and dealers) fall into the range .30 to .32. Moreover, the complete range of average correlations among financial firms in different sectors was .25 to .32.

Overall, since these correlations are significantly different from $+1$, the *necessary* condition for diversification gains from universal banking appears to be supported.

An interesting question that arises from these results is why mean returns across these industries are imperfectly correlated, or alternatively, why their return-risk trade-offs differ. Financial theory suggests that there are two types of risk affecting the overall risk associated with any business firm. These are market or *systematic risk* (so-called market beta risk) and *unsystematic risk*. That is, the return-generating process for firm i's stock is:

$$R_{it} = \alpha + \beta_{im} R_{mt} + \epsilon_{it} , \qquad (7)$$

where, R_{it} = the return on the ith firm's stock,

β_{im} = the systematic risk coefficient on firm i's stock,

R_{mt} = the return on the market index, and

ϵ_{it} = the residual or unsystematic risk component.

This can be rewritten as:

$$\sigma_{it}^2 = \beta_{im}^2 \, \sigma_{mt}^2 + \sigma_{\epsilon it}^2. \tag{8}$$

Hence, the risk of a firm's stock (σ_{it}^2) is higher the greater is its β_m coefficient, that is, its sensitivity to changes in the "market" in general. Also, the greater a firm's unsystematic risk component—($\sigma_{\epsilon it}$) its firm specific risk—and the higher the overall volatility of stock market returns (σ_m^2), the greater is its overall return volatility.

Recent research has argued that an even finer partitioning of risk should be made for financial firms [see Flannery and James 1984; Sweeney and Warga 1986]. In particular, financial firms are likely to be sensitive to both *systematic* changes in interest rates as well as *systematic* changes in the stock market as a whole, for instance due to macroeconomic shocks. This implies that the returns of financial firms are better explained by a "two factor" model rather than the one factor model of equations (7) and (8). In the case of the two factor model, the second factor is the absolute daily change (or shock) to interest rates [Sweeney and Warga 1986].

The two factor return generating model takes the form:

$$R_{it} = \alpha + \beta_{im} R_{mt} + \beta_{iI} R_{It} + u_{it} \tag{9}$$

and in terms of the variance (risk) of returns as:

$$\sigma_{it}^2 = \beta_{im}^2 \, \sigma_{mt}^2 + \beta_{iI}^2 \, \sigma_{It}^2 + \sigma_{uit}^2 , \tag{10}$$

where: β_{iI} = the systematic interest rate risk coefficient of firm i's stock,

R_{It} = the change in interest rates, and

u_{it} = the residual or unsystematic risk component for firm i's stock.[6]

In the context of the two factor model, return risk for the ith firm will also be higher if β_{iI} is large and σ_{It}^2 is high.

Using data for 1984–88 on individual financial firm returns, the daily returns on the value-weighted NYSE–AMEX index (as a measure of R_{mt}) and the daily change in the 12-month Treasury bill offer rate (as a measure for R_{It}), we estimated equation (9) for each firm in each industry group and then took the arithmetic average. This estimation allows us to derive an industry average systematic or market beta coefficient (β_m) and an industry average systematic interest rate beta coefficient (β_I). The results are shown in Table 6–4. Note that the average systematic risk for money center banks is larger than one (the systematic risk of the market index

---

[6]Essentially the residual risk in the one factor model (ϵ_{it}) has been decomposed into an interest rate risk component ($\beta_{iI} \cdot R_{It}$) and an unsystematic risk component (u_{it}).

Table 6–4   Market Betas, Interest Betas, and Standard Errors of the Regressions

	Market Beta[a]	Interest Beta[a]	Percentage (%) of Comp. with Significantly Negative Interest Betas (at 5% level and at 10% level)	Percentage (%) of Comp. with Significantly Positive Interest Betas	Standard Error of the Regression
Money center banks	1.16881 (.04181)	−.00636 (.00523)	33.33 55.56	0 0	.01574
Regional banks	.75391 (.04466)	−.00266 (.00559)	8.33 20.83	0 0	.01682
Life insurance	.81412 (.04261)	−.00275 (.00533)	15.38 23.08	0 0	.01605
Fire & casualty Insurance	.81183 (.03956)	−.00220 (.00495)	12.50 25.00	12.50 12.50	.01490
Security brokers & dealers	1.21848 (.05687)	.00406 (.00711)	0 0	27.27 36.36	.02141

Note: The coefficients reported are the arithmetic means of the coefficients of individual regressions (OLS) of the company returns on an constant, the returns on the value-weighted NYSE-AMEX stock index, and the absolute change in interest rates on 12-month Treasury bills. Dates on which the bond markets were closed while the stock markets were open and the consecutive days are excluded from the sample—a total of 28 days of 1,264 days overall, representing 2.2% of all days on which the stock market was open. The percentages of significantly positive or negative interest betas are based on one-sided T-tests.

[a]Standard errors are in parentheses.

itself) and is more similar to the systematic risk of securities firms than of regional banks. Indeed, by comparison, the average β_m for regional banks, life insurance companies, and fire, marine, and casualty insurers lie in the .75–.81 range.

These results are consistent with the existence of important potential gains from reductions in money center banks' exposure to systematic market risk if they engaged in low-systematic risk universal banking activities such as life and property insurance.

While on a group *average* basis the systematic interest rate risk factor (β_I) was not statistically significant, *within* each group the interest rate risk factor was significant for certain individual firms. Specifically, 5 out of the 9 money center banks stock returns *fell* (significantly at the .10 confidence level) when there was an *upward* shock to daily interest rates.[7] Also, approximately 25% of both the regional banks and life insurance companies showed a similar significant *inverse* or *negative* relationship between positive shocks to interest rates and their stock returns. By comparison, 4 out

[7]Note that a negative β_I is consistent with having more rate sensitive liabilities than assets (or alternatively, that the duration of assets exceeds the duration of liabilities).

of 11 securities firms showed significant *positive* return adjustments to *positive* shocks in interest rates, while casualty insurers showed one significant positive and two negative responses. Thus, there may be some potential gains to be had in diversifying interest rate risk exposure from combining selected money center banks, on the one hand, with selected securities firms, on the other.[8]

Synthetic Minimum Risk Combinations Using Industry Averages

To investigate further the risk-reduction potential from conglomeration into a single universal bank, we undertook a number of additional experiments.

The first set of tests was to take the average industry group risk measures $(\bar{\sigma})$ calculated in Table 6–2 and the average industry correlation measures $(\bar{\rho}_{ij})$ from Table 6–3 and to calculate the *minimum* risk portfolios of activity combinations. That is, *what activity weight* (X_{mc}) should be attached to (money center) banking and what activity weight attached to life insurance (X_{LI}), so as to *minimize* the risk (σ_u) of a *two-activity universal* bank?

As shown in Table 6–5, we can experimentally create 10 synthetic minimum risk two-activity universal banks, 10 synthetic three-activity universal banks, 5 synthetic four-activity universal banks, and a single fully comprehensive five-activity universal bank.[9] The risk-minimizing portfolio of activities is also shown in Figure 6–1 for the five-activity universal bank.

When just two activities are considered, the *minimum* risk combination for money center banks is with casualty insurance $(X_{mc} = .39, X_{CI} = .61)$. However, the lowest risk combination of all is between regional banks and casualty insurance companies. As can be seen from the final two columns of Table 6–5, expanding the permitted range of activities from two to three generally reduces a universal bank's risk (σ) and increases R (return per unit of risk). Thus, in a synthetic three-activity universal bank the minimum risk portfolio for money center banks is $\sigma = .0135$ (versus $\sigma = .01507$ in two-activity case). This minimum risk portfolio would include both regional banking and casualty insurance companies. Note that the lowest $(\sigma = .01296)$ for all possible three activity combinations contains regional banks $(X_{RB} = .31)$, life insurance companies $(X_{LI} = .31)$, and casualty insurance companies $(X_{CI} = .38)$,[10] or approximately one-third in each activity.

---

[8]That is, those banks with negative β_{Is} merging with securities firm's with positive β_{Is}. See also Saunders and Yourougou [1990] for similar findings for synthetic mergers between banks and commercial firms.

[9]The minimum risk portfolio weights were calculated assuming no short sales, that is, that the universal bank could not hold a negative amount of any one activity. The activity weights must sum to one.

[10]The activity combination that produces the highest return per unit of risk is the money center-regional banking-casualty insurance combination.

Table 6-5 Portfolio Weights, Compound Returns, Daily Returns, Standard Deviations Risk Portfolios, and Return/Standard Deviation Ratios

	Money Center Banks	Regional Banks	Life Insurance	Fire & Casualty Insurance	Security Brokers & Dealers	Compound Returns	Daily Returns	Standard Deviation	Return/Std. Dev. Ratio
2-activity Industry	.44610	.55390	0	0	0	.85643	.00063	.01570	.04013
	.43541	0	.56459	0	0	.61837	.00053	.01563	.03391
	.39051	0	0	.60949	0	.91217	.00062	.01507	.04114
	.66314	0	0	0	.33686	.47436	.00050	.01810	.02762
	0	.49071	.50929	0	0	.75130	.00056	.01473	.03802
	0	.44864	0	.55136	0	1.00626	.00063	.01427	.04415
	0	.69414	0	0	.30586	.67104	.00053	.01678	.03159
	0	0	.45611	.54389	0	.81126	.00055	.01435	.03833
	0	0	.70775	0	.29225	.38249	.00041	.01674	.02449
	0	0	0	.74817	.25183	.77488	.00053	.01607	.03298
3-activity Industry	.25616	.36582	.37802	0	0	.74294	.00057	.01382	.04124
	.23485	.34096	0	.42418	0	.93856	.00063	.01350	.04667

.35399	.47231	0	0	.17370	.71065	.00057	.01511	.03772
.23843	0	.34402	.41755	0	.79052	.00057	.01356	.04204
.35158	0	.48269	0	.16573	.51319	.00049	.01509	.03247
.32282	.31206	0	.53267	.14451	.78338	.00057	.01466	.03888
0	.41958	.31100	.37694	0	.86169	.00058	.01296	.04475
0	.39144	.43065	0	.14976	.63920	.00052	.01426	.03647
0	0	0	.47716	.13141	.87340	.00059	.01390	.04245
0		.39623	.47355	.13023	.70534	.00051	.01400	.03643
4-activity Industry .15513	.26293	.26091	.32102	0	.84026	.00059	.01263	.04671
.22078	.33624	.34437	0	.09862	.67028	.00054	.01363	.03962
.20553	.31697	0	.39151	.08599	.86007	.00060	.01334	.04498
.21026	0	.31856	.38702	.08417	.72451	.00054	.01341	.04027
0	.29022	.28690	.34839	.07449	.79757	.00056	.01284	.04361
5-activity Industry .14040	.25200	.24944	.30709	.05108	.79823	.00057	.01258	.04531

Note: Calculations based on mean returns and standard deviations, and average correlation coefficients from Table 6–3.

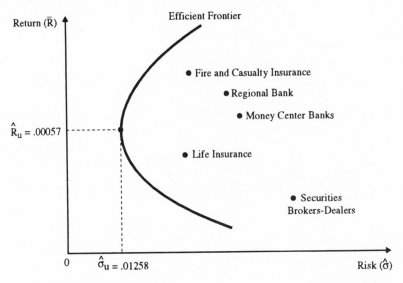

(Positions of the non-efficient sectors are approximate and not drawn to scale.)

Figure 6–1   Minimum risk portfolio for five-activity universal bank. σ the mean return and risk (standard deviation) of individual financial sectors over the 1984–88 period from data in Table 2.

In the four-activity case, the *minimum* risk combination ($\sigma = .01263$) is for the combination of money center banks ($X_{mc} = .16$), regional banks ($X_{RB} = .26$), life insurance ($X_{LI} = .26$), and casualty insurance ($X_{CI} = .32$). Finally, in the full fledged, five-activity universal bank, σ falls to .01258, with the minimum risk combination of 15% money center bank activities, 25% regional bank, 25% life insurance, 31% casualty insurance and 5% securities broker-dealer.[11] This minimum risk level is 38% *lower* than the average risk level for undiversified money center banks alone, in the 1984–88 period, and 33% lower than the average risk level of regional banks over the same period.

Synthetic Merger Combinations Using Industry Averages

It is arguable that the risk reduction identified previously represents only a *potential* risk reduction, and that universal banks will, in general, fail to choose the *minimum* risk portfolio combination of activities—especially since risk minimization does not mean profit maximization. In particular, they may choose a combination of activities that potentially produce *both* higher returns (profits) and higher risks.[12]

---

[11]Interestingly the 5% minimum risk combination for securities activities is not very different from that found in many previous studies of bank activity diversification [see Benston 1989, p. 298].

[12]This may be for strategic opportunity or economy of scope reasons.

To gain an insight into the short-term impact of universal banking, we can analyze the effects of synthetic mergers between firms in different financial industry groups. This is in the spirit of the approach used by both Boyd and Graham [1988] and Brewer, Fortier, and Pavel [1988].

Basically, we assume that a synthetic universal bank is created by merging the equity of firms (as well as their assets and liabilities). As a result, the stock returns for the synthetic universal bank will reflect the weighted sum of current returns of the merging firms—the variance of which is a simulated measure of the risk of the universal bank. It should be noted that this simulation will only provide an idea of the *impact effect* on risk from universal bank creation, since it ignores any potential product-revenue synergies and cost-based economies of scope and scale that result from universal banking. Further, we use existing market values of equity (rather than the book value of assets) to weigh the importance of each activity in the synthetic universal bank on the grounds that the cost and process of mergers involves acquiring another firm's equity in the takeover market.[13]

Our first set of tests uses the *industry* (across firm) average values of daily returns, along with the *average* industry market value of capital (to calculate portfolio weights) in simulating values of risk (σ) and return (R) for the synthetic universal bank.

As can be seen in Table 6–6, many of the conclusions regarding the combinations of activities that best reduce risk are similar to those reached for the minimum risk portfolio simulations. For example, in the case of a two-activity universal bank the lowest risk combination is for money center banks to expand into P/C insurance. In the five-activity case the universal bank activity portfolio optimally contains 33.1% money center banking, 13.6% regional banking, 14.8% life insurance, 22.9% casualty insurance, and 15.7% securities activities. The risk of this type of universal bank (σ) is .01346—compared to the *minimum* risk five-activity universal bank portfolio of .01258 (see Table 6–5).

Merger Simulation Using Firm Data

As a final sensitivity test we undertake a simulated firm-by-firm merger analysis (see Table 6–7). In a world where universal banking is permitted, such banks may be created anew or by mergers among existing firms. In the United States each existing commercial bank has a large number of potential merger partners. For example, Citicorp might merge with Salomon Bros., Inc. or with Merrill Lynch.

Rather than randomly selecting possible merger combinations [see Boyd and Graham 1988; and Brewer, Fortier, and Pavel 1988], it was decided to evaluate the "global" opportunity set of potential mergers in

---

[13]Because of the higher leverage of banks, (measured by either market or book values), using existing asset sizes as portfolio weights would tend to *bias* the portfolio of universal bank towards more banking activities than other activities.

Table 6-6 Compound Returns, Mean Daily Returns, Mean Daily Standard Deviations, and Return/Standard Deviation Ratios of Hypothetical Mergers

	Money Center Banks	Regional Banks	Life Insurance	Fire & Casualty Insurance	Security Brokers & Dealers	Compound Returns	Daily Returns	Standard Deviation	Return/Std. Dev. Ratio
2-activity Industry	.70952	.29048	0	0	0	.79027	.00062	.01683	.03693
	.69076	0	.30924	0	0	.66312	.00057	.01668	.03398
	.59150	0	0	.40850	0	.84792	.00061	.01572	.03907
	.67886	0	0	0	.32114	.48569	.00050	.01810	.02766
	0	.47766	.52234	0	0	.74574	.00056	.01474	.03773
	0	.37218	0	.62782	0	1.01150	.00063	.01437	.04393
	0	.46393	0	0	.53607	.44718	.00045	.01794	.02488
	0	0	.39329	.60671	0	.84236	.00056	.01441	.03892
	0	0	.48622	0	.51378	.26154	.00037	.01778	.02066
	0	0	0	.59348	.40652	.61384	.00048	.01657	.02882
3-activity Industry	.53848	.22045	.24107	0	0	.73043	.00059	.01492	.03921
	.47619	.19495	0	.32886	0	.87142	.00062	.01433	.04334

.53122	.27748	0	0	.25130	.59069	.00053	.01604	.03325
.46766	0	.20936	.32297	0	.78388	.00058	.01430	.04082
.52063	0	.23308	0	.24629	.49883	.00049	.01596	.03094
.46218	0	0	.31918	.21864	.66167	.00054	.01527	.03530
0	.26452	.28926	.44622	0	.87571	.00058	.01303	.04486
0	.30778	.33657	0	.35565	.47912	.00045	.01514	.03000
0	.26025	0	.43902	.30072	.70613	.00052	.01456	.03589
0	0	.27783	.42859	.29358	.59390	.00048	.01458	.03262
4-activity Industry								
.39251	.16069	.17572	.27107	0	.81354	.00059	.01341	.04433
.42916	.17570	.19213	0	.20302	.58134	.00052	.01469	.03548
.38864	.15911	0	.26840	.18385	.71048	.00056	.01421	.03915
.38294	0	.17144	.26446	.18115	.64116	.00053	.01420	.03711
0	.20260	.22154	.34176	.23410	.66978	.00051	.01343	.03804
5-activity Industry								
.33105	.13553	.14820	.22862	.15660	.68552	.00054	.01346	.04038

Note: Weights based on average market values (in $ millions): money center banks: 3430.2162; regional banks: 1404.3090; life insurance: 1535.6415; fire & casualty insurance: 2368.9215; security brokers & dealers: 1622.6873 (at end-1988).

Table 6-7 Compound Returns, Mean Daily Returns, Mean Daily Standard Deviations and Return/Standard Deviation Ratios of Hypothetical Mergers

		Compound Return	Daily Return	Daily Std. Dev.	Return/Std. Dev. Ratio	Minimum Daily Return	Risk Portfolios Daily Std. Dev.
2-activity Industry	M-B-O-O-O	.85409	.00064	.01710	.03743	.00063	.01570
	M-O-L-O-O	.72497	.00060	.01749	.03431	.00053	.01563
	M-O-O-F-O	.83401	.00063	.01669	.03775	.00062	.01507
	M-O-O-O-S	.63240	.00057	.01958	.02911	.00050	.01810
	O-B-L-O-O	.87298	.00061	.01543	.03953	.00056	.01473
	O-B-O-F-O	1.02038	.00066	.01518	.04348	.00063	.01427
	O-B-O-O-S	.73331	.00056	.01812	.03091	.00053	.01678
	O-O-L-F-O	.86888	.00060	.01536	.03906	.00055	.01435
	O-O-L-O-S	.43253	.00045	.01818	.02475	.00041	.01674
	O-O-O-F-S	.76985	.00055	.01753	.03137	.00053	.01607
3-activity Industry	M-B-L-O-O	.81343	.00062	.01555	.03987	.00057	.01382
	M-B-O-F-O	.89303	.00065	.01502	.04328	.00063	.01350
	M-B-O-O-S	.74910	.00060	.01708	.03513	.00057	.01511

M-O-L-F-O	.81144	.00062	.01534	.04042	.00057	.01356
M-O-L-O-S	.65624	.00057	.01738	.03280	.00049	.01509
M-O-O-F-S	.75752	.00060	.01670	.03593	.00057	.01466
O-B-L-F-O	.92834	.00063	.01369	.04602	.00058	.01296
O-B-L-O-S	.73044	.00056	.01579	.03547	.00052	.01426
O-B-O-F-S	.85836	.00061	.01529	.03990	.00059	.01390
O-O-L-F-S	.73316	.00056	.01570	.03567	.00051	.01400
4-activity Industry M-B-L-F-O	.87379	.00064	.01417	.04517	.00059	.01263
M-B-L-O-S	.75889	.00060	.01575	.03810	.00054	.01363
M-B-O-F-S	.83308	.00063	.01527	.04126	.00060	.01334
M-O-L-F-S	.74972	.00060	.01551	.03868	.00054	.01341
O-B-L-F-S	.82431	.00060	.01441	.04164	.00056	.01284
5-activity Industry M-B-L-F-S	.81180	.00062	.01452	.04270	.00057	.01258

Note: The figures are arithmetic means of all possible hypothetical mergers (e.g. M-B-L-F-S: $9 \times 24 \times 13 \times 8 \times 11 = 247{,}104$ possible mergers). The portfolio weights of the individual companies are based on each firm's market value in proportion to the combined market value of the hypothetically merged firm. M = money center banks; B = regional banks; L = life insurance; F = fire & casualty insurance; S = security brokers & dealers.

our sample and the risk characteristics of each. This type of analysis has the advantage of being both disaggregated (firm-level analysis) and comprehensive.

The number of potential mergers is very large. When only two activities are considered, for example, money center (M) and life insurance companies (L), there are 9×13 or 117 possible pairwise inter-*firm* merger combinations. When three activities are considered, such as a joint money center life insurer merging with a regional bank we have $9 \times 13 \times 24$, or 2,808 potential merger combinations. In the case of a full five-activity universal bank we have 9 x 13 x 24 x 8 x 11, or 247,104 possible merger combinations among the existing U.S. financial service firms in our sample.

The results—the average standard deviation of returns—are reported in Table 6–7 along with the returns and risk calculated for the minimum-risk portfolio calculated earlier.

In the two-activity case, the best (lowest risk) merger partners for money centers would be casualty insurers, with $\sigma = .01669$ (compared to .01507 in the minimum risk portfolio). In the three-activity case the lowest risk merger combination would, on average, be between money centers–regional banks–casualty insurers with $\sigma = .01502$ compared to $\sigma = .01350$ in the minimum risk portfolio case. Finally, in the full five-activity case the average $\sigma = .01452$. Again, note that such risk levels are significantly below the average risk level for money center banks (.02024) on a stand-alone basis.

Conclusion

The simulation analysis based on U.S. data suggests that there are potential risk reduction gains from allowing banks to expand their activity-set in a limited fashion—and similarly for nonbank financial firms to expand their set of activities—and that these gains increase with the number of activities undertaken. The main risk-reduction gains appear to arise from banks' expanding into insurance rather than securities activities.[14] Moreover, quite substantial risk-reduction gains as measured by σ and R (return per unit of risk) appear to exist at the most comprehensive level of universal banking when all five areas of financial service activity are combined.[15]

Nevertheless, it is important to end this chapter on some cautionary notes. First, our results may exaggerate the risk-reduction benefits because they ignore many of the operational costs involved in setting up nonbank-

---

[14]Much the same conclusions to these have recently been reached by Boyd, Graham, and Hewitt [1990] using a similar methodological approach.

[15]Such considerations may underlie the big three German universal banks' expansion of their insurance activities under the concept of the *Allfinanz* form of universal banking. This is especially so, given that their interest in insurance appears to have followed periods of weak earnings on their securities activities [see Lewis and Vincent 1988].

ing activities.[16] Second, to the extent that our *ex post* risk measures reflect existing central bank safety nets—which may not exist (at least in the same form) in a world of universal banking and safety net reform—they may tend to underestimate the *ex ante* risk in the future. And last, counteracting the first two considerations, by using existing firm data our simulations cannot account for the possible economies of scope, scale, and other synergies that underlie many of the arguments in favor of universal banking.

At best then, these results of our simulation should be viewed as illustrative of the risk-reduction potential of universal banking.[17]

Appendix

Note: This sample includes all national commercial banks, state commercial banks, life insurance companies, fire, marine, and casualty insurance companies, and security brokers and dealers (including Salomon Bros., Inc.) listed continuously on either NYSE or AMEX over the period 1984–88 with the exception of:

1. Banc Texas Group, Inc.
2. First Wyoming Bancorp (acquired by Keycorp)
3. Horizon Bancorp (acquired by Chemical Banking Corp)
4. Irving Bancorp (acquired by Bank of New York, Inc.)
5. MCorp.
6. Texas American BankShares, Inc.
7. Worthen Banking Corp. (CRSP tape includes several missing returns for this bank)

Daily returns over the sample period (1984–88) were taken from the CRSP tape, which was also the source for the returns on the value-weighted NYSE–AMEX daily stock index.

Interest rates on 12-month Treasuries sampled at daily intervals provided the basis for the interest rate series used in the regressions

Standard and Poor's (S&P) COMPUSTAT tape contained the following information:

1. Number of shares outstanding at year-end
2. Closing stock price at year-end
3. Total assets
4. Common equity (book value)

---

[16]That is, only the financial firms in existence for the full 1984–88 period are considered.

[17]However, it might be noted that White [1986] has produced evidence to show that there were *actual* risk-diversification gains to banks' engaging in securities activities *via* affiliates pre-1933 in the United States, that is, before the Glass-Steagall Act of 1933 required a separation of commercial banking from investment banking (securities activities).

I. Money Center Banks—based on definition of Salomon Bros., Inc.

(stock ticker symbols in brackets)

1. Bank of New York, Inc. (BK)
2. Bank of America Corp. (BAC)
3. Bankers Trust NY Corp. (BT)
4. Chase Manhattan Corp. (CMB)
5. Chemical Banking Corp. (CHL)
6. Citicorp. (CCI)
7. First Chicago Corp. (FNB)
8. Manufacturers Hanover Corp. (MHC)
9. JP Morgan & Co., Inc. (JPM)

II. Regional Banks

1. Amsouth Bancorporation (ASO)
2. Banc One Corp. (ONE)
3. Bank of Boston Corp. (BKB)
4. Barnett Banks, Inc. (BBI)
5. Citizens First Bancorp. (CFB)
6. Continental Bank Corp. (CBK)
7. Equimark Corp Del (EQK)
8. First Fidelity Bancorp. NE (FFB)
9. First Interstate Bancorp. (1)
10. First Pennsylvania Corp. (FPA)
11. First Virginia Banks, Inc. (FVB)
12. Fleet Norstar Financial Group (FNG)
13. Keycorp. (KEY)
14. Mellon Bank Corp. (MEL)
15. NCNB Corp. (NCB)
16. NBD Bancorp, Inc. (NBD)
17. Norwest Corp. (NOB)
18. Republic NY Corp. (RNB)
19. Security Pacific Corp. (SPC)
20. Signet Banking Corp. (SBK)
21. Southeast Banking Corp. (STB)
22. Sterling Bancorp (STL)
23. United Jersey Banks Hackensack (UJB)
24. Wells Fargo & Co. (WFC)

III. Life Insurance Companies

1. Aetna Life & Casualty Co. (AET)
2. American General Co. (AGC)
3. American Heritage Life Investment (AHL)
4. Aon Corp. (AOC)
5. Capital Holding Corp Del (CPH)
6. ICH Corp. (ICH)
7. Jefferson Pilot Corp. (JP)
8. Liberty Corp SC. (LC)
9. Lincoln National Corp Ind. (LNC)
10. Manhattan National Corp. (MLC)
11. Travelers Corp. (TIC)
12. USLife Corp. (USC)
13. Washington National Corp. (WNT)

IV. Fire, Marine, and Casualty Insurance Companies

1. Avemco Corp. (AVE)
2. CIGNA Corp. (CI)
3. CNA Financial Corp. (CNA)
4. Continental Corp. (CIC)
5. Geico Corp. (GEC)
6. General RE Corp. (GRN)
7. Orion Capital Corp. (OC)
8. US F&G Corp. (FG)

V. Security Brokers and Dealers—(including Salomon Bros., Inc., which is listed as Security and Commodity Broker by S&P Index.)

1. Advest Group, Inc. (ADV)
2. American Express Co. (AXP)
3. AG Edwards, Inc. (AGE)
4. Integrated Resources, Inc. (IRE)
5. Inter-Regional Financial Group, Inc. (IFG)
6. Legg Mason, Inc. (LM)
7. McDonald & Co Investments, Inc. (MDD)
8. Merrill Lynch & Co., Inc. (MER)
9. Paine Webber Group, Inc. (PWJ)
10. Quick & Reilly Group (BQR)
11. Salomon Bros., Inc. (SB)

7

Universal Banking and Reform of the Financial Safety Net

One important question, especially in light of the U.S. thrift crisis and widespread proposals for safety net reform, is the implication of U.S. universal banking for the domestic safety net. Does universal banking require major safety net reforms for fear of increasing taxpayer exposure? Or would simply removing regulatory forbearance and too-big-to-fail guarantees—together with firmly implementing bank closure rules— provide sufficient conditions for the introduction of universal banking in the United States? And if, indeed, the safety net can be administered in a manner that avoids an increase in the size of the taxpayers' potential burden, is there any need to restrict the scope of activities in which a (universal) bank can engage?

In this chapter, we begin by reviewing the current structure of the U.S. financial safety net, which is then compared to safety nets existing in "universal banking" systems in other countries. This is followed by an analysis of required reforms to the safety-net structure should universal banking be adopted in the United States. We argue that, regardless of whether universal banking is adopted, a fundamental requirement in any restructured banking and regulatory system involves a credible bank closure rule backed by economically meaningful capital adequacy requirements. The presence of an economically meaningful closure rule not only protects the integrity of the safety net, but is also consistent with reduced exposure of taxpayers.

Evolution of Federal Safety Net

Deposit Insurance

The operation of the traditional U.S. deposit insurance system incurs two major problems.

1. Insurance premiums are only weakly related to the risk of the bank.[1]

2. A belief exists that large banks are "too big to fail" (TBTF)—at least since the Continental Illinois crisis in 1984—and this has resulted in a perception that (potentially at least) large banks can issue debt to liability holders at close to risk-free rates regardless of the quality of their balance sheets. It also suggests that large depositors have little incentive to distinguish among banks according to their asset quality since they enjoy the same (implicit) failure guarantees as the explicit guarantees held by depositors with claims of $100,000 or less.[2]

Thus it is argued [see, e.g., Kane 1985], that large failing banks in the United States have little to lose from continuing to offer increasing amounts of liabilities at close to risk-free rates and investing the proceeds in high-risk assets such as speculative real estate loans. If these investments pay off, the bank makes sizable profits and its net worth is improved. If they fail, stockholders lose what little capital investment they have left in the bank, and the FDIC bears the brunt of the costs of failure. This is usually in the form of financing a *purchase and assumption* merger, or alternatively granting *forbearance*—and/or explicit bank assistance through cash subsidies—so that the bank can continue in operation with negative net worth.

Opponents of allowing universal banking in the United States express the fear that it could lead to the creation of even larger banks and/or encourage them to engage in new areas of business or excessive levels of risk taking. This, opponents claim, would exacerbate any TBTF incentives of bank stockholders to engage in risk-taking behavior—that is, increasing the size of the implicit and explicit guarantees provided by the FDIC and the taxpayer to such banks.[3]

---

[1]Following passage of the FDIC Improvement Act in 1991, the FDIC has allowed a small variation in insurance premiums across banks beginning in 1993. This variation will reflect a bank's capital ratio and supervisory ratings. In 1993, the maximum range of insurance premiums between the lowest and highest risk banks was 9 cents per $100 of deposits.

[2]The FDIC Improvement Act set some limitations on TBTF by reducing the approval of the Boards of the major regulators as well as the President. Nevertheless, the doctrine appears to have been reaffirmed for the very largest banks.

[3]It is of course arguable that banks already have a sufficiently large set of risky investments currently available (if they choose to use them), so that requiring universal banking for increased risk expansion would be unnecessary. See Burnham [1991] who makes the standard case against the expansion of bank powers, and big banks in general, based on the potential expansion of TBTF guarantees.

As we discuss later in this chapter, we believe that there is no *necessary* link between universal banking and the size of deposit insurance subsidies as long as (1) regulators design and credibly enforce appropriate capital standards and that (2) appropriate market and institutional mechanisms are in place to avoid TBTF guarantees being extended *ex ante* to large banking institutions.

The Discount Window

Besides deposit insurance, the discount window has also played an historically important safety net function. The primary role of the Federal Reserve Board's discount window has been to provide liquidity to the banking system in times of panics or liquidity crises. By providing such liquidity, the Federal Reserve is acting as a lender of last resort to the banking system. For example, in both the 1990 Drexel Burnham Lambert crisis and the October 1987 stock market crash the Federal Reserve stood ready to provide loans through the discount window to any commercial bank under liquidity strain.[4]

The size of the subsidy to banks from discount window access is debatable. One possible measure of the subsidy is the difference between the discount window rate and the average federal funds rate, the latter measuring the marginal cost of bank funds/borrowing on the open market. For example, in 1988 the average daily Federal Funds rate was 7.57% and the average discount rate was 6.5%,[5] suggesting a "subsidy" of around one cent per $1 borrowed through the discount window—although any such "subsidy" is likely to have been higher for smaller banks, which pay slightly higher interest rates to borrow federal funds than the largest most creditworthy banks [Stigum 1989].[6] By comparison, in 1991, the federal funds rate-discount window rate spread was reduced to 24 basis points or a subsidy of 1/4 cent per $1 borrowed.

However, this simple spread calculation ignores two explicit and one implicit cost related to borrowing from the discount window.

The first is that, in return for access to discount window loans, banks have to hold noninterest-bearing reserves at the Federal Reserve, thereby reducing the size of any interest-rate subsidy.[7]

The second is that discount window borrowings have to be backed by marketable collateral, thereby excluding excessive borrowing by the ris-

[4]Banks have been major suppliers of finance to securities firms via repurchase agreements and broker–dealer loans.

[5]*Federal Reserve Bulletin*, December 1989, Table 1.14 (Federal Reserve Board of New York discount rate) and Table 1.35.

[6]Also, banks that borrow for more than 30 days in a row from the Federal Reserve are required to pay a higher rate.

[7]The reserve requirement tax was reduced in December 1990 by the removal of reserve requirements on CDs and other nonpersonal time deposits. Nonetheless, a 10% reserve requirement against transaction accounts remains in force.

kiest banks, which presumably would have little or no collateral to post. As long as collateral is appropriately valued, discount window loans are default risk free from the Federal Reserve's perspective.

The third is that excessive borrowings from the discount window are likely to lead to additional surveillance and monitoring by the regulators.

Such costs are similar to an implicit risk premium being added to the discount rate for the borrowing bank [see Buser, Chen, and Kane 1981 for an analysis of implicit risk premiums in a different context].

Thus, it appears that the subsidy element inherent in the operation of the discount window is probably zero or quite small. Nevertheless, an issue that arises with respect to universal banking is that it may well result in demands for expanded access to the discount window, since the range of potential borrowers is likely to expand—to include financial service firms establishing their own universal banking franchises—as is the range of potential financial events covered. Possible discount window reforms to deal with this are discussed later.

Payment System Guarantees

The third aspect of the traditional U.S. safety net is the Federal Reserve's explicit "good funds" guarantee on Fedwire, and any implicit guarantees extended on private wholesale payments systems, such as on the Clearing House Interbank Payments System (CHIPS). Many commentators view the potential exposure of the Federal Reserve, and the risk inherent in the provision of underpriced or "mispriced" guarantees on the wholesale payments networks, as being of a similar (if not greater) importance than the contingent exposure of regulators under the existing system of deposit insurance. In particular, there is a fear that such guarantees may be expanded if banks gain more universal banking powers [see, e.g., Flannery 1988; Humphrey 1987; Saunders 1988; and Eisenbeis 1990].

Estimates in 1991 put the maximum combined dollar value of the daily flow of messages across both the Fedwire and CHIPS networks at close to $2 trillion, far exceeding in importance payments via other media such as cash and checks [see Humphrey 1987]. These payment messages reflect both interbank transactions and transactions made by banks on behalf of large corporate customers.[8] They can be either domestic or international in terms of their origin or destination.

The risk exposure on Fedwire arises because of the nature of the settlement system. A Fedwire payment message might be sent from Bank A (the sending bank) to Bank B (the receiving bank). When Bank B receives the message, it can view the funds message as "good funds" and proceed to on-lend them despite the fact that Bank A will not settle this transaction—with an adjustment to its (reserve) balances at the Federal Reserve—until the close of the banking day. The reason that Bank B can

---

[8]For example, to engage in RPs.

view Fed funds as good funds is because, even if the sending bank (Bank A) were unable to settle the transaction at the end of the day, the Federal Reserve—as the payments system guarantor—would take its place.

The effect of such settlement guarantees, along with incentives to minimize reserve holdings due to the nonpayment of interest on reserves, encourages banks to run daylight overdrafts. That is, Bank A sends payment messages over Fedwire even when it, the sending bank, has zero or negative reserve balances at the time the message is transmitted. Implicitly, by extending a good funds guarantee, the Federal Reserve is providing intra-day credit at zero interest to the sending bank. Moreover, the size of the Federal Reserve's credit risk exposure or implicit subsidy is directly linked to the size of the daylight overdrafts run by banks using Fedwire.

However, as part of a general program to reduce its exposure to daylight overdraft risk—and thus the scale of safety net subsidies on the wholesale payments networks—the Federal Reserve has begun charging an interest rate on peak daylight overdrafts on Fedwire of 25bp ($\frac{1}{4}$ of 1%). This should have the effect of reducing the average peak size of daylight overdrafts and encouraging some banks and their customers to switch to alternative means of settlement.[9]

CHIPS is a private payments network linking 140 domestic and foreign wholesale banks. A traditional concern about the CHIPS network has been its potential exposure to systemic risk.

CHIPS messages are provisional until final payment (settlement) on a net basis by banks through Federal Reserve funds transfers at the end of the day. Thus, if a bank were to fail to settle its net send message transactions at the end of the day, CHIPS could require its send messages and receive messages to be unwound and the whole CHIPS net settlement matrix recalculated excluding that particular bank.

As has been widely recognized,[10] any such unwinding of the payment matrix could result in an increased contagious or systemic risk, with other banks being unable to settle as well. One possible solution to a CHIPS settlement crisis would be for the Federal Reserve to extend discount window loans to ameliorate any settlement problems. As Eisenbeis [1990] has noted, however, this may be undesirable since it amounts to a de facto

---

[9]As a result of these concerns, the Federal Deposit Insurance Corporation Improvement Act (FDICIA) of 1991 required the Federal Reserve to implement a new regulation (Regulation F) under which banks, thrifts, and foreign banks must develop internal procedures or benchmarks to limit their settlement and other credit exposures to depository institutions with which they do business (so called correspondent banks). Under the new (December 1992) rule, banks must normally limit their exposure to an individual correspondent to no more than 25% of the correspondent bank's capital. However, in the case of adequately capitalized banks, this can be raised to 50%, while no set benchmark is required for well-capitalized banks. Thus, the most highly capitalized banks (most solvent banks) will find it easier to transact on the wire-transfer networks—and run daylight overdrafts—than less well capitalized banks.

[10]See Humphrey [1985].

extension of the federal safety net to foreign banking systems and foreign universal banks, given the fact that a large proportion of fund messages on CHIPS reflect transactions in the Euromarkets among foreign banks.[11] Such a policy also leads to an absolute increase in the potential scale of discount window loans. As a result, the Federal Reserve has used moral suasion and the self-interest of the major banks involved to encourage various reforms on CHIPS so as reduce its safety net exposure. These reforms have also collectively worked to reduce systemic risk exposure.

CHIPS settlement risk controls today take a number of forms:

1. Banks self-impose a cross-system debit cap on their total wholesale payment transactions. For the most credit-worthy banks, this means that, as a multiple of primary capital, they can run an aggregate payments system (Fedwire plus CHIPS) overdraft level of 2.25 on any single day and an average level of 1.5 (over a 2-week period).

2. Participants on CHIPS are required to impose maximum bilateral sender caps on the payment send messages received from other participating banks. Thus, if a counterparty is viewed as risky, banks can adjust downward their permitted caps for that bank at the beginning of each business day.

3. In addition to bilateral caps, each bank faces an aggregate sender cap on its payment messages over CHIPS. This aggregate is a percentage (usually 5–6%) of the aggregate of bilateral sender caps imposed by other banks.

4. There have been additional reforms that are turning the provisional nature of payment messages under CHIPS into a network more closely approximating a final settlement payments system. If successful, these reforms will significantly remove the degree of systemic risk inherent on CHIPS, and at the same time lower the scale of any implicit or explicit safety net guarantees.

The essential idea of the scheme, introduced by CHIPS members in 1990, is one of co-insurance. Should a participant on CHIPS fail to settle its net-send obligations at the end of the day, all surviving participants will assume an additional settlement obligation (ASO) proportional to their bilateral credit caps imposed on the failed bank—which reflects each bank's independent credit judgment of that failed bank. To make sure sufficient funds are available, all participants on CHIPS are required to contribute to a collateral fund (held in escrow) from which any such additional settlement payments will be made. This fund had approximately $4 billion in reserves in 1991.

---

[11] It might also be noted foreign banks have direct access to both CHIPS and Fedwire via their branches.

Safety Nets in Countries with Universal Banking

Deposit Insurance

One striking feature of non-U.S. deposit insurance schemes is that most were established after 1960. In other countries, more weight has usually been placed on the central bank and the discount window (or lender of last resort mechanism) than on deposit insurance to stem panics—one of the original reasons for deposit insurance in the United States.[12] One possible reason is that banking systems are generally more concentrated, thus allowing the respective central banks a more prominent "moral suasion" function. In addition, foreign banks are more diversified—along both geographic and product lines—making failures and panics less likely [see, e.g., Benston 1989; Herring and Santomero 1990; and Haraf 1990]. A further reason, commonly advanced, is that the discount window in other countries has historically been used in a more credible manner to stem panics than in the United States [Gilbert and Wood 1986]. In particular, a number of economists [such as Friedman and Schwartz 1963] attribute the U.S. banking panics of the early 1930s to the failure of the Federal Reserve to follow credible lender-of-last-resort policies. That is, the Federal Reserve contracted the monetary base during banking panics rather than expanding it, as would be required of a credible lender of last resort. It can thus be argued that deposit insurance was introduced in the United States as an antipanic policy, in lieu of credible lender of last resort discount window policies.[13]

A question naturally arises as to why, if it has a credible lender of last resort mechanism, the United Kingdom decided to introduce deposit insurance in the late 1970s. The introduction of the U.K. scheme was an outgrowth of a banking crisis among small banks in 1973–74—the so-called secondary banking crisis. The scheme itself has a lower coverage cap than the U.S. scheme (approximately £20,000), as well as a 25% up-front deductible. More importantly, the very rationale of the scheme has more to do with the objective of protecting the wealth of small savers in the case of individual bank failures (such as small secondary banks and, more recently, BCCI), than with acting as a substitute for the Bank of England's lender of last resort discount window as a panic-prevention device [Hall 1989].

In Germany, deposit insurance appears to play an even less visible role than in the United Kingdom. The administration and operation of the scheme is private and noncompulsory for banks. As in the United Kingdom, its primary objective appears to be the protection of small depositors rather than acting as a panic-protection device. As has been frequently

[12]However, the main reason for the introduction of deposit insurance in the United States was to protect small depositors and small banks.

[13]It is arguable that this thesis may be specific to the United States rather than other countries in general. Indeed, central bank policies clearly failed to stem monetary panics and instabilities in Germany in the 1920s and 1930s.

noted, private deposit insurance schemes (on a stand-alone basis) are less likely to offer a credible panic-prevention device compared to publicly administered and operated funds.

The Discount Window

The use of the discount window as a major panic-prevention weapon in universal banking countries should not be construed as implying that it does not (or cannot) have potentially unfavorable moral hazard effects on bank behavior. For example, while it is true that the Bank of England's policies in the banking crisis of 1973–74—through its opening of the discount window—stopped a contagious run spreading from failing secondary banks to the large clearing banks—in association with a scheme to recycle large deposits among the clearing banks—this policy has been criticized as providing a form of TBTF guarantee to the largest U.K. banks, especially National Westminster [Reid 1982].

Thus, a credible discount window policy, while being useful to prevent panics and contagious runs that threaten the banking system, must be able to distinguish between genuine panics and a limited crisis affecting a small group of banks or a single bank. This is no easy task, as the U.K. 1973–74 experience demonstrated. Consequently, a number of observers [e.g., Benston 1989] argue that a blanket TBTF guarantee exists for major banks in most European universal banking systems.

In Germany the discount window has increasingly come to exhibit the type of lender-of-last-resort function advocated by monetary theorists. That is, discount window loans are only available at a penalty cost (a rate of interest higher than the open market rate). The change towards a penalty-rate rule for the so-called Lombard rate dates from 1984. Prior to this, German banks had used the discount window on a revolving credit basis at a below market rate. Since 1984, the Lombard rate has been established as a facility for exceptional bank liquidity needs [see Dudler 1985; and Neumann 1988] with nonexceptional needs being met by central bank controlled repurchase agreements at market rates.[14] It might be noted that, in comparison, the U.S. discount window rate has generally been set below (rather than above) open market rates.

Payment System Guarantees

Most universal banking countries have wholesale payment systems [BIS 1985]. These payment systems are either privately operated—in which case no explicit central bank guarantees exist, as in the Clearing House Automated Payments System (CHAPS) in the United Kingdom—or are operated by the central bank concerned, in which case the potential exists

---

[14]Between 1984 and 1987, up to 50% of the money base was provided by these repurchase agreements. Thus, RPs, rather than the Lombard rate (or more precisely discount window borrowings) have become the major instrument of monetary control.

for similar types of guarantees and subsidies to those on the U.S. Fedwire system.

One universal banking system that has a central bank-operated whole-sale payments network is Switzerland. The Swiss Interbank Clearing (SIC) system, established in mid-1987, has received a great deal of attention since it has been designed explicitly to avoid the type of "good funds" guarantees (subsidies) that appear to exist on the U.S. Fedwire network. The Swiss system's innovation is that a net "send" payments message will not be transmitted unless a bank has a positive reserve balance at the central bank. That is, a bank's payment send-messages have to wait in a line until either the bank adds to its reserves or receives a reserve-adding credit message from another bank. As a result, the Swiss National Bank can operate its system with no risk of daylight overdrafts. Moreover, since the wire transfer system is open 24 hours on banking days, it creates an incentive for banks to synchronize their payment "sends" and "receives" better, so as to avoid delays and gridlock. Finally, since messages are sent on a first in, first out basis, the most important messages can be scheduled earlier in the day. This suggests that it is possible to design a central bank or publicly-owned wholesale payment systems without daylight overdraft risk and safety net guarantees (see below).[15]

Required Reforms in the United States

Sequentially, the problems of the thrift failures, the passage of FIRREA (1989), the Treasury Report [1991] on bank reform, the ensuing debate in Congress, and the passage of the FDIC Improvement Act in 1991, raised important issues relating to both safety net reform and the permitted activities of banks in the United States. Here we examine what, if any, changes are needed in the structure and administration of the U.S. safety net, so that the emergence of universal banking in America does not generate a poten-tial increase in the size of taxpayers' actual and contingent liabilities. The basic conclusions are that: (1) credible bank capital and closure rules must be established, and (2) TBTF guarantees must be eliminated, if the objective standard of no additional taxpayer liability from universal bank-ing activity line expansion is to be met.

We first look at the potential role capital and capital rules would play in a U.S. universal banking system. We then analyze how TBTF guarantees provided by U.S. bank regulators might be replaced with market and institutional mechanisms that both discipline large banks (stockholders, debt-holders, and managers) and, more importantly, avoid systemic risks should the failure of a large universal bank occur in the absence of such guarantees.

---

[15]However, it should be noted the SIC has only around 150 members while Fedwire has around 7,000 [see Vital and Mengle 1988].

Capital Requirements and Universal Banking

While the Treasury Report [1991] on banking reform did not advocate universal banking along either German or British lines—where a bank either undertakes nonbank activities in-house or in direct subsidiaries— (nor were its recommendations accepted), it provided an important framework within which such a debate can take place.

The U.S. Treasury's plan envisaged nonbank activities, such as life and P/C insurance as well as securities activities, taking place within a financial services holding company (FSHC). A FSHC would be very similar to the existing bank holding company structure, in which banks are only affiliated with nonbanking activities via the holding company. Importantly, only FSHCs whose banking subsidiaries are viewed as "well capitalized" would be allowed to engage in expanded nonbank activities.

Specifically, a bank's capital could fall into one of five zones. Banks in Zone 1 are considered to have significantly more capital than is required by regulators and can undertake the whole set of non-bank activities through affiliates of the holding company. Banks in Zone 2 either just meet or are just above the minimum capital standards and may be permitted by the Federal Reserve to engage in some nonbank activities. Banks falling in Zones 3 to 5 are those that fail to meet required capital standards. Banks in Zone 3 would have to file a recapitalization plan, as would banks in Zone 4 which would, in addition, have restrictions placed on their dividend payments. Banks in Zone 5 fall below some critical (non-negative) capital ratio level and would be either closed, merged, or placed into conservatorship.

The Treasury plan embodied several important incentive features. First, it created a positive incentive for banks and their holding company owners to meet high (Zones 1 and 2) capital standards if they wished to expand their nonbanking powers. Indeed, if a bank engaging in nonbank activities were to have its capital ratio fall outside Zones 1 and 2 the FSHC would either have to recapitalize the bank or terminate its nonbank activities [see Treasury Report 1991]. As additional incentives, the firewalls between the bank and its nonbank affiliates would be of the Federal Reserve Act Section 23A and Section 23B funding type, and would not extend to the all-encompassing marketing and resource sharing firewalls that today separates banks from their Section 20 securities affiliates [see GAO, *Bank Powers*, 1990 for a list of some 20 firewalls].

Second, to the extent that a low capital ratio leads to closure at a positive net worth level, bank stockholders face the potential risk of a loss of wealth and bank franchise value on closure. Thus, a credible closure rule at a positive net worth level creates "co-insurance" incentives for stockholders and managers to avoid excessive risk taking, thereby lowering the potential exposure of the deposit insurance fund and the safety net.

Third, bank closure and nonbank activity powers are predicated on the bank's capital position and not that of its parent FSHC (or bank holding company as under the current regulatory regime). This clearly focuses regulatory attention on the question of bank safety and soundness and the need to protect the integrity of the bank's capital.

Fourth, regulation and monitoring of capital adequacy requirements would take place along functional lines. That is, bank regulators would concentrate on monitoring the capital position of the bank, the SEC on the capital position of the securities affiliate and state insurance regulators on the capital position of the insurance affiliate.

Overall, the Treasury plan had a number of attractive features recommending a set of capital maintenance incentives for banks, a clear closure rule,[16] and nonbank activity firewalls that would still allow potential economies of scope to be achieved through cross-marketing and resource (cost) sharing.

However, we believe there were at least three potential areas of weakness in the Treasury plan. First, it did not go quite far enough in that it only permited nonbank activity expansions within a holding company framework and not via bank subsidiaries as in the U.K. universal banking model. Second, the capital zone and closure rules were largely book-value based rather than market-value based. Third, forbearance and TBTF guarantees were still possible for the largest banks. We shall look at these issues in turn.

Bank Subsidiaries and Universal Banking

As is argued elsewhere in this book, and by Herring and Santomero [1990], earnings diversification and economies of scale and scope on the cost side (and possibly on the revenue side as well) are potentially greater for a more integrated universal bank of the U.K. kind, where nonbank activities are carried out through subsidiaries of the parent bank, rather than through separate affiliates as in the holding company model. However, while potential returns may be higher, there may be a greater risk that losses on nonbank activities (e.g., a subsidiary failure) will directly affect a universal bank's safety and soundness since such losses will impose a direct charge on the bank's capital position rather than the holding company's as in an FSHC framework.

Nevertheless, it is evident that the capital zone system conceived of for the FSHC [see also Eisenbeis 1990; and Benston and Kaufman 1988] could easily be extended to the case of universal bank subsidiaries. As under the 1991 Treasury plan and the FDIC Improvement Act of 1991, the focus would be on bank capital adequacy, with only those banks more than adequately capitalized (e.g., those in Zone 1) being allowed to establish direct subsidiaries to engage in insurance and securities activities. As

---

[16]Indeed, the FDIC Improvement Act mandated a capital zoning scheme, including mandatory closure at low capital ratios (2%). This scheme is now operative.

Huertas [1987] has argued, to the extent that a bank's capital is more directly at risk than in a holding company framework, an extra margin of capital—potentially higher than that envisaged in the Treasury plan or under the FDICIA—could be specified to meet Zone 1 requirements.

If a bank's capital were to fall below Zone 1 levels, so that it would be more exposed to losses by its direct subsidiaries, bank stockholders could be required either to add more capital to the bank or to restrict the bank's insurance and securities activities. For example, in case of significant deviations from Zone 1, it might be required to divest and sell its subsidiaries. If necessary, extra protection for the bank could emanate from Rule 23A and 23B-type funding and asset transfer firewalls being extended to intrabank subsidiary transactions. However, to maximize economies of scope and scale as well as earnings diversification potential, marketing and resource-sharing firewalls of the Section 20 type should not be imposed.

Measurement of Capital and Universal Banking

The second issue relates to the measurement of adequate capital. Under the Treasury plan and the recently implemented "prompt corrective action" provisions of the FDICIA, capital zones and capital adequacy are viewed in the context of the risk-based capital asset ratio of the Basel Agreement, which became fully operational in the United States at the end of 1992.[17] While the risk weights under the plan seek, in a rough fashion, to mark-to-market the credit risk of a bank's on and off balance sheet position, no account is taken of interest rate risk or foreign exchange risk. To its credit, the 1991 Treasury plan recognized this weakness and advocated that the capital requirements reflect interest rate risk as soon as a methodology to achieve this could be worked out within the risk-based capital framework.[18] For a capital rules regime to work, and to impose a credible degree of risk control over the stockholders and managers of a universal bank, it is vital that capital ratios reflect market or economic net worth (capital) rather than book-value capital. Otherwise, the same type of perverse risk-taking incentives evident in the thrift crisis of the 1980s may become built into the incentive structures of universal banks.

The imposition of strict, and correctly measured, zonal capital rules for activity line expansions and bank closures also have important implications for the deposit insurance fund. In particular, as long as capital rules approximately reflect the market value of bank net worth, and are imposed without forbearance, the potential exposure of the deposit insurance fund to the risk of nonbank activities will be small, even if these activities are carried out by bank subsidiaries rather than through holding company affiliates. Specifically, a bank will be required to divest itself of nonbank

---

[17]However, they are defined in terms of a simple capital-assets ratio as well.

[18]In fact, the FDIC Improvement Act required interest-rate risk to be operationally reflected in capital requirements in June 1993. The Federal Reserves proposals for risk-weighting are based on the (modified) durations of bank assets and liabilities.

activities at relatively high levels of capital and the bank itself will be closed before its net worth is fully dissipated.

Bank failures that impose substantial costs on the deposit insurance fund under these circumstances can only occur through one or a mixture of three possible causes:

1. A sudden unexpected catastrophic shock to one (or several) bank subsidiaries or to the bank itself, that depletes the banks own capital (e.g., the effects of a major earthquake on life and P/C subsidiaries or a stock market crash on securities and insurance subsidiaries).

2. Fraudulent behavior by the managers and owners of the bank and/or its subsidiaries, such as misrepresenting capital levels.

3. Regulatory failure, such as "unintentional" forbearance through slack monitoring, surveillance, and closure policy enforcement.

While fraud cannot be prevented in any financial system, it can be mitigated, in part, by efficient monitoring and regulation on the part of regulators, external bank auditors (accounting firms), and credit rating agencies. Furthermore, the potential exposure of bank subsidiaries or the bank itself to catastrophic risk can be exaggerated, given the presence of a broad array of risk management techniques and instruments. As discussed in Chapter 4, both life and P/C insurers tend to hedge catastrophic risks through reinsurance markets, while major losses on securities underwriting (such as a stock market collapse) can be hedged by taking offsetting positions in the index futures and options markets.

Finally, to the extent that bank insurance premium payments are inversely related to bank capital ratios, as under the 1993 risk-based premium system, there will be incentives to maintain higher capital standards than under a flat premium system.[19]

Too Big to Fail and Universal Banking

The third issue of relevance regarding required U.S. reforms concerns the failure of the Treasury plan and the FDIC Improvement Act to eliminate forbearance totally, and thus scrap TBTF guarantees for the largest banks. Despite the implementation of capital-zoning discipline, many observers, including the Treasury and Congress, appear to doubt that closure could be imposed on the largest banking organizations for fear that this could set off a series of systemic or contagious runs on other banks. Indeed, the bigger the bank, the greater is the fear of runs and systemic collapse. As a result, forbearance and TBTF guarantees may be magnified in any future U.S. universal banking system that contains larger banks with more nonbank activity lines than in the past [see Burnham 1991]. This raises the question of how feasible it is to require regulators to forgo, *ex ante*, and in

---

[19]These incentives are small, however, under the current (1993) scheme; the "deductible" for good behavior is a relatively small 9 basis points.

a credible fashion, a willingness to bail out or guarantee the debt-holders (and perhaps equity-holders) of large universal banks should they get into difficulty; furthermore, how large are TBTF subsidies?

First, we first examine how large a subsidy TBTF guarantees really provide to the biggest banks. We then go on to evaluate market and institutional mechanisms now available to deal with large bank failures, absent TBTF guarantees, without significant increases in systemic or contagion risk to the banking system and financial markets as a whole.

Size of TBTF Guarantees

There is considerable disagreement regarding the extent to which TBTF guarantees benefit large banks today. Any factual evidence consistent with the existence of pervasive TBTF guarantees would include (1) an increased market share of banks for savings; (2) an increasing share of bank assets held by the very biggest U.S. banks; and (3) an absence of risk premiums in the markets for (large) bank uninsured deposits, debt, and equity. In fact the evidence to date tends to be largely inconsistent with the supposed existence of sizable TBTF subsidies.

First, aggregate flow of funds data show that the share of commercial bank assets in the total assets of financial institutions has been falling over time. For example, from a 57.3% share in 1946 commercial bank assets fell to a 38.6% share in 1970 and a 31.2% share in 1990. By contrast, pension funds and mutual funds have increased their collective shares of financial institution assets from 3.3% in 1946 to 16.3% in 1970 and to 28.6% in 1990. This is in spite of the fact that the Pension Benefit Guarantee Fund has been technically insolvent for much of this period [Kaufman 1988] and money market mutual funds are either uninsured or are backed only by private insurance guarantees.

Second, the share of large U.S. bank assets as a percent of either domestic or global bank assets has been shrinking. For example, in 1990 the top 5 banking organizations in the United States held 13.1% of domestic bank assets compared to 14% in 1970. And nationwide concentration ratios tend to be lower in banking than those found in either life or P/C insurance. As discussed in Chapter 2, at the end of 1991, no U.S. bank measured by asset size was in the world's top 20 banks. This compares to three U.S. banks in the top 20 in 1980 and seven out of the top 20 twenty in 1970.

Third, risk premiums clearly show up in the costs of large banks' debt and equity, thereby reflecting the underlying exposures of the bank concerned. In an investigation of interest rates paid by 58 large banks for their uninsured deposits, James [1987] found these rates to be significantly dependent on bank leverage, loan-loss provisions, and stock return variance. Similarly, Hannan and Hanweck [1988] found large CD rates to be significantly (inversely) related to the ratio of bank income to assets and the bank's capital asset ratio. With regard to subordinated debt, Gorton and Santomero [1990] found that implied variance in bank bond rates significantly reflected risk measures directly derived from bank balance sheets. A study by Avery, Belton, and Goldberg [1988] of bank bond yield spreads, by contrast, found similar risk variables to have no explanatory power. James [1988], Cargill [1989], Grammatikos and Saunders [1990], Cornell and Shapiro [1986], and Smirlock and Kaufold [1987] have all found bank stock returns (and risk) to be highly sensitive to a bank's relative exposure to LDC loans. Brewer and Lee [1986] found that bank systematic risk coefficients (or betas) were significantly related to bank balance sheet variables such as the capital assets ratio. Interestingly, much of this empirical work analyzes bank interest rates and returns in the post-1984 period, that is, after the Continental Illinois reorganization, which many view as the first clear statement of the de facto TBTF guarantee for large banks.

Potential Failure Resolution for Large Universals

While it is arguable that some market discipline does (and will continue to) exist for large banks, even in the absence of credible threats of closure and discipline to their largest depositors and claimholders, it is interesting to speculate how feasible it would be to close—either by transfer of insured depositors, a modified payoff, or liquidation—future U.S. universal banks without a dramatic increase in banking and financial market systemic risk.

One obvious institutional barrier to discipline via closure through a transfer of insured depositors or a modified payoff—in which uninsured depositors take an upfront haircut or loss on their deposits (equal to the expected loss of the FDIC) and their remaining deposits plus all insured deposits are then transferred to another bank—is that there may be very few banking organizations willing or able to acquire a failing universal bank of multibillion dollar asset size. This raises the question of how feasible it would be to close and liquidate the assets of a major universal bank without imposing large transactions costs and systemic risks on other participants in the financial markets.

Haraf [1990, 1991] has pointed out that an important case study already exists on how to liquidate a large "universal-type" institution and what the systemic risk consequences of such a liquidation might be. The case in point is the bankruptcy and liquidation of the Drexel Burnham Lambert Group in 1990, with $28 billion of assets (equivalent to a top 25 U.S. bank holding company). Drexel was an unregulated holding company that included four subsidiaries—two regulated and two unregulated. These were (1) Drexel Burnham Lambert, Inc. (DBL), a broker dealer regulated by the SEC; (2) Drexel Burnham Lambert Government Securities (GSI), a government securities dealer regulated by the Federal Reserve; (3) DBL Trading Corporation, which engaged primarily in foreign exchange and commodities trading; and (4) DBL International Bank, NV of Curacao, through which Drexel conducted much of its international banking operations.

While the DBL securities affiliate and the GSI affiliate were generally profitable, and financed their operations largely through bank loans and RPs, the parent holding company financed its inventory of junk bonds (and other assets) mainly through bank loans and the commercial paper market.

When the rating agencies downgraded Drexel's commercial paper to below investment grade, the firm found it almost impossible to borrow on the CP market, and its bank creditors demanded repayment of loans. To prevent the Drexel holding company raiding its profitable brokerage and government securities subsidiaries, the SEC and the Federal Reserve moved to protect these subsidiaries. As a result, Drexel was left with bankruptcy as its only option. Thereafter DBL and GSI, the Drexel brokerage and securities subsidiaries, began to liquidate their assets in order to pay off their liability holders. While both subsidiaries had a positive net worth, liquidation was hampered, but not prevented, by imperfections in the payment, clearance, and settlement systems for cash, securities, and other assets. For example, market participants were often reluctant to surrender securities to Drexel because of the time lag between delivery of such instruments and payment, and because of doubts about the ability of Drexel to settle its transactions over the wire networks. Eventual liquidation was in fact achieved, and all liability claimholders of DBL and GSI were paid in full.

The importance of the Drexel case is not only that a liquidation of a major universal-type financial institution was feasible, but that it occurred without significant apparent systemic risk or disruption to the financial system. This was accomplished in spite of existing institutional imperfections in the wholesale payments systems and securities clearance and settlement systems. It suggests that current and proposed reforms to the payments, clearance, and settlement systems should actually work to make future universal bank liquidations easier, with a lower risk of disruption and contagion to the financial system at large.[20]

Reform of Payment, Clearance, and Settlement Systems

As discussed earlier, significant strides have been made in recent years to iron out imperfections in the wholesale payments networks. Moves towards charging interest on daylight overdrafts on Fedwire, capping the exposures of individual banks, and reforms to CHIPS that bring the system closer to "payment message finality," are viewed as efforts to ameliorate settlement or daylight overdraft risk on these systems. Further, as Baer

---

[20]However, it is arguable that there is a crucial difference between the Continental Illinois and Drexel cases. This was the exposure of a large number of small bank correspondents to losses should Continental have been closed and liquidated. However, estimates suggest that correspondent losses would only have been in the 2–5 percent of deposit range, moreover, such concerns should not inhibit the closure of a big bank. Indeed, if "subsidies" are believed to be "socially" necessary for the small bank correspondents, a more efficient mechanism would have been to give them direct subsidies such as through the tax system, etc., rather than indirect subsidies via Continental Illinois.

and Evanoff [1990] argue, payment system risk could be further reduced by more frequent settlement of transactions, such as allowing 24-hour interbank payment transfers, and netting across foreign currency payment networks. While such institutional changes have yet to materialize, they provide alternative institutional mechanisms that can help to control systemic payment risks. They offer an important alternative to blanket TBTF guarantees.

In addition to institutional improvements in the wholesale payment networks, reforms are underway in a number of countries to bolster the clearance and settlement systems for both primary and derivative securities. A report by the Group of Thirty [1989] has provided an important framework for such reforms. It had seven major recommendations.

1. Each country should have a centralized securities depository (CSD) structured to include a parallel or linked payments system, dematerialize securities, and minimize delivery problems on settlement.

2. Netting systems for securities, rather than individual settlements of trades, should be encouraged.

3. There should be synchronization between the delivery of securities and payment for securities—so-called delivery versus payment (DVP).

4. Payments for the same securities trading in different markets should be made consistent by adopting "same day" funds conventions.

5. Settlement should occur a maximum of 3 days after a trade (T + 3).

6. Securities lending and borrowing (e.g., short sales) should be encouraged to expedite settlement of securities transactions.

7. Each country should adopt a standardized system of securities message transfers.

As progress is made toward these goals, and as the market and institutional technology for transferring funds, settling, and clearing trades improves, transaction and systemic disruption costs from unwinding or liquidating the assets and liabilities of a large universal bank will tend to decrease. This in turn increases the cost of TBTF solutions to large bank problems relative to the costs of large bank liquidations, and makes its justification as a policy device more difficult to accept [see also Morgan Guaranty 1993].

Other Required Reforms Under Universal Banking

While U.S. banking reform proposals largely concentrate on the implications of greater universal banking powers for the deposit insurance and payment system components of the safety net, there is also the issue of its potential implications for the discount window.

The Discount Window

To the extent that universal banking is structured either through direct bank subsidiaries or through affiliates, problems at those affiliates/subsidiaries may affect the willingness of depositors to renew deposits and/or result in their requiring higher liquidity premiums on funds deposited. To the extent that such problems are temporary, the discount window may be called into play as a source of liquidity. Intraorganizational contagion effects of this sort may occur either because of direct transactions between a bank and its subsidiary—subject to any funding firewalls—or from informational contagion in which bank managers are placed in the same category as the subsidiaries managers by liability-holders.[21]

Since the activity-scope of a universal bank will, by definition, be broader than that of a traditional commercial bank, the range of potential events that might result in intraorganizational contagion is likely to expand—whether informational or institutional in terms of their source. For example, a parent universal bank with life insurance and P/C insurance subsidiaries may face funding pressures if these subsidiaries happen to suffer major losses in an earthquake or hurricane. A question thus arises as to whether additional safety net subsidies will accrue to universal banks through the discount window mechanism.

As discussed earlier, the subsidy element in the discount window has been small or nonexistent in the United States, partly because of the collateralized lending requirement and partly because any interest rate spread subsidy is offset by implicit interest payments to the Federal Reserve in the form of noninterest-bearing reserve requirements. Despite this, there still may be a concern that a small safety net subsidy could remain under the discount window mechanism and that this may be magnified by any increased potential scope for event risk under universal banking.[22]

The structure and management of the discount window mechanism under German universal banking is instructive here. In order to make its discount window truly a lender of last resort facility and to eradicate any net interest rate spread subsidies, we have noted that the German discount (Lombard) rate has consistently been set above money market rates since 1984. Other universal banking countries such as Canada adopt a floating rate mechanism whereby the discount window rate varies with money market rates plus a spread.

In order to negate any subsidy element totally, either a fixed (but adjustable) discount rate—set at a penalty level above market rates—or a floating discount rate with a spread above market rates could be instituted by the Federal Reserve. Either policy would allow the discount window to

---

[21]See Saunders [1985] and Flannery [1986] for further discussion of intraorganizational contagion effects.

[22]It could be argued that a subsidy is desirable if there are social costs to bank illiquidity (e.g. runs) that exceed private costs.

be there in times of fundamental "need," as in a liquidity crisis, without providing any potential profit or subsidy opportunity for universal banks.

Conclusion

This chapter has sought to analyze the implications of a shift to universal banking in the United States for bank safety and soundness and the federal safety net: deposit insurance, the discount window, and payment system guarantees. Our overall conclusion is that universal banking and the ability of banks to undertake a broader range of activities are fully consistent with a safe and sound banking system and the absence of new taxpayer exposure as long as suitable regulatory, institutional, and market mechanisms are set in place.

In the aftermath of the U.S. thrift crisis, it has been argued that greater universal banking, with its implied nonbank activity expansions, may impose an increased threat to the federal safety net and require significant reforms in the structure of the safety net itself before universal banking can be allowed.

In this chapter, we have argued that central to protecting the safety net and minimizing any subsidies should be a (universal) bank's capital and a credibly enforced bank closure rule based on the market value of capital or a close variant thereof. Specifically, we have argued that increased bank stockholder and manager discipline will be imposed if a capital-zoning system, approved under the FDIC Improvement Act, were implemented (with some amendments) within a universal bank subsidiary framework. This would mean that only the best capitalized banks would be allowed to operate subsidiaries that engaged in nonbank activities such as life insurance, P/C insurance, and securities activities.

An essential feature of the incentive structure of such a system would be that closure is enforced without forbearance and regardless of bank size, before capital (net worth) of the bank is fully dissipated. While concerns about systemic risk associated with closing and liquidating large universal banks remain, we suggest that market, information, and institutional mechanisms are developing the technology and infrastructure to ameliorate the potential scale of any adverse contagion and systemic effects.

Along these lines, significant changes in wholesale payment systems have been made to reduce the scale and size of the Federal Reserve's exposure to daylight overdrafts. Similarly, improvements are underway in national and global settlement and clearance systems for securities (and derivative products) that bode well for lowering the transactions costs and other institutional frictions relating to the unwinding of the asset and liability positions of a large universal bank in cases of failure.

Our analysis suggests that universal banking of the U.K. bank-parent, nonbank subsidiary type can be instituted with a minimum degree of (funding) firewalls as long as credibility over the implementation and enforcement of capital zoning rules is maintained (without forbearance) by the regulators. Such a structure also has a number of advantages over the holding company form of universal banking. By allowing a greater degree of integration between a bank and its nonbank subsidiaries, and thus increasing the potential to generate earnings diversification benefits for the bank, the safety and soundness of the bank can be enhanced, as discussed in Chapter 5. And the potential for generating economies of scope both on the cost and revenue sides for the universal bank would be increased. Both diversification effects and economies-of-scope effects serve to reduce the probability that the safety net will be called into play.

8

Towards a Rational and Competitive Regulatory Structure

Global economic and financial interdependence has fundamentally and permanently changed economic and financial life in the United States. Many of today's policymakers grew up at a time when U.S. international trade was perhaps 3% of GNP. Today it is four times that. They were taught that fiscal deficits did not matter much and could easily be funded domestically. Now foreign savings are largely relied upon to cover excess federal spending. They learned that U.S. interest rates could be set at will by the Federal Reserve. Today American monetary policy is conducted with a wary eye on the Bundesbank and the Bank of Japan. They were convinced that U.S. financial institutions were world-class competitors and would inevitably stay that way, only to see many of them in full retreat. The world has changed.

Unfortunately, perceptions sometimes change more slowly than reality. The U.S. steel and automobile industries remained contemptuous of their emerging foreign rivals long after the handwriting was on the wall. Fiscal policies in the 1980s were conducted as if they had few international implications. Adaptation of the American banking and financial system remained largely impervious to the changing structural realities in modern money and capital markets. Protagonists representing large and small commercial banks, savings institutions, securities firms, insurance underwriters and brokers, and finance companies sought to enhance and protect their parochial interests with little regard for the interests of the nation as a whole. The regulators and the courts had to be relied upon to validate market realities as best they could.

The Congress, which has the mandate to set the boundaries and parameters for a financial system that ultimately serves the national interest, has dithered and tinkered for over 60 years, responsive as it has been to special interests.

For many years this probably did not matter much. In the 1980s, however, it began to matter a great deal, especially as Britain, Canada, Australia, France, and other countries began to make serious efforts at financial liberalization and reform, and as the EC began the design and implementation of a new regional financial structure as part of the 1992 single market initiatives. Even Japan moved steadily toward financial liberalization—under pressure from trading partners, to be sure—and began seriously considering major structural reforms. As of April 1993, subsidiaries of the 10 Japanese trust banks can underwrite and deal in government and corporate bonds, underwrite (but not distribute) equity-linked securities, and manage investment trusts such as mutual funds. The same limited privileges may be extended to Japan's commercial banks in 1994. At the same time, securities firms are allowed to set up trust-banking subsidiaries to deal in investment trusts and currency instruments. Indications are that further deregulation may occur in 1995 or 1996, depending on the results of these initial steps. The United States meanwhile continues to be mired in politicized decisions, inaction, and fire-fighting made necessary by serious design flaws that had crept into the financial system in the 1930s.

Clearly, what is needed in the United States is a blueprint for a financial system that fundamentally serves the national interest by promoting efficiency in resource allocation, capital formation and economic growth, financial stability, and global competitiveness of financial firms themselves and those who use their services. It can be argued that the U.S. system, as it has evolved, has underperformed against all of these benchmarks. If true, far-reaching reforms are clearly called for—reforms that permit *economic* rather than *political* considerations to determine the organizational forms through which financial services can best be carried out.

In particular, the German, Swiss, and Japanese economic experience during recent decades has raised important issues as to what can be done to improve U.S. performance in a global competitive context. A key area—the one that has been the focus of this study—is the institutional design of a country's financial system. The Germans, Swiss, and British have pursued several different forms of universal banking, whereas the United States has relied largely on a functionally separatist and geographically fragmented approach.

Overview

The major theme of this study has been an examination of the case for and against universal banking in the United States, focusing on three key areas—efficiency, stability, and competitiveness.[1]

An optimal institutional design should serve to maximize social welfare gains in selecting any specific institutional arrangement. While it is impossible to describe precisely the nature and functional form of the "social welfare" objectives pursued by U.S. legislators and regulators in attempting to carry out their mandate from the public, it seems reasonable to argue that important features of that function would likely include: (1) increasing the static efficiency with which the financial system does its job; (2) increasing the dynamic efficiency and creativity with which it performs; and (3) lowering the risk of instability embedded in the system.

In the first part of this study, the relative performance of the U.S. banking system was compared to that of other countries. Based on various measures of efficiency and performance, such as return on equity/assets and growth, the U.S. banking system has in some respects appeared to perform poorly compared to systems characterized by some form of universal banking. An attempt was made to understand the origins of this performance differential. Specifically, enhanced profitability from a more universal banking design might come from either cost or revenue synergies. We presented an analysis of the cost functions of the world's largest banks which suggested that over some size ranges of banks there appear to be economies of super-scale to be gained from an institution's evolving into a moderately large-sized universal bank. However, there were few apparent cost synergies (or economies of scope) from joint production of multiple financial services. Recent empirical analysis suggests that the profitability/efficiency scope gains inherent in universal banking may lie more on the revenue-generating side than on the cost side (see Berger, Hancock, and Humphrey [1992]).

This kind of analysis raises the question as to what type of revenue synergies would be generated should U.S. banks be allowed to produce multiple financial services for their clients with a minimum of "firewalls."

The first revenue synergy would clearly arise from the enhanced ability of managers to shift resources freely into those activities in greatest demand by consumers, rather than being constrained by regulation to oversupply or undersupply various financial services. Moreover, increased resource flexibility would potentially lead to a more *dynamic* financial services industry in terms of the range and type of new and often innovative financial products produced.

The second area of synergy would derive from the joint marketing and

---

[1] For studies on efficiencies through greater competition in property/casualty insurance, see Angoff [1988] and Joskow [1973]. Studies concerning efficiencies through lower distribution costs include Joskow [1973] and Pauly, Kunreather, and Kleindorfer [1986].

selling of financial services. Many financial products, such as mortgage loans and mortgage (credit) life insurance, or auto loans and auto insurance, are strong complements. By allowing a single financial services firm to originate and sell these products, transactions costs, search costs, and other obstacles faced by consumers would be reduced by their ability to engage in one-stop shopping for financial products. Not only would universal banks benefit from cross-product demand, but social welfare savings would be achieved from a reduction in the transaction and search costs that are currently expended by consumers and other users of financial services.

Assessment of the experience with universal banking abroad also refutes the notion, frequently mentioned, that allowing universal nationwide banking will eventually spell the end of community banking and insurance. Even in Germany, which has essentially no restrictions on what universal banks can do, either within the bank itself or through subsidiaries, this has not occurred. There is a long tradition of powerful and prosperous local players in the financial services industry—with the *Grossbanken* having less than 8% of all branches and 10% of banking assets in the country during 1990. This compares with 44% of branches and 21% of assets in the case of savings banks and 40% and 12%, respectively, in the case of rural and urban cooperative banks. While there is no comparable tradition in the United States, there is no reason why community banks cannot form cooperative networks that would combine centralized processing "factories" and wholesale financial market capabilities with the kind of product differentiation, local market knowledge, and personal services that are the traditional strengths of community banks. Modern technologies, brought to the market by vendors like Electronic Data Systems (EDS) and IBM, should make this a viable form of financial organization in the future.

The same is true of insurance. Since although life insurance is only a recent addition to the German banking scene—and P/C insurance remains to be added to the banks' portfolios—the returns and benefits from *Allfinanz* are not yet in. Despite some initial successes, it remains an open question whether commission agents and proprietary sales forces can be replaced by fixed-point distribution with significant cost savings and quality improvements. British universal banks, on the other hand, have had much more extensive insurance experience, ranging from brokerage by banks like National Westminster to underwriting by Lloyds Bank. Yet proprietary sales forces of firms like Allied Dunbar and commission brokers—required under the U.K. Financial Services Act to sell the "best available" product to meet the client's needs—continue to do well in terms of market share.

Again, there is no reason why independent insurance agents should be unable to hold their own against in-bank insurance sales teams, just as they do today against the direct sales forces of insurance companies and against remote distribution via mail. Competition and the pressure for efficiency and creativity will of course intensify, but this pressure is the source of gains from adding a new set of competitors from a different strategic group to the insurance underwriting and distribution industry.

The second part of this book examined the risk aspects of universal banking, including its potential impact on the federal safety net (deposit insurance, the discount window, and payment system guarantees). Some argue that universal banking should not be pursued if a reasonable probability exists that it will promote instability in the banking system and/or the potential failure or bailout costs to the nation's taxpayers. The first issue concerns the question of how risky universal banking is. The second concerns both risk and the regulatory policies that should be pursued in order to minimize any adverse impacts of universal banking on taxpayers without negating the potential revenue/cost synergies identified in the first part of this book.

To understand the inherent riskiness of a nascent U.S. universal banking system, various risk-simulation experiments were conducted in this study, including a number of possible mergers between currently functionally separate banking, insurance, and securities firms. These simulations strongly indicate the existence of risk-diversifying effects of financial service conglomerates. Moreover, since they ignore future dynamic effects of such mergers, these results represent a *lower bound* on eventual risk-reducing (return-increasing) gains from multiproduct operations.

In general, these results are consistent with those of previous authors—small but identifiable risk-diversification gains would be associated with combinations of banking and securities activities, and far greater risk-reduction gains would derive from the joint provision of banking and insurance products, both P/C and life.

While empirical evidence suggests that there will indeed be (on average) risk-reduction gains from U.S. universal banking, the existence of moral hazard attributable to a mispriced federal safety net cannot be ignored.

Moral hazard may, for example, induce some newly universal banking firms to alter their product mixes towards assuming risks that are excessive from a social welfare perspective. In our view, the answer to such a problem lies not in prohibiting universal banking, but rather in redesigning and reforming the federal safety net in order to make it a more coherent and economically rational system—one in which excessive risk taking is punished and not rewarded. Indeed, banks today (without universal banking) already have a sufficiently risky set of products available should they desire to take excessively risky positions. Indeed, virtually all banking failures in recent decades have been related to classic commercial banking operations.

Our belief is that at the center of a redesigned U.S. banking system—one that permits universal banking—should be a well-defined *closure rule* based on the *market value* of the capital position of the bank. If the market value of a bank's capital or net worth begins to fall due to losses from excessive risk-taking or nonbank activities, the bank should be closed before its capital position is fully dissipated. A bank closure rule that is activated when the market value of capital is positive and that is pursued without serious error or forbearance (discretion) by regulators is fully consistent with a universal banking system with no nonbank activity constraints and no new safety net liabilities—contingent or otherwise—imposed on taxpayers. It is our view that the early-closure and capital rules implemented under the FDIC Improvement Act go some way towards meeting these goals.

Moreover, the imposition of capital-based closure rules relegates the structure, pricing, and operation of the deposit insurance contract to second-order importance from a policy prospective. This is because, as long as banks are closed *before* net worth is negative, neither depositors nor the deposit guarantee fund will lose on closure—bank assets can be liquidated and depositors fully compensated from the proceeds of the liquidation.

Concerns about the structure of deposit insurance are only relevant should regulators enforce a capital-based closure rule *with error* due to delays, regulator mismanagement, or fraud. In our view, such real-world problems or imperfections can best be met by reforming the deposit insurance system (something that is valuable in and of itself, that is, whether or not universal banking is adopted). Specifically, the deposit insurance contract should have its premiums linked to the risk of bank failure. It should also subject large depositors to up-front losses in cases of failure equal to any costs borne by regulators in pursuing post-failure merger and failure resolutions the so-called "modified purchase and assumption" method. The 1991 FDIC Improvement Act, while mandating a risk-based deposit insurance premium scheme, failed to eliminate fully TBTF guarantees.[2]

The combination of a binding bank capital closure rule and a risk-based deposit insurance contract should more than assuage regulator and taxpayer concerns regarding potential increases in safety net exposure emanating from the advent of U.S. universal banking.

Implications for Policy

Based on the analysis contained in this study, we believe that the Glass-Steagall and Bank Holding Company Acts should be modified or repealed so as to allow U.S. banks to select a "universal" institutional structure should they choose to do so in response to the realities of the marketplace. We have examined in detail the two alternative institutional models of universal banking: (1) *integrated* universal banking, in which all financial activities such as commercial and retail banking, insurance, and securities are undertaken by separate departments within a universal bank and (2) the *subsidiary* form of universal banking, in which the parent bank undertakes commercial banking services and has separately capitalized subsidiaries to engage in nonbank activities, such as insurance and securities activities.

---

[2]However, a number of restrictions were imposed on the use of TBTF guarantees to try to limit these guarantees to exceptional cases. Moreover, the costs of TBTF bailouts could be passed on to other banks rather than being borne by the FDIC and the taxpayer.

At present, no country in the developed world has a fully *integrated* universal banking system. The closest example is Germany, which allows banking and securities activities to take place in house—in departments of the universal bank parent—but requires that insurance, mortgage banking, and certain other activities take place in subsidiaries of the parent. The *subsidiary* form most closely approximates that prevailing in Britain.

In theory, a fully integrated universal bank would be most desirable in a wholly transparent world, where regulators could impose and implement a nondiscretionary "market value of capital" bank closure rule without error. A totally universal bank would potentially maximize cost and revenue synergies in-house without imposing new safety net costs (contingent or otherwise) on the taxpayer.

In the imperfect real world, it is likely that:

1. Regulators will sometimes make errors in monitoring and surveillance of risk taking in banking, securities, and insurance.

2. There may be difficulties in applying a single (market value of capital) rule to a universal bank due to fractured and inconsistent financial accounting methods across the various types of activities.[3]

3. Regulators may not agree on a single agency/regulator for universal banks, especially given the history of functional regulation and bureaucratic turf battles in the United States.

4. Developing a fairly-priced single (incentive-compatible) integrated universal bank insurance contract that would simultaneously protect small depositors, securities customers, and insurance policyholders would be extremely difficult.

These concerns are real ones. While the fully integrated universal bank represents a conceptually desirable institutional design we believe that, for the United States, the subsidiary form of universal banking is probably the most desirable and politically realistic. It would provide substantial benefits to the U.S. economy, compared to the existing separate systems, and it can be applied in a way that maintains functional regulation.

It is our view, therefore, that the U.K. subsidiary model represents the best practical universal banking approach for the United States. This is because it represents an organizational arrangement that can support important static and dynamic gains, and at the same time is reasonably able to handle the four regulatory imperfections just identified.

First, the costs or errors caused by regulators underestimating and monitoring the risks of securities/insurance activities can best be controlled by requiring that these nonbank activities (or the most risky among them) take place in separately capitalized subsidiaries of the bank. Consequently, bank capital is in part protected from major unexpected losses in these areas.

---

[3]Although the problems of applying market-value accounting rules are significantly greater in banking than in securities activities.

Second, the practical problem of having to apply market value accounting rules—or a single such rule—across all areas of a fully integrated financial services firm can be ameliorated in the short term by allowing the universal bank parent and its securities and insurance subsidiaries to abide by existing accounting standards such as GAAP or SAP. However, over the longer term, a transition could be made towards a single (market value) accounting standard for the parent bank and its subsidiaries.

Third, the U.K. model dovetails directly into the historical functional design of financial services regulation in the United States. Consequently, banking authorities could remain the primary regulators of the universal bank parent, while the SEC and (state) insurance commissions remain the primary regulators of the securities and insurance subsidiaries, respectively. It would be desirable that these regulators coordinate their polices and that eventually a single lead regulator would emerge to oversee U.S. universals on a fully consolidated basis.

Finally, the U.K. universal banking model is fully consistent with the continued existence of separate deposit insurance funds for the (small) depositor, the securities account holder, and the insurance policyholder. That is, a federal insurance fund could continue to guarantee deposits at the parent bank, SIPC could insure securities account holders at the securities subsidiary, and state insurance guarantee funds could provide a similar service for small policyholders insurance subsidiaries.

This model, while requiring some separation of activities between parent and subsidiaries, does not require the type of firewalls that are uniquely evident in the U.S. bank holding company structure, that is, between Section 20 securities subsidiaries and their bank and other affiliates. Universal banks should be allowed to maximize their ability to cross-market financial services, subject to normal constraints on exploiting any potential conflicts of interest. In addition, within binding capital-based closure rules the parent bank should be free to move excess capital resources—those in excess of regulated minimums—between the parent bank and its subsidiaries as the patterns of demand for financial services shift over time. Such an organizational form would maximize resource flexibility and market responsiveness, within limits imposed by risk insulation, regulatory structure, and accounting system constraints.

The 1991 Treasury plan, for all its potential blemishes and implementation problems, was a welcome addition to the debate on financial reform in the United States. Through a relatively transparent, clean structure of separately capitalized subsidiaries, it limited exposure of taxpayers to losses and at the same time promoted a more level playing field. It streamlined the regulatory structure and moved toward the goal of regulation by function. And it went some way towards eliminating both line-of-business and geographic barriers to domestic competition, thus opening the door for nationwide universal banking and the potential for the kinds of scale and scope economies discussed in this book—and for the potential for greater international financial services competitiveness in an environment where

U.S. banks have the kind of freedoms domestically that have long been enjoyed by many of their foreign rivals.

In the American tradition, however, lobbyists well-armed with special interest arguments and Political Action Committee (PAC) contributions had long been geared up for the battle that followed. Members of Congress not directly involved in these issues generally found the whole matter complex and arcane, and of little immediate interest to their constituents, working in a political environment where all financial institutions tend to be lumped together under a black hat—identified in the minds of many voters with an unbroken string of "accidents" associated with the oil patch, LDCs, real estate, highly leveraged transactions, junk bonds, and the S&Ls during the decade of the 1980s. According to one observer, "Following the mess Congress made of deregulating the thrifts, there is little reason to think it will do better this time. Congressmen have a fading appetite for bank reform, and would be happy with merely refilling the deposit-insurance fund."[4] This is basically what happened.

In all of the confusion, the benefits of restoring a level playing field and symmetry between risks and returns—while creating a more internationally competitive financial system—were largely lost. However, while the Federal Deposit Insurance Corporation Improvement Act (FDICIA) passed in 1991 certainly did not deliver the kind of wholesale reforms that were proposed by the U.S. Treasury, it was not a complete void. Most importantly, it embodied the concept of "early closure" of troubled banks (based on their capital ratios) which, as we have already suggested, is a critical component of safety and soundness provisions intended to protect taxpayers and the "safety net" from the risks of universal banking. Moreover, it linked expanded bank powers to the level of their capital ratios. Although it presupposes substantially upgraded supervision, if early closure for banks can be successfully implemented it would remove one important obstacle to universal banking in the United States—since the lines of business engaged in by other affiliates of the bank's holding company became immaterial to the costs of the safety net and taxpayer's loss exposure. It would, therefore, permit exploitation of potential economies of scale and scope without running the risk that the FDIC will have to bail out the nonbanking activities of the holding company.

We have argued in this book that the time for universal banking in the United States has arrived. Without such a system the U.S. banking system will continue to perform below its potential and will ill serve the nation's interest. Moreover, in the global market for financial services, the United States is likely in many ways to lag behind its European and Japanese competitors. A first-rate economic power needs a first-rate financial system.

[4]*Economist*, 2 February 1991, 14.

Annex Summary of Laws Affecting Domestic Activities of Commercial Banks in Major Industrialized Countries

	Japan	European Community (EC)	West Germany	U.K.
Principal regulators of commercial banks	Ministry of Finance (MOF) Bank of Japan		Federal Banking Supervisory Office (FBSO) Deutsche Bundesbank	Bank of England
Branching restrictions geographic	None.	None for EC-based banks, which can branch Communitywide effective no later than 1 January 1993. Banks not based in the EC may branch only as permitted by each country's supervisory authorities.	None.	None.
regulatory	Price authorization by MOF required. Number of new branches limited by MOF.	EC-based banks must notify their home state supervisory authorities.	Notification to the FBSO and the Bundesbank required.	Prior notice to the Bank of England required.
Scope of permissible activities securities	Japanese banks are limited to (1) purchasing and selling securities for customer accounts or for the investment purposes of the bank; (2) underwriting and dealing in commercial paper and government, government-guaranteed and municipal securities; (3) dealing on behalf of institutional clients. Non-	The Second Banking Directive (SBD) permits an EC-based bank to engage in securities activities anywhere in the EC to the extent permitted by the bank's home state supervisor. An Investment Services Directive has been proposed.	Unrestricted.	Unrestricted powers. Activities usually conducted through subsidiaries of parent bank. Firms carrying on securities activities are regulated by the Securities and Investment Board (SIB) and by self-regulatory organizations (SROs)

Annex (Continued)

	Japan	European Community (EC)	West Germany	U.K.
	Japanese banks may conduct securities activities through 50%-owned affiliates.			
Insurance	Not permitted.	Permitted only if permitted by the bank's home state supervisor and by the bank country where the bank proposes to engage in the activity.	Unrestricted powers. Activities generally conducted through subsidiaries of parent banks.	Unlimited powers. Activities usually conducted through subsidiaries of parent banks.
Industrial investments	Limited to holding 5% interest.	SBD forbids a bank from investing more than 15% of its own funds in a nonfinancial company; such investments are limited in the aggregate to 60% of the bank's capital.	Unrestricted powers. Activities generally conducted through subsidiaries of parent banks.	Permitted subject to consultations with Bank of England.
Restrictions on the structure of banking operations	Japanese banks must be corporations; foreign banks are exempted. Bank holding companies are prohibited.	None. However, in countries where access to organized securities markets is restricted to nonbanks, banks can obtain access through wholly-owned financial services subsidiaries.	Banks may not be organized as sole proprietorships.	Banks may not be organized as sole proprietorships.
Capital requirements	Statutory minimum of 1 billion yen for city banks, regional banks, trust	Proposed directive provides uniform risk weights for EC banks, with one	Banking Act requires "adequate" capital as determined by principles	Banks incorporated in the U.K. must have a minimum capital of £1

	Japan	EC	Germany	United Kingdom
(capital requirements, continued)	banks, and branches of foreign banks and 10 million yen for long-term credit banks and the specialized foreign-exchange bank.	exception: West German and Danish banks may weigh commercial loans secured by real estate at 50% instead of 100% until 1 January 1996.	issued by the FBSO, in agreement with the Bundesbank. Initial capital of a least DM 10 million is expected.	million. There is no minimum capital requirement for branches of foreign banks. The Bank of England established minimum capital for each bank to reflect its own circumstances.
Deposit protection scheme	Deposit Insurance Corporation.	In place in all member states by end-1990.	Deposit Protection Fund.	Deposit Protection Fund.
Administration and membership	Mixed public–private control: mandatory.		Private: voluntary. Most banks are members.	Mixed public–private control: mandatory.
Maximum protection per depositor	10 million yen (U.S. $69,000).		30% of bank's capital and disclosed reserves.	75% of £200,000 (75% of U.S. $34,000).
Annual cost/premiums	0.012% of deposits (1989)		0.03% of deposits (1988).	Depends on payments made by Fund in prior year.
Special features	Unlike most schemes, includes coverage for deposits of foreign branches of domestic banks. Excludes deposits of Japanese branches of foreign banks.		Unlike most schemes, includes coverage for deposits in foreign branches of domestic banks.	
Reserve requirements	Yes: Interest-free.		Yes: Interest-free. 4.15–12.1% from 1 February 1987.	Yes, for banks with more than £10 million in sterling liabilities

Annex (*Continued*)

	Japan	European Community (EC)	West Germany	U.K.
				(excluding interbank deposits) maturing in less than 2 years. (0.45% of eligible liabilities as of September 1988).
Mergers	Require MOF approval.	Effective 21 September 1990, approval by EC merger-control commission generally required if companies have combined worldwide revenue of ECU 5 billion (U.S. $6.0 billion) (1/10th of assets used instead of revenue for banks and insurance companies)	Subject to control by German Cartel Office.	Subject to review of U.K. Monopolies and Mergers Commission.
Acquisitions of rank stock	Companies are prohibited from acquiring more than 5% of the stock of a Japanese bank.	SBD provides that crossing thresholds of 20, 30, and 50% requires disclosure to the home country of the company whose stock is being acquired. The home country can oppose the acquisition if it is not satisfied with the acquirer's suitability.	No regulatory approvals required.	Crossing the 15, 50, and 75% thresholds requires prior notice to the Bank of England, which may reject the acquisition if it determines that the acquirer is not a "fit and proper" person or company.

Consumer protection laws					
Consumer credit	Yes.	Yes.	Directive proposed in 1986.	Yes.	Yes.
Advertising	Yes.	Yes.	Directive proposed.	Yes.	Yes.
Other	Interest rate on consumer loans required.		Proposed directive forbids discrimination in mortgage credit on basis of nationality. Recommendations introduced relating in electronic payment and credit cards.		Consumer Credit Act 1974 regulates consumer loans of £15,000 (U.S. $25,000) or less (excluding loans secured by real estate). Discrimination in granting credit on the basis of race, color, or national origin is prohibited.
Restrictions on foreign banks					
Entry	Official national treatment policy: statutory requirements for reciprocal national treatment in practice, foreign banks have been limited by MOF to a few branches each.	An EC-based bank subsidiary of a non-EC institution is eligible to utilize the SBD's "single banking license" provided that the institution's home country offers EC institutions "national treatment offering same competitive opportunities as are available to domestic institutions."		No restrictions on the establishment of German subsidiaries of foreign banking institutions. Licenses may be refused to branches of foreign banks if the bank's home countries do not offer German banks national treatment.	Entry may be either through a branch or by the establishment of a subsidiary. A foreign branch or subsidiary may not conduct investment business without authorization under Financial Services Act.
Other	Deposits of Japanese branches of foreign banks			Subsidiaries of foreign banking institutions have	Treasury Ministry may revoke authorization to do

Annex (Continued)

	France	Italy	Canada	U.S.
	are not insured. Certain foreign banks have been granted licenses to establish trust banking subsidiaries and to hold up to 50% of the stock of securities affiliates branching.		the same powers as German banks. Foreign branches are ineligible to underwrite government bonds or manage DM-denominated bonds.	business in U.K. or restrict activities if the bank's home country discriminates against U.K. persons in investment, insurance, or banking business.

	France	Italy	Canada	U.S.
Principal regulators of commercial banks	Banking Commissions Committee on Bank Regulation. Committee on Credit Institutions.	Ministry of Treasury; Interministerial Committee for Credit and Savings (CICR). Bank of Italy.	Office of the Superintendent of Financial Institutions (SFI).	Federal Reserve Board; bank holding companies; state member banks; consumer protection regulations. Comptroller of the Currency (national banks), Federal Deposit Insurance Corporation (FDIC)-insured banks. State banking regulators (state-chartred banks).
Branching restrictions geographic	None.	None.	None.	Interstate branching allowed only to the extent permitted by state law

		...regulatory	Scope of permissible activities
		Notification to the Banking commission required.	Unrestricted powers.
		Authorization by Bank of Italy required.	Unrestricted powers except that banks are not permitted to execute transactions on exchanges.
	None for widely-held banks and for U.S.-owned Canadian bank subsidiaries. Prior authorization required for other banks.		Unrestricted powers when conducted through subsidiaries of parent banks.
	(McFadden Act). Interstate branching by national banks is generally not permitted. However, bank holding companies may own bank subsidiaries in more than one state if expressly permitted by state law (Douglas Amendment).	Authorization by federal or state agencies required.	May underwrite and deal in government securities & deal in other debt & equity securities provided that (1) the activities are conducted in a bank holding company subsidiary; (2) the revenues of such activities do not exceed 10% of the total revenues of the subsidiary; and (3) bank affiliates are insulated by appropriate fire walls.

Annex (Continued)

	France	Italy	Canada	U.S.
Insurance	Unlimited powers. Activities usually conducted through subsidiaries or affiliates.	Not currently permitted.	Not permitted. Government has proposed unlimited activities through subsidiaries of parent banks.	Restricted powers for national banks. Powers for state banks vary according to state law. Bank holding companies generally limited to credit-related insurance activities.
Industrial investments	Permitted subject to regulatory approval of interest in excess of 10%. Banks cannot own more than 20% of nonfinancial companies.	Permitted on a nonpermanent basis in connection with merchant banking securities.	Limited to holding 10% interests.	Generally limited to holding 5% interests.
Restrictions on the structure of banking operations	All banking establishments must operate through a corporation, a general partnership, or through a branch office. Foreign banks may operate in France in any of these forms.	New commercial banks must be stock corporations or incorporated partnerships.	There are no bank holding companies. Securities activities by banks must be conducted through subsidiaries.	Acquisition of banks is generally through bank holding companies. Activities may be conducted through bank holding companies if the Federal Reserve Board determines that the activity is "so closely related to banking or managing or controlling banks as to be a proper incident thereto."

	France	Italy	Canada	United States
Capital requirements	Minimum capitalization of FF 15 million for banks (including branches of foreign banks) with local assets under FF 1.2 billion and FF 30 million for banks with greater assets. The regulatory authorities usually request higher capital amounts for new banks.	As a general matter, a minimum capital of L 25 billion is required. (This is the minimum for branches of foreign banks.) The Bank of Italy establishes a minimum capital for each institution on a case-by-case basis. The bank issued new capital ratios in late 1986, effective in late 1990.	The Bank Act requires "adequate" capital. Capital requirements are traditionally specific to each individual bank. Banks are expected to meet the minimum interim target of 7.25% for local capital by 31 October 1990 and 8% by 31 October 1992.	For national banks, minimum capital of $1 million generally required by Comptroller of the Currency. Current capital-to-asset ratios are 5.5% primary capital and 6% total capital. The Basle Agreement ratios are currently being implemented.
Deposit protection scheme	Deposit Guarantee Fund.	Deposits Protection Scheme	Canada Deposit Insurance Corporation.	Federal Deposit Insurance Corporation.
Administration and membership	Private: voluntary.	Private: voluntary. Almost all commercial banks are members.	Government: mandatory.	Government: mandatory for almost all banks.
Maximum protection per depositor	FF 400,000 (U.S. $70,000).	100% of final L 300 million (U.S. $161,000) 90% of next L 800 million (up to U.S. $605,000); 80% of next L 2 billion (up to U.S. $2.5 million).	C$60,000 (U.S. $50,000).	U.S. $100,000.
Annual cost/premiums	None. Contributions based on the bank's local deposits are assessed only when the Fund makes payments to depositors.		0.001% of insured deposits (February 1990).	0.12% of insured deposits for most banks (rate for 1990). Increased to 0.15% in 1991.

	France	Italy	Canada	U.S.
Special features	Participating banks have entered into an agreement providing that they will reimburse depositors of a failed bank up to the specified limit. Certificates of deposits and foreign currence deposits are excluded from coverage.	The scheme is organized as a voluntary bank consortium.	Unlike most schemes, includes coverage for interbank deposits.	Required for branches of foreign banks if they accept more than a *de minimis* amount of deposits less than U.S. $100,000. Unlike most schemes includes coverage for interbank deposits.
Reserve requirements	Yes. Interest-free deposits based on a percentage of short-term loans, deposits, resources, and off-balance sheet liabilities: 3.0% of time deposits (as of 1989).	Yes. Interest-bearing (5.5% as of 1989) deposits: 22.5% of deposits as of February 1989.	Yes. Interest-free deposits equal to 10% of demand deposits: 2–3% of time deposits (1988).	Yes. Interest-free 3–10% on transaction accounts: 0% on short-term time deposits.
Mergers	Require prior authorization by the Banking Commission.	Require prior approval of Bank of Italy.	Require approval of Minister of Finance.	Require prior approval of appropriate federal agency (Bank Merger Act). May be challenged by the Department of Justice. State banks may also need state approval.
Acquisitions of rank stock	Crossing the 5% threshold requires prior notification to the Committee on Credit Institutions.	Acquisition of more than 2% of the voting stock of a bank, as well as subsequent increases or	Domestic banks must be widely held. There is 10% ceiling on group and individual ownership,	Crossing 10 or 25% threshold generally requires prior notification. any company acquiring

	(continued)			
(continued from prev. page)	Crossing the 10, 20, and 33-1/3 % thresholds or obtaining a "controlling interest" requires the prior approval of the Committee.	decreases in excess of 1%, must be disclosed to the Bank of Italy.	except on newly incorporate banks. Total holdings by nonresidents (other than U.S. residents) may not exceed 25%, with no individual owning more than 10%	25% or some lesser amount that constitutes control requires prior approval. Bank holding companies are required to obtain prior approval to acquire 5% or more of a bank's shares.
Consumer protection laws				
Consumer Credit	Yes.	None as of 1980.	Yes.	Yes.
Advertising	Yes.	Yes.	Yes.	Yes.
Other	Banks are prohibited from seeking new customers by "undignified" methods, such as distributing advertising circulars and making house-to-house visits. Banks are required to show the amount of their paid-in capital and reserves on all letters, publications, and advertisements.		Banks may not charge for cashing government checks.	Community Reinvestment Act requires supervisory agencies to assess banks' records of meeting the credit needs of the bank's entire community, including low- and moderate-income neighborhoods. Among other laws (the Federal Reserve Board administers more than a dozen) are the Equal Credit Opportunity Act and the Home Mortgage Disclosure Act.
Restrictions on foreign banks				
Entry	Entry is through the establishment of branches. Non-EC banks whose home countries do not have	Entry is through Canadian bank subsidiary, not a	None. National treatment standard, except in	

Annex (Continued)

	France	Italy	Canada	U.S.
	treaties of establishment with France may be required to obtain a commercial card for their non-EC officers which authorizes the banking subsidiary to employ foreign nationals. In addition, non-EC banks may be denied access if the bank's home country does not grant French banks reciprocal access.	of subsidiaries. The minimum capital for a new foreign branch is L 25 million. Foreign banks' home countries must offer Italian banks access to the home countries markets in order to do business in Italy. (Reciprocal national treatment.)	branch. "Similar competitive opportunity" reciprocity requirements.	obtaining primary dealer status, which requires reciprocal national treatment.
Other		As of 15 December 1989, new banks will be authorized provided they meet minimum capital, management, and operations requirements.	Non-U.S. foreign banks may not hold more than 12% of all domestic bank assets. Beyond the first office, non-U.S. foreign bank subsidiaries may not open additional branches without the prior permission of the Minister of Finance.	

Data: Compiled by Organization for Economic Cooperation and Development, (OECD), 1990.

Note: Although the information contained in this table is based on sources believed to be reliable, the preparers disclaim any expertise in the banking laws and regulations of foreign countries or international organizaitons. Because banking laws and regulations are constantly changing, not all information may be current. In addition, presentation of this material in this format substantially oversimplifies the nature of the respective regulations.

References

Aigner, Dennis, C. A. Knox Lovell, and Peter Schmidt. "Formulation and Estimation of Stochastic Frontier Production Models." *Journal of Econometrics* 6 (1977): 21–37.

Aliber, Robert Z. "International Banking: A Survey." *Journal of Money, Credit and Banking* 16 (November 1984): 661–678.

Altman, E. I. "Measuring Corporate Bond Mortality and Performance." *Journal of Finance* 44 (September 1989): 909–921.

Ambrose, J. M., and J. A. Seward. "Best's Ratings, Financial Ratios and Prior Probabilities in Insolvency Prediction." *Journal of Risk and Insurance* 55 (1988): 229–244.

American Bankers Association. *Federal Deposit Insurance: A Program for Reform.* New York: American Bankers Association, March 1990.

Angoff, J. "Insurance Against Competition: How the McCarren-Ferguson Act Raises Prices and Profits in the Property–Casualty Insurance Industry." *Yale Journal of Regulation* 5 (Summer 1988): 397–416.

Arthur Andersen & Co. *European Capital Markets: A Strategic Forecast.* London: Economist Publications Ltd., 1990.

Asquith, P., and E. H. Kim. "The Impact of Merger Bids on the Participating Firm's Security Holders." *Journal of Finance* 37 (December 1982): 1209–1228.

Asquith, P., D. W. Mullins and E. D. Wolff. "Original Issue High Yield Bonds: Aging Analyzes of Default, Exchanges and Calls." *Journal of Finance* 44 (September 1989): 923–952.

Asquith, P., and D. W. Mullins. "Equity Issues and Offering Dilution." *Journal of Financial Economics* 15 (1986): 61–89.

Avery, R. B., T. Belton, and M. A. Goldberg. "Market Discipline in Regulating

Bank Risk: New Evidence from Capital Markets." *Journal of Money, Credit and Banking* 20 (November, 1988): 597–610.

Babbel, D. F. "Insuring Banks Against Systematic Credit Risk." *Journal of Futures Markets* 9 (1989): 487–505.

Babbel, D. F., and K. B. Staking. *The Market Reward for Insurers That Practice Asset/Liability Management*. Goldman Sachs, New York: November 1989.

Baer, H. L. and E. Brewer. "Uninsured Deposits as a Source of Market Discipline: Some New Evidence." *Economic Perspectives*, Federal Reserve Bank of Chicago, September/October 1986.

Baer, H. L., and D. D. Evanoff. "Payments System Risk in a Global Economy." *Federal Reserve Bank of Chicago Working Paper*, 12 August 1990.

Bailey, Elizabeth E., and Ann F. Friedlander. "Market Structure and Multiproduct Industries." *Journal of Economic Literature* 20 (September 1982): 1024–1048.

Bank for International Settlements (BIS). *Payment Systems in Eleven Developed Countries*. Rolling Meadows, Ill.: Bank for International Settlements, 1985).

———. *Recent Innovations in International Banking*. Basel: Bank for International Settlements, 1986.

Bank of England. *The Single European Market: Survey of the U.K. Financial Services Industry*. London: Bank of England, 1989.

Banque Nationale Suisse. *Les Banques Suisses en 1989*. Zurich: Orel Fussli Verlag, 1990.

———. *Bulletins Mensuels* (various issues).

Baumol, William J., J. C. Panzer, and R. Willig. *Contestable Markets and the Theory of Industry Structure*. New York: Harcourt Brace Jovanovich, 1982.

Benston, G. "The Federal Safety Net and the Repeal of the Glass-Steagall Act's Separation of Commercial and Investment Banking." *Journal of Financial Services Research* 2 (October 1989): 287–306.

Benston, G. J. *The Separation of Commercial and Investment Banking: The Glass-Steagall Act Reunited and Reconsidered*. Oxford: OVP, 1990.

Benston, G., and G. G. Kaufman. *Risk and Solvency Regulation of Financial Institutions: Past Policies and Current Options*. Monograph Series, no. 1988–1, Salomon Brothers Center for the Study of Financial Institutions, New York University, 1988.

Benston, G., Hanweck, and D. Humphrey. "Scale Economies in Banking." *Journal of Money, Credit and Banking* 14 (1982): 435–456.

Benston, George, A. Berger, G. Hanweck, and D. Humphrey. "Economies of Scope and Scale." *Conference Proceedings*. Federal Reserve Bank of Chicago, 1983.

Berger, Allen, and David B. Humphrey. "The Dominance of Inefficiencies Over Scale and Product Mix Economies in Banking," Board of Governors of the Federal Reserve System, Woruing Paper, November 1990.

Berger, Allen, Diana Hancock, and David B. Humphrey. "Bank Efficiency Derived from the Profit Function." *Journal of Banking and Finance* 17 (1993): forthcoming.

Berger, Allen, G. Hanweck, and D. Humphrey. "Competitive Viability in Banking." *Journal of Monetary Economics* 20 (1987): 501–520.

Berger, Allen, William C. Hunter, and Stephen G. Timme. "Efficiency of Financial Institutions." Board of Governors of the Federal Reserve System, Working Paper, April 1993A.

Berlin, Mitchell, Kose John, and Anthony Saunders. *Universal Banking: Should Banks Hold Equity in Borrowing Firms?* Working Paper, no. 92-45, Salomon Brothers Center for the Study of Financial Institutions, New York University, August 1992.

Bertrand, Olivier, and Thierry Noyelle. "Changing Technology, Skills and Skill Formation: The Policy Implications of the OECD/CERI Comparative Study of Financial Service Firms." Paris: Organization for Economic Cooperation and Development, 1986. Mimeo.

Best's *Aggregates and Averages: Life–Health*. New Jersey: Oldwick, 1989.

Best's *Aggregates and Averages: Property–Casualty*. New Jersey: Oldwick, 1989.

Birchler, Urs W., and Georg Rich. "Switzerland." In George C. Kaufman, ed. *Banking Structures in Major Countries*. 1992.

Black F., M. H. Miller and R. A. Posner. "An Approach to the Regulation of Bank Holding Companies." *Journal of Business* 51 (July 1978): 379–412.

Blenkarn, Don. *Canadian Financial Institutions*. Report of the Parliamentary Standing Committee on Finance, Trade and Economic Affairs. Ottawa, November 1985.

Bloch, Ernest. *Inside Investment Banking*. 2d ed. Homewood, Ill.: Dow-Jones Irwin, 1989.

Boyd, J. H., and A. J. Rolnick. "A Case for Reforming Federal Deposit Insurance." *Federal Reserve Bank of Minneapolis Annual Report*, 1988.

Boyd, J. H., and S. L. Graham. "The Profitability and Risk Effects of Allowing Bank Holding Companies to Merge with Other Firms: A Simulation Study." *Federal Reserve Bank of Minneapolis Quarterly Review*, Spring 1988, 3–20.

Boyd, John H., and Stanley L. Graham. "Bank Holding Company Diversification into Nonbank Financial Services: A Simulation Study." Federal Reserve Bank of Minneapolis Working Paper 378, January 1988.

Boyd, John H., and Stanley L. Graham. "Risk Regulation, and Bank Holding Company Expansion into Nonbanking." *Federal Reserve Bank of Minneapolis Quarterly Review*, 10 (Spring 1986): 2–17.

Boyd, John H., Gerald A. Hanweck, and Pipat Pithyachariyakul. "Bank Holding Company Diversification." *Proceedings of a Conference on Bank Structure and Competition*, Federal Reserve Bank of Chicago, 1980, 102–121.

Boyd, J. H., S. L. Graham, and G. Hewitt. "Bank Holding Company Mergers with Non-Bank Financial Firms: Effects on the Risk of Failure." *Federal Reserve Bank of Minneapolis* Working Paper, 1990.

Breeden, Richard C. "Testimony Concerning Financial Services Modernization." *U.S. Securities and Exchange Commission*, 11 July 1990.

Brewer III, Elijah. "A Note on the Relationship Between Bank Holding Company Risk and Nonbank Activity." Federal Reserve Bank of Chicago Staff Memorandum 88–5, 1988.

Brewer, E., and C. F. Lee. "How the Market Judges Bank Risk." *Economic Perspectives*. Federal Reserve Bank of Chicago, November/December 1986.

Brewer, E., D. Fortier, and C. Pavel. "Bank Risk from Non-Bank Activities." *Economic Perspectives*. Federal Reserve Bank of Chicago, July/August 1988, 14–26.

Burnham, J. B. "Banking Reform without Bailouts." *CSAB*, Washington University, September 1991.

Buser, S., A. Chen, and E. J. Kane. "Federal Deposit Insurance, Regulatory Policy and Optimal Bank Capital." *Journal of Finance* 35 (March 1981): 51–60.

Cable, J. "Capital Market Information and Industrial Performance: The Role of West German Banks." *Economic Journal* 95 (1985): 118–132.

Cable, J., and M. J. Dirrheimer. "Hierachies in Markets: An Empirical Test of the Multi-Divisional Hypothesis in West Germany." *International Journal of Industrial Organization* 1 (1983): 12–43.

Calomiris, Charles W. *The Costs of Rejecting Universal Banking*, University of Illinois, Working Paper, February 1993.

Campbell, Katherine. "Old Ways May Endure." *Financial Times*, 5 June 1990.

———. "Vanguard Against Change." *Financial Times*, 19 June 1990.

Cargill, T. "Camel Ratings and the C.D. Market." *Journal of Financial Services Research* 3 (December 1989): 347–358.

Caves, Richard, and Michael Porter. "From Entry Barriers to Mobility Barriers: Conjectural Decisions and Contrived Deterrence to New Competition." *Quarterly Journal of Economics* 91 (May 1977): 241–262.

Cherin, A. A., and R. C. Hutchins. "The Rate of Return on Universal Life Insurance." *Journal of Risk and Insurance*, 52 (1985): 691–711.

Chicago Fed Letter. "Lender Liability Under Environmental Law." No. 49, September 1991.

Clark, Jeffrey A. "Economies of Scale and Scope at Depository Financial Institutions: A Review of the Literature." Federal Reserve Board of Kansas City, September/October 1988.

Clarke, R. N., F. Warren-Boulton, D. D. Smith, and M. J. Simon. "Sources of Crisis in Liability Insurance: An Economic Analysis." *Yale Journal of Regulation* 5 (Summer 1988): 367–398.

Conference of State Bank Supervisors. *Comments on Federal Deposit Insurance Reform*. Washington, D.C., 9 March 1990.

Cooper, Kerry, and Donald R. Fraser. *Bank Deregulation and the New Competition in Financial Services*. Cambridge, Mass.: Ballinger, 1986.

Cornell, B., and A. C. Shapiro. "The Reaction of Bank Stock Prices to the International Debt Crisis." *Journal of Banking and Finance*, 10 (1986): 55–73.

Corrigan, E. Gerald. "Reforming the U.S. Financial System: An International Perspective." *Federal Reserve Bank of New York Quarterly Review*, Spring 1990.

Cowell, M., and W. Hoskins. Aids, HIV, Mortality and Life Insurance. Chicago: Society of Actuaries, 1987.

Crane, Dwight B., and Samuel L. Hayes III. "The New Competition in World Banking." *Harvard Business Review* 60 (July–August 1982): 88–94.

Cumming, Christine M., and Lawrence M. Sweet. "Financial Structure of the G-10 Countries: How Does the United States Compare?" *Federal Reserve Bank of New York Quarterly Review*, Winter 1987–88, 14–24.

Cummins, J. D., and J. F. Outreville. "An International Analysis of Underwriting Cycles in Property–Liability Insurance." *Journal of Risk and Insurance* 53 (1986): 246–260.

Cummins, J. D., and S. E. Harrington. "The Impact of Rate Regulation in U.S. Property–Liability Insurance Markets: A Cross Sectional Analysis of Individual Firm Loss Ratio." *Journal of Risk and Insurance* 54 (January 1987): 50–62.

Cyert, R. M., and J. G. March. *A Behavioral Theory of the Firm*. Englewood Cliffs, N.J.: Prentice-Hall, 1963.

Delamide, Darrell. "The Deutsche Bank Juggernaut Will Keep on Rolling." *Euromoney* (January 1990): 32–36.

Department of Justice, Tort Policy Working Group. *An Update on the Liability Crisis*. Washington, D.C., March 1987.

Dermine, Jean, ed. *European Banking After 1992* Second edition. Oxford: Basil Blackwell, 1993.

Dodd, P. "Merger Proposals, Management Discretion and Stockholder Wealth." *Journal of Financial Economics* 8 (June 1980): 105–137.

Dudler, H. J. "Changes in Money-Market Instruments and Procedures in Germany." Paper presented at the Bank for International Settlement, Basel, November 1985.

EC Commission. *Proposal for a Council Directive on Investment Services in the Securities Field*. Brussels: Commission of the European Communities, COM(88) 778 - SYN 176, 16 December 1988.

———. *Proposal for a Second Council Directive on the Laws, Regulations and Administrative Provisions Relating to the Taking-up and Pursuit of the Business of Credit Institutions*. Brussels: Commission of the European Communities, COM(87) 715, 16 February 1988.

Economic Council of Canada. *A Framework for Financial Regulation*. Research report, Ottawa, 1987.

Economist. "A Survey of Europe's Capital Markets," 16 December 1989.

Eisemann, P. C. "Diversification and the Congeneric Bank Holding Company." *Journal of Bank Research* (Spring 1976): 68–77.

Eisenbeis, R. A. "Commentary." In W. S. Haraf and R. M. Kushmeider, eds. *Restructuring Banking and Finance Services in America*. Washington, D.C.: American Enterprise Institute, 1988).

———. "Restructuring Federal Deposit Insurance and the Federal Safety Net." Paper prepared for the Academic Consultant's Seminar, Federal Reserve Board of Governors, 6 March 1990.

Federal Reserve Board. Testimony Presented to the Subcommittee on Bank Competitiveness, House Banking Committee, U.S. Congress, March 1990.

Feketekuty, Geza. "International Trade in Banking Services: The Negotiating Arena." Washington, D.C.: Office of the United States Trade Representative, 1987. Mimeo.

Felgren, S. D. "Banks as Insurance Agencies: Legal Constraints and Competitive Advances." *New England Economic Review* (September/October 1985): 34–49.

Fields, Joseph A. and Knoll B. Murphy. "An Analysis of Efficiency in the Delivery of Financial Services: The Case of Life Insurance Agencies." *Journal of Financial Services Research* 2 (1989): 343–356.

Fieleke, Norman S. "The Growth of U.S. Banking Abroad: An Analytical Survey." In *Key Issues in International Banking*. Boston: Federal Reserve Bank of Boston, 1977.

Flannery, M. J. "Contagious Bank Runs, Financial Structure and Corporate Separateness Within a Bank Holding Company." In *Proceedings of a Conference on Bank Structure and Competition*. Federal Reserve Bank of Chicago, 1986.

———. "Payments System Risk and Public Policy." In W. S. Haraf and R. M. Kushmeider eds. *Restructuring Banking and Financial Services in America*. Washington, D.C.: American Enterprise Institute, 1988, 261–287.

———. "Pricing Deposit Insurance when the Insurer Observes Bank Risk with Error." Working Paper, University of North Carolina, Chapel Hill, October 1988.

Flannery, M. J., and C. M. James. "The Effect of Interest Rate Changes on the Common Stock Returns of Financial Institutions," *Journal of Finance* 39 (1983): 1141–1153.

Forbes. "Who's Where in the Industry Groups," 8 January 1990, 246–247.

Forster, F. Douglas, and S. Viswanathan. "A Theory of Interday Variations in Volumes, Variances and Trading Costs in Securities Markets," Duke University Working Paper, September 1989.

Friedman, Milton, and Anna Schwartz. *A Monetary History of the United States, 1867–1960.* Princeton, N.J.: Princeton University Press, 1963.

General Accounting Office. *Bank Powers: Activities of Securities Subsidiaries of Banking Holding Companies.* GAO/GGD, 90-48. Washington, D.C., March 1990.

———. *Bank Powers: Issues Relating to Banks Selling Insurance.* GAO/GGD, 90-113. Washington, D.C., September 1990.

———. *Insurance Regulation: Problems in the State Monitoring of Property/Casualty Insurer Solvency.* GAO/GGD, 89-129. Washington, D.C., September 1989.

———. *Insurance Regulation: The Insurance Regulatory Information System Needs Improvement.* GAO/GGD, 91-20. Washington, D.C., November 1990.

———. *Insurer Failures: Property/Casualty Insurer Insolvencies and State Guaranty Funds.* GAO/GGD, 87-100. Washington, D.C., July 1987.

———. *Property and Casualty Insurance: Thrift Failures Provide Valuable Lessons.* GAO/T - AFMD - 89-7, Washington, D.C., April 1987.

Gibrat, R. "On Economic Inequalities." In *International Economic Papers.* Vol. 7. New York: Macmillan, 1957, 53–70.

Giddy, I. "Is Equity Underwriting Risky for Commercial Bank Affiliates." In I. Walter, ed. *Deregulating Wall Street.* New York: John Wiley & Sons, 1985, 145–169.

Gilbert, R. A., and G. E. Wood. "Coping with Bank Failures: Some Lessons from the United States and United Kingdom." *Federal Reserve Bank of St. Louis Quarterly Review*, December 1986, 5–14.

Gilligan, Thomas, and Michael Smirlock. "An Empirical Study of Joint Production and Scale Economies in Commercial Banking." *Journal of Banking and Finance* 8 (1984): 67–78.

Gilligan, Thomas, Michael Smirlock, and William Marshall. "Scale and Scope Economies in the Multi-Product Banking Firm." *Journal of Monetary Economics* 13 (1984): 393–405.

Gnehm A., and C. Thalmann. "Conflicts of Interest in Financial Operations: Problems of Regulation in the National and International Context." Paper prepared for the Swiss Bank Corporation, Basel, 1989.

Goldberg, L. F., G. A. Hanweck, M. Keenan, and A. Young. "Economies of Scale and Scope in the Securities Industry." University of Miami Working Paper, March 1990.

Goldberg, Lawrence G., and Denise Johnson. "The Determinants of U.S. Banking Activity Abroad." *Journal of International Money and Finance* 9 (1990): 123–137.

Goldstein, Steven, James McNulty, and James Verbrugge. "Scale Economies in the Savings and Loan Industry Before Diversification." *Journal of Economics and Business* 39 (1987): 199–208.

Gorton, G., and A. M. Santomero. "Market Discipline and Bank Subordinated Debt." *Journal of Money, Credit and Banking* 22 (February 1990): 119–128.

Grammatikos, T., and A. Saunders. "Additions to Bank Loan-Loss Reserves: Good News or Bad News?" *Journal of Monetary Economics* 25 (March 1990): 289–304.

Gray, H. Peter, and Jean M. Gray. "The Multinational Bank: A Financial MNC?" *Journal of Banking and Finance* 5 (1981): 33–63.

Greene, William H. *Econometric Analysis*. New York: Macmillan, 1990.

———. *Limdep*. New York: Economic Software, Inc., 1990.

Greenspan, Alan. "Testimony Before the Committee on Banking, Housing and Urban Affairs, U.S. Senate." Board of Governors of the Federal Reserve System, 12 July 1990.

Gropper, Daniel M. "An Empirical Investigation of Scale Economies for the Banking Firm, 1979–1986." *Journal of Money, Credit and Banking*, 23, 4 (November 1991): 718–727.

Group of Thirty. *Reciprocity and the Unification of the European Banking Market*. New York: Group of Thirty, 1989.

———. *Securities Clearance and Settlement Study*. New York and London: Group of Thity, 1989.

Grubel, Herbert G. "A Theory of Multinational Banking." *Banca Nazionale del Lavoro Quarterly Review* 123 (December 1977): 349–363.

Gutfreund, John H. *The State of the U.S. Financial Services Industry*. Testimony Before the Subcommittee on Securities, U.S. Senate Committee on Banking. New York: Salomon Brothers, 1990.

Hall, M.J.B. "The Deposit Protection Scheme: The Case for Reform." *National Westminster Bank Review* (1989): 45–54.

Hannan, T. H., and G. A. Hanweck. "Bank Insolvency Risk and the Market for Large C.D.'s." *Journal of Money, Credit and Banking* (1988): 208–211.

Haraf, W. S. "The Collapse of Drexel Burnham Lambert: Lessons for Banks Regulators." *Regulation* 15 (Winter 1991): 22–25.

———. "Commentary: The Corporate Structure of Financial Conglomerates." *Journal of Financial Services Research* (December 1990): 499–507.

Harrington, S. E. "Prices and Profits in the Liability Insurance Market." In R. E. Litan and C. Winston, eds. *Liability: Perspectives and Policy*. Washington, D.C.: The Brookings Institution, 1988, 45–54.

Harrington, S. E., and J. Nelson. "A Regression Based Methodology for Solvency Surveillance." *Journal of Risk and Insurance* 53 (1986): 584–605.

Hayes III, Samuel, A. M. Spence, and D.V.P. Marks. *Competition in the Investment Banking Industry*. Cambridge, Mass.: Harvard University Press, 1983.

Heggested, A. A. "Riskiness of Investments in Nonbank Activities by Bank Holding Companies." *Journal of Economics and Business* 28 (Spring 1975): 219–223.

Hermalin, B. E. "The Negative Effects of Lender Liability." *Federal Reserve Bank of San Francisco Weekly Letter* no. 91-32, 20 September 1991.

Herman, Edward S. *Conflicts of Interest: Commercial Bank Trust Companies*. New York: Twentieth Century Fund, 1975.

Herring, R. J. and A. M. Santomero. "The Corporate Structure of Financial Conglomerates." *Journal of Financial Services Research* 4 (December 1990): 471–497.

Hindley, Brian, and Alasdair Smith. "Comparative Advantage and Trade in Services." *World Economy* 7 (June 1984): 369–389.

Hockin, Thomas. "New Directions for the Financial Sector." *Report of the Minister of State for Finance Tabled in the House of Commons.* Ottawa, 18 December 1986.

Holthausen, Robert W., Richard W. Leftwich, and David Mayers. "The Effect of Large Block Transactions on Security Prices: A Cross-Sectional Analysis." *Journal of Financial Economics* 19 (1987): 237–268.

Huertas, T. F. "Redesigning Regulation: The Future of Finance in the United States." Jackson Hole, Wyo., Federal Reserve Bank of Kansas City Conference, 22 August 1987.

Humphrey, D. B. "Payments Finality and Risk of Settlement Failure." In A. Saunders and L. J. White, eds. *Technology and the Regulation of Financial Markets.* Lexington, Mass.: D.C. Heath and Co., 1985, 97–120.

———. "Payments System Risk, Market Failure and Public Policy." In E. H. Salomon, ed. *The Payments Revolution.* Boston: Kluwer Nijhoff, 1987.

Hunter, W. C., and S. G. Timme. "Technology Change in Large U.S. Commercial Banks." *Journal of Business* 64 (1991): 287–312.

Independent Bankers Association of America. *Protecting the Federal Deposit Insurance System.* Washington, D.C.: Independent Bankers Association of America, February, 1990.

Insurance Information Institute. (III). *Property/Casualty Insurance Facts.* New York: Insurance Information Institute, 1990.

———. *Reinsurance Fundamentals and New Challenges.* 2d ed. New York: Insurance Information Institute, June 1989.

International Monetary Fund (IMF). *The European Monetary System in the Context of the Integration of European Financial Markets.* Washington, D.C.: International Monetary Fund, 1989.

Ippolito, R. A. "The Effects of Price Regulation in the Automobile Insurance Industry." *Journal of Law and Economics* 22 (October 1979): 55–89.

J. P. Morgan, Inc. *Rethinking Glass-Steagall.* New York, J. P. Morgan, Inc., 1984.

James, C. "Empirical Evidence on the Implicit Government Guarantees of Bank Foreign Loan Exposure." *Carnegie-Rochester Conference Series* 30 (1989): 129–162.

———. "Loan Sales and Stand-by Letters of Credit." *Journal of Monetary Economics* (November 1988): 395–422.

———. "Some Evidence on the Uniqueness of Bank Loans." *Journal of Financial Economics* 19 (1987): 217–236.

Jensen, Michael, and Richard Ruback. "The Market for Corporate Control: The Scientific Evidence." *Journal of Financial Economics* 11 (April 1983): 5–50.

Jessee, M., and S. Seelig. *Bank Holding Companies and the Public Interest.* Lexington, Mass.: Lexington Books, 1977.

Johnson, Rodney D., and David R. Meinster. "Bank Holding Companies: Diversification Opportunities in Nonbank Activities." *Eastern Economic Journal* 1 (October 1974): 1453–1465.

Joskow, P. L. "Cartels, Competition and Regulation in the Property–Liability Insurance Industry." *Bell Journal of Economics and Management Science* 4 (1973): 375–427.

Kallberg, Jarl S., and Anthony Saunders. *Direct Sources of Competitiveness in Banking Services.* New York: Salomon Brothers Center for the Study of Financial Institutions, 1986. Mimeo.

Kane, E. J. "Competitive Financial Reregulation: An International Perspective." In

R. Portes and A. Swoboda, eds. *Threats to International Financial Stability.* London: Cambridge University Press, 1987.

——. *The Gathering Crisis in Federal Deposit Insurance.* Cambridge, Mass.: MIT Press, 1985.

Kaufman, George G. "The Federal Safety Net: Not for Banks Only." *Economic Perspectives,* 11, November/December 1987, 19–27.

Keeton, W. R. "The Treasury Plan for Banking Reform." *Economic Review.* Federal Reserve Bank of Kansas City, May/June 1991.

Kellner, S., and G. Frank Mathewson. "Entry, Size Distribution, Scale and Scope Economies in the Life Insurance Industry." *Journal of Business* 56 (1983): 25–44.

Khoury, Sarkis J. *Dynamics of International Banking.* New York: Praeger, 1980.

Kim, H. Youn. "Economies of Scale and Scope in Multiproduct Financial Institutions." *Journal of Money, Credit and Banking* 18 (1986): 220–226.

Kim, Moshe. "Banking Technology and the Existence of a Consistent Output Aggregate." *Journal of Monetary Economics* 18 (1986): 181–196.

Klein, Michael A. "A Theory of the Banking Firm." *Journal of Money, Credit and Banking* 3 (1971): 205–218.

Koenig, Peter. "Has the U.S. Got the Bottle for a Fight?" *Euromoney* (January 1990): 46–52.

Kolari, James, and Asghar Zardhooki. *Bank Cost Structure and Performance* Lexington, Mass.: D.C. Heath and Co., 1987.

Krozsner, Randall S., and Ragharam G. Rajan. "Is the Glass-Steagall Act Justified?" Graduate School of Business, University of Chicago, Working Paper, October 25, 1992.

Krümmel, H. K. "German Universal Banking Scrutinized." *Journal of Banking and Finance* 4 (1980): 33–55.

Kryzanowski, Lawrence, and Gordon S. Roberts. "Market Value Measures of Canadian Bank Solvency." Paper presented at the Northern Finance Association, Montreal, 21–23 September 1990.

Kryzanowski, Lawrence, and Nancy Ursel. "Market Reaction to Canadian Bank Takeover Announcements of Canadian Investment Dealers and Announcement Timing." *Journal of Financial Services Research* (1993, forthcoming).

Kuffel, F. "RRG's Premium Volumes Growing." *Journal of Commerce,* 379 (21 March 1989): 13A.

Lamm-Tennant, J., and L. Starks. "Alternative Ownership Structure Hypotheses: A Test of Risk Implications." Villanova University, Villanova, Pa., 1990. Mimeo.

Lamm-Tennant J., L., Starks, and L. Stokes. "Solvency Surveillance: An Empirical Evaluation of the Property–Liability Industry." Villanova University, Villanova, Pa., 1990. Mimeo.

Lawrence, Colin. "Banking Costs, Generalized Functional Forms, and Estimation of Economies of Scale and Scope." *Journal of Money, Credit and Banking* 21, no. 3 (1989): 368–379.

Lawrence, Colin, and Robert Shay. "Technology and Financial Intermediation in the Multiproduct Banking Firm: An Econometric Study of US Banks." In *Technological Innovation, Regulation and the Monetary Economy.* Cambridge, Mass.: Ballinger, 1986.

Leigh-Pemberton, Robin. "Economic Policy Perspectives on Financial Market Regulation and Supervision: A U.K. View." Bank of England, 1990. Mimeo.

———. "Europe 1992: Some Monetary Policy Issues." *Economic Review*, September/October 1989): 3–8.

Levich, Richard M. "Financial Innovation in International Financial Markets." In M. Feldstein, ed. *The United States in the World Economy*. Chicago: University of Chicago, Press, 1988.

Levich, Richard M., and Ingo Walter. "The Regulation of Global Financial Markets." In T. Noyelle, ed. *New York's Financial Markets*. Boulder, Colo.: Westview Press, 1988.

Lewis, S., and W. Vincent. "West German Universal Banks: The Banks Dependence on the Securities Markets in Revealed." Salomon Bros. European Equity Research, New York: 18 February 1988.

Lim, J., and A. Saunders. "IPO's and Venture Capitalists: A Test of the Dynamic-Strategy Hypothesis." Stern School of Business, Working Paper, February 1990.

Litan, R. E. *What Should Banks Do?* Washington, D.C.: The Brookings Institution, 1987.

Litan, Robert E. "Assessing the Risks of Financial Product Deregulation." Paper presented to the American Economics Association in New York, December 1985.

Lockwood, L. J., Apilado, V. P., and J. E. Gallo. "Expanded Securities Underwriting: Implications for Bank Risk and Return." University of Texas-Arlington, Working Paper, March 1991.

Loderer, C. F., D. P. Sheehan, and G. B. Kadlec. "The Pricing of Equity Offerings." *Journal of Financial Economics* 29 (1991): 35–57.

Longstreth, Bevis, Ivan E. Mattei, and David P. Mason. "U.S. Bank Reform: Getting Beyond the Oxymoron." New York University Salomon Center, May 1992. Mimeo.

Macey, Jonathan R., M. Wayne Marr, and S. David Young. "The Glass- Steagall Act and the Riskiness of Financial Intermediaries." Tulane University, New Orleans, La., November 1987. Mimeo.

Markwell, Christopher. "Banking and Insurance: Marrying Corporate Cultures." Paper presented at the International Insurance Society, Paris, 11 July 1990.

Mayers, D., and C. W. Smith, Jr. "On the Corporate Demand for Insurance: Evidence from the Reinsurance Market." *Journal of Business*, 63 1990, 19–40.

Mehr, R. I., and S. G. Gustavson. *Life Insurance Theory and Practice*. 4th ed. Austin, Tex.: BPI, 1987.

Mei, Jiam-Ping, and A. Saunders. *Performance of Insurance Companies in Real Estate Investments*. Paper presented at the Conference on the Dynamics of the Insurance Industry, New York University Salomon Center, May 20–21, 1993.

Meier, J. J. *The Political Economy of Regulation: The Case of Insurance*. Albany: SUNY Press, 1988.

Meinster, David R., and Rodney D. Johnson. "Bank Holding Company Diversification and the Risk of Capital Impairment." *The Bell Journal of Economics* 10 (Autumn 1979): 683–694.

Merrick, J. J. "Portfolio Insurance with Stock Index Futures." New York University Salomon Center, Working Paper no. 434, New York, August 1987.

Merrill Lynch. "Insurance Companies Investments in High Yield Bonds," 2 March 1990.

Mester, L. "Efficient Production of Financial Services: Scale and Scope Economies." *Business Review*. Federal Reserve Bank of Philadelphia, January/February 1987, 15–25.

————. "A Multiproduct Cost Study of Savings and Loans." *Journal of Finance* 42 (1987): 423–445.

————. "Traditional and Nontraditional Banking: An Information-Theoretic Approach." *Federal Reserve Board* Working Paper no. 90-3, Washington, D.C., February 1990.

————. "Traditional and Nontraditional Banking: An Information-Theoretic Approach." *Journal of Banking and Finance* 16 (1992): 545–566.

Molinari, S. L., and Kibler, N. S. "Broker–Dealers' Financial Responsibility under the Uniform Net Capital Rule—A Case for Liquidity." *Georgetown Law Journal* 72, no. 1 (1983): 1–37.

Morgan Guaranty Trust Company. "America's Banking Market Goes International." *Morgan Economic Quarterly*, June 1986.

————. *Cross-Border Clearance and Settlement: Beyond the G-30 Recommendations*, Brussels: Morgan Guaranty Trust Company, 1993.

Murray, John D., and Robert S. White. "Economies of Scale and Economies of Scope in Multiproduct Financial Institutions." *Journal of Finance* 38 (June 1983): 887–902.

Nathan, A., and E. H. Neave. "Competition and Contestability in Canada's Financial System: Empirical Results." 22 *Canadian Journal of Economics* (August 1989): 576–594.

Neu, C. R. "International Trade in Banking Services." Paper presented at a National Bureau of Economic Research/Centre for Economic Policy Research Conference on European–U.S. Trade Relations, Brussels, June 1986. Mimeo.

Neumann, M. J. "Implementation of Monetary Policy in Germany." Paper presented at the Federal Reserve, Washington, D.C., 26–27 May 1988.

New York State Banking Department. "Briefing Papers on Financial Conglomerates, Large Credit Exposure, and Market Risk." International Conference of Banking Supervisors, Frankfurt, 10–12 October 1990.

Newman, H. "Strategic Groups and the Structure-Performance Relationships." *Review of Economics and Statistics*, August 1978.

National Organization of Life and Group Health Associations (NOLGHA). "Life and Health Insurance Company Insolvencies and Impairments." 1975–Sept. 1989, Mimeo.

Noulas, Athanasios G., Subhash C. Ray, and Stephen M. Miller. "Returns to Scale and Input Substitution for Large U.S. Banks." *Journal of Money, Credit and Banking* 22 (1990): 94–108.

Office of Technology Assessment, U.S. Congress. *International Competition in Banking and Financial Services*. Washington, D.C.: Office of Technology Assessment, July 1986. Mimeo.

Officer, Dennis T., and William J. Boyes. "The Behavior of Brokerage Firm Shares." *Financial Analysts Journal* 40 (1984): 41–46.

Organization for Economic Cooperation and Development (OECD). *Trade in Services in Banking*. Paris: Organization for Economic Cooperation and Development, 1983.

Page, Daine, and Neil M. Soss. "Some Evidence on Transnational Banking Structure." In *Foreign Acquisitions of US Banks*. Washington, D.C.: U.S. Government Printing Office, for the Office of the Comptroller of the Currency, Department of the Treasury, 1982.

Panzar, John C., and Robert D. Willig. "Economies of Scope." *American Economic Review* 71 (May 1981): 268–272.

Pastre, Olivier. "International Bank-Industry Relations: An Empirical Assessment." *Journal of Banking and Finance* 5 (March 1981): 65–76.

———. *Multinationals: Banking and Firm Relationships*. Greenwich, Conn.: JAI Press, 1981.

Patel, J. M. "Corporate Forecasts of Earnings per Share and Stock Price Behavior." *Journal of Accounting Research* 14 (1976): 246–276.

Pauly, Mark, Howard Kunreuther, and Paul Kleindorfer. "Regulation and Quality Competition in the U.S. Insurance Industry." In *The Economics of Insurance Regulation: A Cross-National Study*. Joerg Finginger and Mark V. Pauly, eds. New York: St. Martin's Press, 1986, 65–110.

Pecchioli, R. M. *Internationalization of Banking*. Paris: Organization for Economic Cooperation and Development, 1983.

Petre, Peter. "Merger Fees that Bend the Mind." *Fortune*, (20 January 1986): 18–23.

Pozdena, Randall J. "Do Banks Need Securities Powers?" *Federal Reserve Bank of San Francisco Weekly Letter*, 89–52, 29 December 1989.

Rappaport, E. B. "Insurance Company Solvency." CRS Report for Congress, July 1989.

Reid, M. *The Secondary Banking Crisis, 1973–1975*. London: Macmillan, 1982.

Reinsurance Association of America. *Reinsurance Underwriting Review: 1989 Premiums and Losses*. New York: Reinsurance Association of America, April 1989.

Ritter, Jay R. "The 'Hot Issue' Market of 1980." *Journal of Business* 57 (1984): 215–240.

Roeller, Wolfgang. "Die Macht der Banken." *Zeitschrift fuer das Gesamte Kreditwesen*, 1 January 1990.

Roll, Richard. "The Hubris Hypothesis of Corporate Takeovers." *Journal of Business*, 59 (April 1986): 197–216.

Rybczynski, T. N. "Corporate Restructuring." *National Westminster Bank Quarterly Review*, August 1989, 18–28.

Sagari, Sylvia B. "The Financial Services Industry: An International Perspective." Ph.D. diss., Graduate School of Business Administration, New York University, 1986.

Sagari S., and G. Udell. "Bank Examination and Deposit Insurance Reform: A Proposal." *Journal of Accounting, Auditing and Finance* (forthcoming).

Santomero, A. "The Capital Issue in Perspective." Paper presented to the Federal Reserve Board of Governors, March 1990.

Saunders, A. "Bank Holding Companies: Structure, Performance and Reform." In W. Haraf and R. M. Kushmeider, eds. *Restructuring Banking and Financial Services in America*. Washington, D.C.: American Enterprise Institute, 1988.

———. "Conflicts of Interest: An Economic View." In *Deregulating Wall Street*, Ingo Walter, ed. New York: John Wiley & Sons, 1985, 207–230.

———. "The Separation of Banking and Commerce." *Journal of Banking and Finance* (1994, forthcoming).

———. "Why Are So Many New Stock Issues Underpriced?" *Federal Reserve Bank of Philadelphia Business Review*, March–April 1990, 3–12.

Saunders, Anthony, and Ingo Walter. "International Trade in Financial Services: Are Bank Services Special?" Paper presented at a symposium on New Institutional Arrangements for the World Economy, University of Konstanz 1987. Mimeo.

Saunders, Anthony, and M. Smirlock. "Intra- and Interindustry Effects of Bank Securities Market Activities: The Case of Discount Brokerage." *Journal of Financial and Quantitative Analysis* 22 (December 1987): 467–481.

Saunders, A., and P. Yourougou. "Are Banks Special: Some Evidence from Stock Market Returns." *Journal of Economics and Business,* 1990, 171–182.

Schipper, Katherine, and Abbie Smith. "A Comparison of Equity Carve-Outs and Seasoned Equity Offerings: Share Price Effects and Corporate Restructuring." *Journal of Financial Economics* 15 (1986): 153–186.

Schipper, Katherine, and Rex Thompson. "The Impact of Merger- Related Regulations on the Shareholders of Acquiring Firms." *Journal of Accounting Research* 21, no. 1 (1983): 184–221.

Scholes, Myron, and Joseph Williams. "Estimating Betas from Non-Synchronous Data." *Journal of Financial Economics* 5 (1977): 309–327.

Schwartz, R. A. *Equity Markets.* New York: Harper Business Books, 1991.

Shaffer, Sherrill. "A Revenue-Restricted Cost Study of 100 Large Banks." Federal Reserve Bank of New York, February 1990. Mimeo.

———. "A Restricted Cost Study of 100 Large Banks" Federal Reserve Bank of New York Working Paper, 1988.

———. "A Test of Competition in Canadian Banking." Federal Reserve Bank of Philadelphia, April 1990. Mimeo.

Schaffer, Sherrill, and Edmond David. "Economies of Superscale in Commercial Banks." *Applied Economics* 23 (1991): 283–294.

Smirlock, M., and M. Kaufold. "Bank Foreign Lending, Mandatory Disclosure Rules, and the Reaction of Bank Stock Prices to the Mexican Debt Crisis." *Journal of Business,* 60 (1987): 347–364.

Smirlock, Michael, and Howard Kaufold. "Bank Foreign Lending, Mandatory Disclosure Rules, and the Reaction of Bank Stock Prices to the Mexican Debt Crisis." *Journal of Business* 60 (1987): 347–364.

Smith, Roy C., and Ingo Walter. *Global Financial Services.* New York: Harper, 1989.

———. "Bank-Industry Linkages: Models for Eastern European Industrial Restructuring." In Christian de Boissieu (ed.), *The New Europe: Evolving Economic and Financial Systems in East and West.* Amsterdam: Kluwer, 1993.

Spindler, J. Andrew, Jonathan T. B. Howe, and David F. Dedyo. "The Performance of Internationally-Active Banks and Securities Firms Based on Conventional Competitiveness Measures." Federal Reserve Bank of New York, May 1990. Mimeo.

Steinherr, A., and C. Huveneers. "Universal Banking: A View Inspired by German Experience." Paper presented at the University of Bocconi, Milan, 10 March 1989.

Stigum, M. *The Money Market.* 3d ed. Homewood, Ill.: Dow-Jones Irwin, 1989.

Stoll, H. R., and R. E. Whaley. *Expiation Day Effects of Index Options and Futures.* Monograph series no. 1986-3. Salomon Brothers Center for the Study of Financial Institutions, New York University, 1986.

Stover, Roger D. "A Reexamination of Bank Holding Company Acquisitions." *Journal of Bank Research* 13 (Summer 1982):101–108.

Sweeney, R. J., and A. D. Warga. "The Pricing of Interest-Rate Risk:Evidence from the Stock Market." *Journal of Finance,* 41 (June 1986): 393–410.

Swiss Bankers Association. "Answers to the International Survey of Banking and Financial Services by the American Bankers Association." Basel, January 1990. Mimeo.

Teece, David J. "Transactions Cost Economics and the Multinational Enterprise: An Assessment." *Journal of Economic Behavior and Organization* 7 (March 1986): 21–45.

Thomas, Hugh, and Ingo Walter. "Foreign Direct Investment and International Trade in Financial Services." U.N. Centre on Transnational Corporations Working Paper, New York, December 1989.

———. "The Introduction of Universal Banking in Canada: An Event Study." *Journal of International Financial Management and Accounting* (1992): 42–49.

Tillman, H. T. "Insurance and Credit Tie-Insurance: Myth or Reality." *Banks in Insurance* (January 1986): 1–5.

Toronto Stock Exchange. *1989 Official Trading Statistics.* Toronto: Toronto Stock Exchange Press, 1989.

Travlos, N. "Corporate Takeover Bids, Methods of Payment and Bidding Firms Stock Returns." *Journal of Finance,* 42 (1987): 943–963.

Tschoegl, Adrian E. *The Regulation of Foreign Banks: Policy Formation Outside the United States.* New York: Salomon Brothers Center for the Study of Financial Institutions, New York University, 1981.

———. "Size, Growth and Transnationality Among the World's Largest Banks." *Journal of Business* 56, no. 2 (1983): 187–202.

U.S. Comptroller of the Currency. *A Critical Evaluation of Reciprocity in Foreign Bank Acquisition.* Washington, D.C.: U.S. Government Printing Office, for the Office of the Comptroller of the Currency, 1984.

———. *Foreign Acquisition of US Banks: Motives and Tactical Consideration.* Washington, D.C.: U.S. Government Printing Office, for the Office of the Comptroller of the Currency, 1982.

———. *US Banks' Loss of Global Standing.* Washington, D.C.: U.S. Government Printing Office, for the Office of the Comptroller of the Currency, 1984.

U.S. Department of the Treasury. *Report to the Congress on Foreign Government Treatment of U.S. Banking Organizations.* Washington, D.C.: Department of the Treasury, [1979], 1984.

———. *Modernizing the Financial System: Recommendations for Safer More Competitive Banks.* Washington, D.C.: Department of the Treasury, February 1991.

U.S. House of Representatives. *Insurance Company Failures.* Subcommittee Hearings of the Committee on Energy and Commerce, Serial no. 101–38, April 1989.

Vaughan, E. M. *Fundamentals of Risk and Insurance.* 5th ed. New York: John Wiley, 1989.

Vital, C., and D. L. Mengle. "SIC: Switzerland's New Electronic Interbank Payment System." Federal Reserve Bank of Richmond, November/December 1988, 12–27.

Wall, Larry D. "Insulating Banks from Nonbank Affiliates." *Economic Review.* Federal Reserve Bank of Atlanta, September 1984, 18–28.

———. "Nonbank Activities and Risk." *Economic Review.* Federal Reserve Bank of Atlanta, October 1986 19–34.

Walter, Ingo. *Barriers to Trade in Banking and Financial Services.* London: Trade Policy Research Centre, 1985.

———. *Global Competition in Financial Services.* Cambridge, Mass.: Ballinger–Harper & Row, 1988.

———. *The Secret Money Market.* New York: Harper Collins, 1990.

———., ed. *Deregulating Wall Street.* New York: John Wiley, 1985.

————. "The Battle of the Systems: Control of Enterprises in the Global Economy." *Journal of International Securities Markets* 6 (Winter 1992): 309–324.

Walter, Ingo, and Takato Hiraki, eds. *Restructuring Japan's Financial Markets.* Homewood, Ill.: Business One/Irwin, 1993.

Walter, Ingo and H. Peter Gray. "Protectionism in International Banking." *Journal of Banking and Finance,* 7 (December 1983): 597–609.

Walter, Ingo, and Roy C. Smith. *Investment Banking in Europe: Restructuring for the 1990s.* Oxford: Basil Blackwell, 1989.

White, E. N. "Before the Glass-Steagall Act: An Analysis of the Investment Banking Activities of National Banks." *Explorations in Economic History* 23 (1986): 33–55.

White, L. J. "Marking to Market Recognizes Realities." *American Banker* 154 12 December 1989, 6.

————. "The Value of Market Value Accounting for the Deposit Insurance System." *Journal of Accounting, Auditing and Finance* (forthcoming).

Witt, R. C. and P. R. Aird. "The Competitive Nature of Property–Liability Reinsurance Markets: An Economic Overview." Department of Finance, Working Paper no. 89/90–2–13. University of Texas at Austin, April 1990.

————. "An Overview of Reinsurance and the Reinsurance Markets." Department of Finance, Working Paper no. 89/90–2–10, University of Texas at Austin, April 1990.

Wyler, Georg. "The Swiss Banks: History, Legislation and Major Banking Groups." Union Bank of Switzerland Working Paper, 1986. Mimeo.

Yannopoulos, George N. "The Growth of Transnational Banking." in Mark Casson, ed. *The Growth of International Business.* London: Allen & Unwin, 1983.

Yoshioka, Kanji, and Takanobu Nakajima. "Economies of Scale in Japan's Banking Industry." *Bank of Japan Monetary and Economic Studies* 5 (September 1987): 35–70.

Index

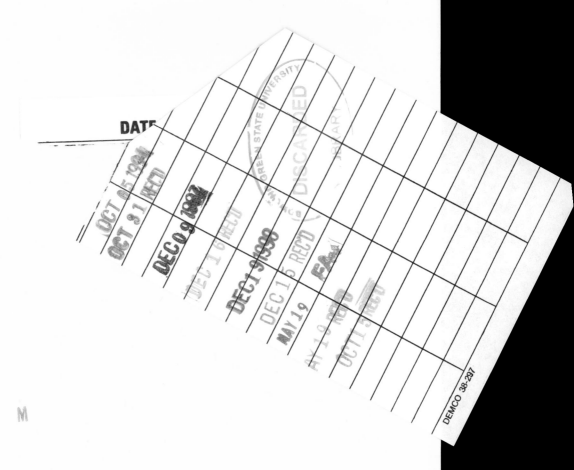